Ways of Writing

Ways of Writing

*The Practice and Politics
of Text-Making in
Seventeenth-Century
New England*

David D. Hall

PENN

UNIVERSITY OF PENNSYLVANIA PRESS

PHILADELPHIA

Published by
University of Pennsylvania Press
Philadelphia, Pennsylvania 19104-4112

Printed in the United States of America on acid-free paper

10 9 8 7 6 5 4 3 2 1

Library of Congress Cataloging-in-Publication Data

Hall, David D.
    Ways of writing : the practice and politics of text-making in seventeenth-century New England / David D. Hall.
        p.   cm.—(Material texts)
    Includes bibliographical references and index.
    ISBN 978-0-8122-4102-0 (alk. paper)
    1. Book industries and trade—New England—History—17th century.   2. Authorship—Social aspects—New England—History—17th century.   3. Transmission of texts—New England—History—17th century.   4. New England—Intellectual life—17th century.   I. Title.
Z473.H23   2008
381′.45002097409032—dc22

                                                            2008011500

In memory of
Roland Andre Delattre
sans pareil

CONTENTS

PREFACE

THE INVITATION to deliver the Rosenbach lectures at the University of Pennsylvania prompted the writing of this book, a much expanded version of the three lectures I gave to an informed and responsive audience in February 2007. The pleasure of being invited to participate in a longstanding series was far exceeded by that of spending a week with a thriving community of faculty and students. I thank in particular Peter Stallybrass, the most generous of hosts, and the staff of special collections in Van Pelt Library, especially John Pollack, who undertook the unenviable task of "local arrangements." It was an honor to be introduced on successive afternoons by three friends who have also been intellectual companions for many years: Robert St. George, Roger Chartier, and James Green; I have acknowledged Roger Chartier in the past for his goodwill and example as a thinker, but I thank him again for comments and citations he provided during the course of the lectures.

The book that follows bears some of the marks of social authorship I describe at length for the colonists. Three chapters were greatly improved by Lawrence Buell's astute comments, and I have benefited from the observations of Matthew Brown, Leah Price, James Simpson, and Roger Thompson on other parts of the manuscript. Kristin Gunst helped prepare the copy text, and Linford Fisher and Lydia Willsky assisted with some of the research. An unexpected boon was the gift from his granddaughter Kim Buell of Sidney Arthur Kinder's *Cambridge Press Title-pages, 1640–1665*. The making of my book has depended to a remarkable degree on the editorial and archival skills of the "antiquarians" who, in the nineteenth and early twentieth centuries, edited or brought into print a host of seventeenth-century documents, often providing annotations of unusual breadth, as in the unsung John Davis's notes for his 1826 edition of Nathaniel Morton's *New Englands Memoriall* (1669). James Savage, Charles Deane, Samuel G. Drake, Williston Walker (an academic historian), and the many others whose accomplishments filled volume after volume of the *Collections* of the Massachusetts Historical Society and similar series have served me well. This book is especially indebted to the meticulous bibliographical scholarship of Thomas J. Holmes. I have also relied on the generations of librarians and cataloguers at the American Antiquarian Society who assembled its library and, more recently, raised bibliographical knowledge of early American imprints to a new level of precision. Much of my research was done during the academic year 2004–5 when I was Mellon Distinguished Scholar in Residence at the Society. There I benefited once again from the skills of those who work in readers' services, and my quest for quantitative information about Cotton Mather was generously satisfied by Alan Degutis and Kathleen Haley. I am grateful to the libraries that have granted permission to reproduce illustrations of material in their collections: the Houghton Library, Harvard University and, especially, the Massachusetts Historical Society. In quoting from seventeenth-century sources I have expanded most contractions, eliminated italics, and, in general, substituted modern equivalents for the letters *y* and *u*.

This book stands on its own, but readers seeking a broader understanding of early American cultural history and the history of the book may want to consult what I wrote about literacy and related matters in *Worlds of Wonder, Days of Judgment: Popular Religious Belief in Early New England* (1989) and the chapters about seventeenth-century books and writers I contributed to *The Colonial Book in the Atlantic World* (2000), coedited with Hugh Amory. The pages that follow register the influence on me of questions about the making of texts during the English Renaissance as debated and described by Harold Love, David McKitterick, David Scott Kastan, Marcy L. North, Margaret Ezell, Peter Stallybrass, and many others. I have also benefited from the extensive scholarship on "literature and politics," though not able in what follows to analyze any single text as intricately as sometimes happens in that body of work. Within the field of early American literature, I have been informed in particular by the contributions of David Shields, Matthew Brown, the late Sargent Bush, and Winfried Herget. The influence on me of my late friend and colleague Hugh Amory is evident in the efforts I make in these pages to transform bibliographical information into cultural and political history.

A life time spent reading in and about the seventeenth century has repeatedly taught me that the past is always open to fresh questions. The research for this book has taught me another lesson, that we still know relatively little about the bibliographical histories of a great many printed texts and even less about the histories of texts that circulated in handwritten copies. What I say about these topics is merely a beginning, a means, I hope, of encouraging others to explore the histories of writing and bookmaking and, not least, the practices of petitioning and political debate among the colonists.

* * *

On the eve of February 20, when I was to give the first of the Rosenbach lectures, I learned that someone of great significance in my life, Roland Delattre of Minneapolis, had been diagnosed with a malignant brain tumor. He would die a little less than two months later. I dedicate this book to him to honor a singular friendship that began in 1959 and, although strong from its outset, deepened significantly in the past twenty-five years. A fellow lover of all things French, he was my beau ideal as an ethical person and in how he expressed and lived a joy for life.

Hannah Jones has been a sustaining presence from the moment I began this book, and was so especially during the week we spent together in Philadelphia as the lectures were unfolding. Far-removed though she is in her own interests from seventeenth-century New England, she has been an ever-reliable reader and critic, for which I offer heartfelt thanks.

CHAPTER ONE

Contingencies of Authorship

The Protestant Vernacular Tradition, the Book Trades, and Technologies of Production

WRITERS ABOUNDED in seventeenth-century New England. From the moment of colonization and constantly thereafter, hundreds of people set pen to paper in the course of their lives, some to write letters that others recopied, some to compose sermons as part of their life work as ministers, dozens to attempt verse, and many more to narrate a remarkable experience, provide written testimony to a civil court, participate in a controversy, or keep some sort of records—and of these everyday forms of writing there was no limit.[1] As in other early modern societies, so in New England the curve of productivity rose sharply at one end and, at the other, dipped to a single poem or personal narrative. The story of text-making in New England must also encompass writers whose work never interested any printer or copyist and the few who deliberately refrained from sharing what they wrote.[2]

Every colonial writer knew of two different modes of publication, each with its distinctive benefits and limitations. One was to entrust a manuscript to a printer who would set type and impose it on sheets of paper that were bound up into a book. The other was to make handwritten copies or have others make copies, possibly unauthorized. Among the colonists the terms "publishing" and "book" referred to each of these technologies.[3] Publishing could also mean reading aloud—publishing in the sense of declaring or declaiming, as happened frequently with proclamations a colony government sent to each local community.

This book is about the making and transmission of texts in the seventeenth century, some fashioned into printed books, others existing in handwritten copies. Any history of text-making opens out into a history of practices and meanings, first and foremost the practices of the book trade for printed books, but also the patterns of decision-making about anonymity, title pages, dedications, prefaces, errata, and "fair copy" that many who were not connected with the book trades helped determine. In deciding any feature of a printed or handwritten book, the colonists drew on a repertory of social custom they owed to their English background. Similarly, the colonists drew on religious and political frameworks of meaning that were familiar currency in England. Acknowledging these all-important continuities, I also try to identify points of difference, though I do so without regarding them as constituting a proto-"American" version of text-making.[4]

The most important continuity may have been that text-making was always a collaborative process. A central goal of this book is to restore to visibility the intermediaries without whom no manuscript would have circulated or book been printed.[5] As the examples and case studies that follow will indicate in abundance, printers and booksellers sometimes behaved as though they had license to redo a manuscript that reached them. So did the people on whom every seventeenth-century colonial writer depended, though especially those whose work was published in far-away London. Seeking out the evidence of these interventions, I have relied on the material aspects of printed books, in particular the elements of "pretext" or "paratext" that, remarkably often, inform us about the provenance and condition of a copy text.[6] Another goal, and perhaps the more surprising to those of us unfamiliar with it, is to reclaim the importance of scribal publication, the technology that writers as productive as John Winthrop and William Bradford preferred, that satisfied many others, and that figured as the medium of debate in political and religious controversies for much of the seventeenth century. Indeed, the prevalence of handwritten texts is the key to understanding how dissent could be expressed in a society that placed a high value on consensus. Reclaiming its utility also displaces the oft-told story of print as a technology that brought scribal publication to a crashing halt.[7]

Beyond these two acts of recovery, I tell stories of text-making in the service of three larger arguments. One of them has long been the meat and drink of early New England studies, that writing and publishing were constantly political. For many others who have shown this to be the case, the politics of text-making was rooted in efforts to describe the colonists' "errand into the wilderness" and the internecine disputes that erupted soon after they arrived. As Udo Hebel has emphasized, the first of these was always international, for the colonists had to defend themselves against English critics, some to their left, others to their right, who complained about the policies of the founders.[8] Taking these versions of politics for granted, my goal is to extend our understanding of them by showing how they were manifested in the particularities of text-making—for example, the ministers' refusal to share the major texts of the Antinomian controversy, an episode I narrate in Chapter 2, and the decision to dedicate the Algonquian translation of the New Testament (Cambridge, 1661) to Charles II. As I try to demonstrate in Chapter 5, the everyday world of politics, the world we know so well for early Massachusetts from John Winthrop's journal-history, looks different if we take seriously the uses of scribal publication. Texts were political in and of themselves, but the possibilities for sharing handwritten books or manifestos also affected the nature of politics.

In general, political situations influenced what people put on paper or refrained from writing, how others handled their manuscripts, and why writers angered each other. As the temperature of the Quaker movement cooled in late seventeenth-century England, the men who, after his death, edited George Fox's journal, curtailed the fervency of his early entries lest he seem guilty of "enthusiasm." In the first printing of Nathaniel Morton's *New Englands Memoriall* (Cambridge, 1669), he inserted a marginal note (p. 110) directed at the local religious radicals known as Gortonists, "Horrible Familism and Blasphemy, as if they were spoken by, and differ little from the cursed doctrine of their grand Leader Henry Nichols," that disappeared from the second, printed in 1721.[9] Though such acts of revision were pervasive, it is perplexing that few traces remain of the changes made to colonial texts for political reasons. Some writers curbed their frankness or eliminated material deemed too controversial to publish, but these acts of self-censorship remain elusive, just as writers wanted them to be. Writers also tangled with each other—famously Roger Williams and John Cotton in the 1640s, and almost as famously, Cotton Mather and Robert Calef in the 1690s. Others, too, wrote in order to dispute another person's version of affairs, as John Mason did in his belated memoir of the Pequot War of 1637.[10] But I am interested less in these well-told episodes than in the controversial aspects of the "New England Way," the factionalism that erupted during moments like the Antinomian controversy, and the contested relationship with the English empire.

A second argument takes its point of departure from the "sociology of texts," an approach to the history of transmission that represents it as ceaselessly introducing variations, few if any with unimpeachable authority. To foreground this possibility, as I do in what follows, is to associate my study of writing and writers in seventeenth-century New England with the tenor of recent work on the English Renaissance—Shakespeare and company, as it were. The theme or perhaps the discovery that drives this scholarship is the recognition that texts remain "unfixed, always open to revision." The same proposition drives the impulse to "unedit the Renaissance" by jettisoning the methods and assumptions of the major school of Anglo-American bibliography at mid-century, the New Bibliography. The men and women who fashioned the New Bibliography labored to recover the history of printing office practices, the better to understand the making of a printed text. This knowledge in hand, editors attempted to reconstruct the copy text used by printers as the author had intended it. These efforts focused on the great writers of the English Renaissance, Shakespeare in particular. These were writers everyone regarded as central to the making of the English literary tradition as well as being masterful in their own right—that is, authoritative or canonical.[11]

But which of their plays, poems, and books have descended to us in versions we can confidently regard as authoritative? Though we owe almost everything we know about the printing of English books in the seventeenth century to the exacting scholarship associated with the New Bibliography, most of its strategies for answering this question have been called into question. We hear that questioning in every evocation of "indeterminacy" and each dismissal of authorial intention. Denouncing "the fantasy of literary autonomy," the Shakespeare scholar David Kastan has enumerated the advantages of doing so: "Focus on the documentary particularities of a text frees our reading from the fantasy of literary autonomy. It demystifies the act of writing, clarifying the actual conditions of creativity, locating the text within a network of intentions, within which the author's, however dominant, are still only some among many—and intentions, it should be noted, that are incapable of producing the book itself."[12] What Kastan is proposing is that literary scholars should rethink the continuum of author-text-canon as it was construed in the New Bibliography. The key to this continuum was the overlapping authority of canon, text, and author. But for Kastan and others of his persuasion, authority has been radically de-centered, the canon re-opened, and authorial control superseded by "a network" of people and agencies all of whom—and especially everyone who undertook the role of editor—participated in the work of making texts.[13]

In the pages that follow, I bring something of the same perspective to colonial writing and writers. Something, not everything, because the condition of New England texts then and now is different in certain respects from the condition of Shakespeare's plays. A crucial difference is that neither in the seventeenth nor the twentieth century did a definitive canon of colonial texts emerge.[14] The reasons why no such canon exists are several, beginning with the fact that no New England writer regarded his or her texts in this light, whereas certain writers (or their editors) of the English Renaissance did—the playwright Ben Jonson, for one, who assembled his plays into a collection printed in the grand format of folio (1616), and the two friends of Shakespeare who put together the First Folio of 1623. To make this point another way, no New England writer sorted through his or her corpus of work in order to differentiate the excellent from the so-so or good versions from those that were badly transmitted, with the sole exception, perhaps, of Thomas Hooker, who set himself to rewriting the sermons that became *The Application of Redemption* (London, 1656).[15] Nor did any coterie of connoisseurs take on this function, as often happened for English poets.[16] A writer as major as Cotton Mather is a case in point, for he treated much of what he published with astonishing indifference, a practice he carried over to texts by other writers he incorporated into books of his own. The writers who immigrated from England in the 1630s behaved in the same way. If we ask which of John Cotton's London-printed books he supervised in the sense of preparing copy text, the answer may be five or six out of fifteen. For Hooker, the answer may be no more than one out of the seventeen editions of his sermons published in England by 1640. No canon in our own time, no canon in the seventeenth century, and among the colonists, no firm understanding of "author" that conflated it with the authority of a particular printed (or manuscript) text—these circumstances help to explain why the reaction against the New Bibliography is without parallel in the field of "early American literature." Another impediment has been the kinds of texts the colonists produced, the sermons, elegies, autobiographies, and histories that resist being incorporated into the category of "literature," a gesture the colonists themselves refused to make.

Nonetheless, the questions that animate recent scholarship on the English Renaissance are questions worth asking of colonial writers and writing, if only because the answers can be surprising. We know a good deal about text-making in early New England thanks to a handful of scholars.[17] But mine is the first attempt to juxtapose those accomplishments with the newer

attention to such matters as scribal publication, the practice of social authorship, the purposes of the paratext, the meaning of anonymity, and the contours of transmission. Because I do so as a historian, my scope in principle is
everything that was written in the New England colonies, and because I am
a historian I foreground how the colonists themselves understood the sociology of texts and its implications for any writer's authority. Instead of insisting
on indeterminacy, I sketch in Chapters 3 and 4 a counterpoint of anxiety and
indifference about authenticity.[18] Instead of rejecting authorial intention, I
take stock of several versions of intentionality that figured in the making of
texts. Doing so has led me to the words "private" and "public" as they were
used among the colonists. It mattered a great deal to some writers that their
texts, though possibly published in handwritten copies, remain private. Nor
was every printed text automatically deemed public. The nuances of private
and public served as a critical framework for text-making, a framework that
may deserve more attention than the concept of indeterminacy.

A third argument concerns the consequences of the Protestant vernacular
tradition for the practices of writing and text-making. Here I follow the lead
of John N. King, John R. Knott, Barbara Kiefer Lewalski, Barbara A. Johnson, and many others who have demonstrated the significance of a particular
kind of Protestantism for writers and readers in early modern England.[19] I
describe that tradition more specifically in the next two sections of this chapter and suggest its role at later points in this book as well. I do so as a
historian exempt from a long-running debate among students of the English
Renaissance as to whether a John Bunyan or John Milton—in effect, anyone
touched with the disease of "Puritanism"—should be accorded the same
praise as a Sidney, a Donne, or a Shakespeare. Were this distinction attempted for New England writers, there would be little left to discuss. High
or low, learned or unlearned, virtually every colonist who put pen to paper
was employing literary strategies associated with the Puritan version of the
Protestant Reformation.

In early seventeenth-century England, the writers who worked within
the Protestant vernacular tradition relied on London printers and booksellers
to produce and distribute most of what they wrote. Some of their contemporaries were suspicious of the book trades and hesitated to trust what they
wrote to the rhythms of the market lest their texts acquire the taint of commerce. Godly writers voiced the same anxiety, but it would be a serious
mistake to insist on some fundamental antagonism between the vernacular
tradition and the market for printed books.[20] Any assertions of this kind must

ignore the role of sponsored printing in New England and the modest size of
editions (see below); of more importance, it ignores the fragmenting of the
English book trade into market sectors, with Nonconformist booksellers
printing Nonconformist authors for Nonconformist readers, and the like.[21]
Fortunately for the colonists, the diversity within the trade worked to their
advantage, for godly books were considered highly "vendible," sought out by
like-minded readers who wanted instruction and counsel on how to become
good Christians.

* * *

Why did so many of the colonists write? The simplest answer is that people
wrote because literacy in the sense of knowing how to read was almost univer-
sal, and literacy in the sense of knowing to write, though much less common
among women, was shared by a majority of the adult men. Social history
helps to explain the ways in which the culture of these people relied on
written texts. It did so in courtrooms where judges were guided by printed
or handwritten laws, and in churches where the rituals of preaching, praying,
and singing relied on the Bible and printed translations of the Hebrew
psalms. Writing was utilitarian in more mundane sites like the household,
where children rehearsed a catechism, a parent read aloud from notes of last
Sunday's sermon, and the elderly or dying crafted wills. In this setting, parents composed legacies in prose and poetry for their children that evoked the
significance of being in covenant with God and acknowledged his providential care; in this setting, people solicited poetry from friends or well known
writers to honor someone who had died. That colonies, towns, and churches
practiced participatory forms of government made for other forms of writing,
like record-keeping, petitions, and proclamations posted in a public place.
Commercial life accounted for a host of documents, as did the sharing of
news, which commonly happened in letters. Keeping in touch with English
allies and the English government was another reason for writing.[22]

Yet social history carries us only so far in explaining why so many people
wrote. A fuller answer must encompass the politics of writing in the seventeenth century, a politics that had two dimensions for the colonists. The first
was their religious identity, itself inescapably political in the context of early
modern English history. To be a Puritan, as some of the colonists called
themselves and the name that, by the nineteenth century, was commonly
used in referring to the immigrants, was to take sides in an acutely divisive

controversy rooted in the unfinished nature of the English Reformation. Was the Church of England fully Reformed or a hybrid institution? Did its standing as a true church depend on whether its structure and practices were aligned with Scripture, or was Scripture to be supplemented by "reason" and church history? How bothersome were its inadequacies—the unlearned or nonresident clergy, the ill-informed laypeople who were being admitted to the sacraments of baptism and the Lord's Supper? To Puritans the answers to these questions were self-evident: the Church had fallen short of purging the vestiges of Catholicism, to the point of imperiling its legitimacy; Scripture, and especially the apostolic letters, should be normative; and the condition of laypeople and clergy cried out for strong measures to reshape each. To be sure, Puritans spoke in different voices at different times in dealing with these issues. But the people who immigrated to New England, and especially the clergy who played so large a role in supervising the new society, were nearly as one in "desir[ing] to worship God in spirit, and in trueth," willing to undergo a difficult journey in order to "enjoy the libertye, not of some ordinances of god, but of all, and all in Puritye."[23]

Religion got the colonists into trouble before the founding generation moved from England and complicated their dealings with the homeland for the rest of the seventeenth century. As an English correspondent of the Winthrops pointed out in 1632, "there are here a thousand eyes watching over you to pick a hole in your coats."[24] The Massachusetts Bay Company had secured a charter from Charles I, but the leaders of the new colony were reluctant to acknowledge the king's authority once they reached New England and, for the most part, ignored the commercial and political policies of the Commonwealth. During the 1640s, the ministers in the colonies participated in an often angry debate with ministers in England and Scotland who, though broadly Reformed in their own politics, regarded the "Congregational Way" of the colonists as dangerously radical. Many in England would have agreed with what Nathaniel Ward said of English opinion of the immigrants: "We have beene reputed a colluvies [sic] of wild Opinionists, [who] swarmed into a remote wildernes to find elbow room for our phanatick Doctrines and practices."[25] Fresh difficulties arose after the monarchy was restored in 1660, for the failure of the Puritan Revolution prepared the way for a sharp reaction against the reforming ambitions and cultural style of people like the colonists. That reaction weighed heavily on the English ministers and laypeople who in 1662 refused to acknowledge the authority of an unpurified Church of England; thereafter, excluded from the national

church, these Nonconformists were intermittently persecuted or severely constrained in what they could practice. Though the colonists were able to protect most of their distinctive system of church and state, they found
themselves tarred with the brush of sedition and sectarianism because so little
was done to fall in line with English laws and regulations. Insist though the
Massachusetts government did to Charles II that "we left not our native
country upon any dissatisfaction as to the constitution of the civil state," the
General Court never welcomed the officers of Charles II or James II and
people rose up against an instrument of royal governance, the Dominion of
New England, in 1689.

Religion also got the colonists into trouble in their own space, for the
people who immigrated in the 1630s, though agreeing on certain principles,
found much to quarrel about. Unanimity eluded them in deciding how
churches should be organized or Baptists and Quakers treated once these
groups appeared on the scene. At moments like the Antinomian controversy
of the mid-1630s and the agitated debates of the 1660s about baptism, differences turned into long-lasting hostility. The much reiterated lament of
"declension" was also divisive, put to use in different ways by different inter-
preters.[26]

All of this politics provoked people to choose sides and write, be it in
defense of the "Congregational Way," a task that accounts for a large share
of what the minister John Cotton published, be it by insisting on a certain
version of declension, which motivated Increase Mather for much of his
career, be it by denouncing the Christianized Indians in the wake of King
Philip's War, as Mary Rowlandson relished doing in *The Sovereignty & Goodness of God* (Boston, 1682). To write and publish was also to invite censure
from others; writing begat writing, or as contemporaries remarked, to publish
was to be "exposed" to criticism and reprisal. Thus it happened that William
Hubbard and Increase Mather wrote competing histories of King Philip's
War and, depending on which branch of the Massachusetts General Court
named the preacher of the annual election sermon, such texts became partisan
responses to previous sermons. Always, the politics of writing was rooted in
the complexities of the colonists' situation: the presence of competing tendencies within Puritanism itself, the ever problematic relationship with the
English state, and the divergent interests, at once political and economic, of
the four Puritan colonies as they dealt with problems like the presence of
Native Americans.

Writing in New England was political for an entirely different reason that also helps explain the eagerness of people to write. Because of their Puritanism the immigrants had already been participating in a literary tradition that arose in the wake of the Protestant Reformation, a tradition associated with John Calvin and the Reformed wing of that far-reaching movement. For Calvin and his heirs, the purpose of writing was what it had become for St. Augustine after he converted, to teach the essentials of true religion in a style that all could understand. The model for true speech and writing was the "humble style" of Jesus, an unlearned man who, as understood by many English Protestants, had never employed a formalized rhetoric of the kind St. Augustine was teaching at the moment he converted. Another model was Scripture, especially the apostolic letters and the prophetic books of the Old and New Testaments. From Scripture descended the principle that speech and writing should be vehicles of the Holy Spirit: the "letter" was of human doing, but through it moved the "Spirit" (2 Corinthians 3:2–3, 6). A predicate for spiritual writing was spiritual preparation beforehand, a connection dramatized by uneducated English men and women who, under the influence of the Quaker movement, became fluent speakers and writers. Quaker or Puritan, the men and women who took up writing were encouraged to do so by the principles of the Protestant vernacular tradition. This tradition was vernacular in a double sense, first by enjoining writers to make sense to everyday people and to do so using simple language; and second, by presuming that every person touched by faith was empowered to express his or her experiences of divine grace. Thus it happened that hundreds if not thousands of men and women in early New England narrated in speech and writing the inner experiences of grace and that others put on paper their observations of divine providence. Lay people wrote in abundance because the vernacular tradition regarded such experiences as useful to anyone who affiliated with the godly; writing was an act of "service," the motive the young minister Increase Mather gave for publishing a life of his father.[27]

From the moment the vernacular tradition emerged in the middle of the sixteenth century, it was contending against other representations and practices of writing. What the literary historian Nigel Smith says of writing during the period of civil war and Commonwealth in England holds more generally: "cultural polarization was endemic; literature was one of the major ways by which the disease of division spread."[28] The Humanist reiteration of the classical tradition, which any one attending Oxford or Cambridge was taught, was a seductive alternative. Court culture of the kind that flourished under James I and Charles I was less appealing, though always a rival. The differences between these two and the vernacular tradition was in part a matter of themes and genres: epic, lyric, plays, and histories centered on national glory or great leaders versus histories centered on God's providence or the warfare between Antichrist and the godly, poetry influenced by the Psalms, and sermons describing the difficult, stress-filled passage out of sin and offering strategies for self-examination.

Sometimes these differences were blurred, as when Puritan writers re-sorted to satire or drew on the classical tradition for tropes and literary de-vices. More often, however, writers and readers in New England (and their cultural counterparts in England) were being told how wrong the alternatives were—how vainglorious, how deceitful, how alien to the task of serving God. In the midst of a treatise on the right ways to pray, Thomas Cobbet, the minister in Lynn, Massachusetts, who came to New England in 1637, paused to indict the "hypocrisie" of so much speech and writing:

> Hypocrites are Stage-players, which albeit they are illiterate Dunces many of them, yet will be high-flown sometimes in their Expres-sions, their Mouth speaketh great swelling words when they speak to Men or God, or else they fail of their use and aime, Jude. 16. And in all affectation there is some Hypocrisie . . . Sincerity will account those Gentile-like esteemed flourishes of Rhetorical Ingeminations, but vaine Repetitions, Matt. 6.6,7. not expecting that the Lord should be moved by any such-like vanity.

In Cobbet's reckoning, the godly prayed and wrote in an utterly different manner: "The Lips of the Saints in their Prayer, are as a Thred of Scarlet, not stuffed out with the gowty Rhetorick of Man (for it is in comparison of the high and holy Language of the Spirit, no better) but with the pure-spun spiritual eloquence of God, Cant. 4.3."[29] The people who crowded St. Mary's in Cambridge to hear John Cotton preach a sermon experienced this differ-ence first-hand when he shifted to the "plain style," not the more elaborated mode of rhetoric some in the congregation were expecting.[30]

Social history also figured in the differences between the vernacular tradi-tion and its rivals. Humanism was a child of the university and Court culture of the Crown and who or what it favored. Each of these, but especially Court culture, employed patronage to support writers, musicians, actors, painters, and architects. All who sought such patronage (and many did who never received it) were acutely aware of the vagaries of royal policy and the intrigues that threatened each favorite of the Crown or members of the aristocracy, some of whom were also patrons. Any writer who turned toward the Court and aristocracy was turning away from the commercial marketplace in books. By default, writers who adhered to the vernacular tradition relied upon the book trades. Its appetite for godly books, though occasionally constrained by economic circumstances, was both large and enduring. The robust market for the Bible and translated versions of the Psalms is a good example, for English readers bought up hundreds of thousands of copies of each in the decades between 1570 and 1640. In this context, the decision to prepare and print a fresh translation of the psalms soon after the colonists reached New England made sense. Indeed *The Whole Booke of Psalmes, Newly translated* (Cambridge, 1640; revised, 1651) won a place among its many competitors. The market for godly books also explains why so many writers sent their manuscripts to England despite the risks of having them published at long range, and why a remarkable proportion made their way into print.[31]

Yet another aspect of social history concerns the connections between writing and hierarchy. The vernacular tradition displaced most of the traditional hierarchies that writing involved, substituting a geography of dispersed production and distribution for a geography of a cosmopolitan center, and substituting the sociability of like-minded Protestants for the coteries that practiced literary connoisseurship. Like all such acts of displacement, the undoing of hierarchy within the vernacular tradition was incomplete and inconsistent. Three versions of control or constraint persisted within the tradition, two of them almost as ancient as writing itself, the third a response to the upheavals of the 1640s and 1650s in civil war England. During those years, unlettered men and women turned themselves into preachers who claimed the authority of the Holy Spirit. Forewarned of what was coming by the prophesying of Anne Hutchinson in the mid-1630s, the colonists insisted at every turn that intangible Spirit and tangible Word (the Bible) were inseparable, the one always communicated through the other in an orderly and orthodox manner.[32] A second version of control concerned women, who were not supposed to cross the line between the private and the public. Some Englishwomen did, of course, as did a handful of colonists. Nothing is known, however, of the "many bookes" written by Ann Yale Hopkins after she arrived in New England in 1637, books that troubled her high-status husband, who thought she had "gone out of her waye and callinge, to meddle in suche things as are proper for men." Another high-status woman, the wife of the governor of New Haven Colony, Thomas Eaton, was also speaking her

mind in "writeings" that her husband and others regarded as "of concern-
ment to the jurisdiction"; they do not survive.[33] A third constraint was
learnedness and its rhetorical opposite, illiteracy. Clergy who brought to their
work the skills and expectations they learned at Cambridge, Oxford, or Harvard could lapse into disdain for the literary skills of ordinary people like the
shoemaker-turned-Baptist John Russell and the mason John Goodwin, whose
story of diabolical possession in his household was incorporated into Cotton
Mather's *Memorable Providences, Relating to Witchcrafts and Possessions* (Boston, 1689), prefaced by Mather's remark, " 'Tis in his own Style; but I suppose a Pen hath not commonly been managed with more cleanly Discourse
by an Hand used only to the Trowel; and his Condition hath been such, that
he may fairly have Leave to speak."[34]

Underlying all of these constraints, and possibly of more importance in
the long run, was a geography of writing that favored the small group of
ministers who served churches in Boston and its vicinity. From Mather's
house in the north end it was a short walk to the booksellers who clustered
around the town market. The distance between Boston and Northampton,
where Solomon Stoddard was town minister, helps to explain why in 1685
the yet-unpublished Stoddard wrote Increase Mather to report that "a small
treatise" was on its way "to the presse," and to ask that the better situated
Mather "doe me the kindnesse, to join with me to write an epistle to it: I
live in a remote corner and am much unknown; it may be a few wordes from
your selfe may gain it the greater acceptance." No such preface appeared in
Stoddard's *The Safety of Appearing at the Day of Judgment* (Boston, 1687),
perhaps because Mather was still smarting from a dispute he had with Stoddard in 1679.[35] Over time, the geography of writing—and undoubtedly the
factor of personal ambition and perhaps of personal means—was revealed in
the large number of ministers or lay people who had one text of theirs
printed, the even larger number of ministers who never published anything
in printed form, and the small group who published a significant number of
texts.[36] Far more accessible and encouraging than most other modes of culture in the seventeenth century, the vernacular tradition was always caught
up in constraints both old and new.

* * *

Everyone who wrote in seventeenth-century New England could choose between two different technologies of publication. Or, it may be that someone

else did the choosing. The decision to prefer scribal (handwritten) publication was easy to make, for the expense of making a few copies was minimal. Another advantage was avoiding all aspects of the commerce in texts and the piracies this commerce could entail; except for clerks and professional scriveners, no one in New England ever sold handwritten copies or charged others for making them. In principle if not always in fact, an authorial original was available to correct (or challenge) the copies in circulation. But printing had its own advantages. Edward Holyoke, who came to New England in the 1630s, described one of them in the preface to *The Doctrine of Life*, printed in London in 1658: "Some in New England have seen this frame of mine, and have desired that it might be made more common by printing, and indeed I cannot write so many Copies, as to communicate it to you and to that generation, except it be by Printing."[37] Anyone wanting a large number of copies, as Holyoke did to make his book "more common," turned to printing. John Eliot cited a similar circumstance in explaining why *The Dying Speeches of Several Indians* (1683–85?) was "printed, not so much for publishment, as to save charge of writing out of copyes for those that did desire them."[38] The minister John Norton added a third reason, that books allowed the "writer [to be] always at hand, attending the capacity of the Reader." Likening the distribution of books to the sowing of seed in a field, Norton commended printing as long lasting and therefore "more effectual" than speech.[39] The technology was useful to civil governments and churches too; the handwritten catechisms written out for individual congregations and groups of Native Americans were replaced with printed versions, and handwritten codes of law gave way to printed books. Some English writers valued printing because it curtailed the circulation of unauthorized handwritten or "imperfectly and surreptitiously printed" versions. Thomas Browne arranged for the printing of *Religio Medici* in 1643 precisely for this reason. So, it seems, did John Woodbridge when he carried a manuscript collection of his sister-in-law's verse to London to have it printed.[40] One way or another, the colonists figured out what they wanted done with their texts, which may have been to decide that no one else should see them. But what writers wanted was not always what happened. The history of text-making in early New England is also a history of texts that languished on someone's table, never copied or accepted by a printer. It is a history as well of texts that were published in print long after someone had died.

Why were some texts never reproduced? No general answer holds, but the individual stories are enlightening. The passage of time could be an obstacle if a manuscript owed its being to a long-ago event or controversy. Size and pertinence were others. Richard Mather, the minister in Dorchester, labored over "A Plea for the Churches of Christ in New England," a six-hundred-page response to an English critic of New England-style Congregationalism, William Rathband. But his opponent died and another colonist published a response, so Mather set his "Plea" aside, to survive in a family archive rich in manuscripts of many kinds. Long after Richard's death in 1669, his son Nathaniel Mather, who returned to England in 1647 and became a minister in Dublin, reminded his brother Increase that by their father's will he had "an interest in his Manuscripts; viz. a 5th part of them, as my Brother Sam had two fifths. And by his will I had all his [Samuel's'] Manuscripts." Nathaniel must have thought there was valuable material in this archive, for he asked his brother to forward "some of my father's. I cannot name any, tis so long since I left N.E. But I remember hee did write an answer to Mr. Rathband, and by what you say in his life I gather hee wrote something for the Congregationall way, as differing from the Presbyterian on one hand and Brownism on the other." Nathaniel was already rescuing another family manuscript, Samuel's lengthy analysis of "types" in the Bible that a Dublin bookseller would bring out in 1683. He knew or guessed of other manuscripts he regarded as candidates for publication, wondering in the same letter to Increase, "Why . . . nothing of Mr. Mitchell's [was] printed" and asking what had become of a "body of Divinity" by the first-generation minister Samuel Stone.[41]

Much admired though he was, nothing of Jonathan Mitchell's routine preaching to his Cambridge congregation was published until after he died in 1668. As for Stone, long after his death in Hartford, Connecticut in 1663 his "Body of Divinity" was still interesting another generation of colonists, for two handwritten copies survive, one of them a carefully done version dating from 1697 that may have been intended as copy text for a printer. The oddest feature of a family copy and putative original, which Stone's son Samuel Jr. had inherited, was how much the son thought it was worth. At a time when no printer in New England was paying for a manuscript, Sam Jr. remarked that someone had offered him sixty pounds for the "Body of Divinity." Meanwhile a much shorter manuscript and certainly one with a wider utility, a catechism Stone had prepared for his congregation, was printed in 1684 by Samuel Green "for John Wadsworth of Farmington"—a gesture of private printing, for the Wadsworths were related to Stone.[42]

The promise but also the pitfalls of state sponsorship were singularly evident in the failure of another substantial manuscript to appear in print. When William Hubbard set to work in the late 1670s on a history of New England, he knew that a book of the size he intended would need financial support, which he hoped to get from the Massachusetts General Court. Indeed the Court proved willing to entertain the possibility, moved to do so, perhaps, by the willingness of the Plymouth government to subsidize the printing of Morton's *New Englands Memoriall.* Hubbard's political connections also helped. When he approached the Court in 1679 about the manuscript, the government appointed a small committee to consider whether it should sponsor the book. Three years later, Hubbard shared the completed manuscript with the committee, only to be told that the government would do nothing until he had transcribed "it fairely into a booke, that it may be the more easely perused." As an inducement, he was offered fifty pounds. The following spring, after he had hired two or more copyists, the Court voted to pay him half of that sum, with the rest deferred. The draft version did indeed fall short of the "fair copy" that printers expected, with chapter headings indicated as marginalia and the spacing of the whole extremely cramped. The copyists' was a much more legible text, though filled with mistakes Hubbard attempted to correct. But for reasons that cannot be recovered, the manuscript would remain unpublished until the nineteenth century.[43]

When subsidies were wanting, the economics of the book trade stood in the way of some manuscripts passing into print. These economics were on Edward Taylor's mind when he wrote Increase Mather in 1683 to solicit his support for having a manuscript printed by the Boston trade. In counterpoint, as it were, to the material condition of Hubbard's "Generall History," Taylor was unusually specific about the state of the manuscript and the person responsible for its clarity: "I am desirous to inquire after your advice and direction concerning the printing a Manuscript of Mr. Daniel Denton's, who settled with the Church at Stamford . . . he having fully prepared a small treatise by his own hand, about 353 pages in 8, for the Press, before he dyed, stiled a Divine Soliloquy." Taylor recommended both the contents and style of the work, itemizing its four sections and describing them as "Piously, Solidly, Pathetically, and Practically handled in good Language." Only then did he share the news that "a Press hath been sought after for it, by his son now with us, but the price Mr. Forster [John Foster, the sole Boston printer] demanded discouraged the owner as being above his ability." Two years after Foster's death, Taylor was still hoping that someone in Boston would undertake the job: "Mr Sherman and Mr. Higginson, who have perused it, incorage its printing, and also think it will carry itselfe through the Press." Whether Mather agreed to read the manuscript, as Taylor suggested he do, is not known, but the trade never bit.[44]

A writer's reputation could help get a book printed, but it never opened every door. John Davenport was well known on both sides of the Atlantic, but his sermon series on the Psalms bumped around the London trade for two or three decades before vanishing into oblivion. So did some of the manuscripts of Thomas Hooker's Hartford sermons.[45] Despite the great success of Michael Wigglesworth's retelling of the last judgment, *The Day of Doom*, privately printed in Cambridge (or possibly in London) in 1662 and much reprinted thereafter, no one undertook to print "Gods Controversy with New England," which survives only in a manuscript with a title page of his artless design.[46] Letters seeking private patronage, which gradually became common practice among the colonists, were variously successful—often for Cotton Mather, but not for Samuel Stow, the minister in Middletown, Connecticut, who wrote such a letter in 1689 to Wait Winthrop, his near neighbor. "I make bold . . . to inform your Honour of a greate attempt that I have been labouring to write," Stow told Winthrop, "an Essay to call the Jewes, tho' som look at it as a ridiculous thing to attempt such a thing; yet I know that wise and understanding ones that are men of wisedom to know the times, what ought or may be done in the fear of God and for the sake of the honour and glory of God and the salvation of souls, will judge otherwise." This flattery (or bait) was followed by gestures of concession, for Stow asked that Winthrop and Samuel Willard of Boston make whatever improvements they wished in the manuscript: "What I have don, I have sent it for your Honour and the Reverend Mr Willard to peruse and censure as ye shall see cause. And if, Sir, you judge the labourer worthy of any thing, it being for a publick designe and work you may, I doubt not, in you[r] wisdom and prudence promote it; if it be not performed by the author so takingly, let others that can do beter mend it." Stow was not finished pleading his case. As though he were addressing a bookseller in Boston or London, he declared that others were assuring him the manuscript would have wide appeal: "I look at it, if such a work by God's blessing succeed, all Christians will be desirous to be reading the books . . . yea, as Capten Allyne, of Hartford, said to me . . . while at our towne upon a visit, there are many things good and usefull for Gentiles as well as Jews." The last we hear of the book is in a letter from Samuel Sewall some years after Stow's death; "His manuscript of the

Jews is in your hand," Sewall wrote a friend, "to do with it as you see cause, being well assured you will do nothing amiss."[47]

The unluckiest writer in seventeenth-century New England may have been Daniel Gookin, for none of his book-length texts were published in any form by the time of his death in 1687. A man of means (though according to John Eliot he died poor) and a magistrate in the Massachusetts government, Gookin served as superintendent of the colony's Praying Indians, a role that made him well known to the officers of the New England Company in London, the charitable foundation that supported the missionary John Eliot. The knowledge and sympathies Gookin acquired in his role as superintendent resulted in three substantial manuscripts and the outline of a fourth, a history of New England. The earliest to be completed (c. 1674) was "Historical Collections of the Indians in New England," also entitled "Indians converted," which he envisaged as one section of a longer history of New England. An elaborate outline is all that survives of this second project; according to family legend, the manuscript was destroyed in a fire in the middle of the eighteenth century. A third was "An Historical Account of the Doings and Sufferings of the Christian Indians in New England in 1675, 1676 and 1677," a sorrowfully specific description of how the Christian Indians had been mistreated by the many colonists who ignored their professions of loyalty. Gookin wrote the "Sufferings" in the immediate aftermath of King Philip's War (1675–76), during which his concern for the Christian Indians had nearly resulted in his being drowned by a hostile group of colonists. A year or two later, he was at work on a more politically correct manuscript, a "Narrative of troubles with the Manquaoy Indians" (title supplied). Gookin shared each of these manuscripts with Robert Boyle, the governor of the New England Company, expecting no doubt that Boyle would arrange for them to be printed in England. For the "Narrative" he tried harder. John Eliot wrote to Robert Boyle in November 1680 reporting that "We are in great affliction by the Mauquaoy Indians" and that their recent attacks were recorded in "a narrative whereof major Gookin presented to lord Culpepper, who was affected with it. Also he presented a copy thereof to Sir Edmund Andros, who was likewise affected with it, though it is said, that he might have prevented it." Eliot noted, too, that "Major Gookin intendeth to present your honour with a copy of the same narrative." One by one these manuscripts disappeared until rediscovered a century or more later, when copies with an English provenance came to light.[48]

Other colonists were more fortunate, though not always in their lifetime.

After someone with a reputation for writing (or preaching) died, a friend or family member may have rummaged for a manuscript worth publishing. Shortly after the death of Thomas Shepard II, the minister in Charlestown, another minister wrote Increase Mather wondering "whither he [Shepard] had any thing provided for the presse. I hope his friends wil not be wanting to search, that so if there be, right may be done both to him and to the world."[49] Certainly there was no prejudice within the Boston book trade against manuscripts by writers who had died, including manuscripts that had lain unattended for many years. The most delayed may have been a sermon John Cotton preached in Salem in June 1636, published finally in 1713. John Davenport's *The Power of Congregational Churches Asserted and Vindicated, In Answer to a Treatise of Mr. J. Paget,* printed in London in 1672 two years after Davenport died, appeared long after he had tangled with Paget while both were living in the Netherlands; according to the "M.N." who signed the preface, it would have been published in the 1650s had a manuscript Davenport sent to London not gone to the bottom of the sea in a shipwreck.[50] These were among the extremes. For living authors, delays were also a fact of life, some of them intentional, as when Increase Mather held back his fiery election sermon of 1677 from immediate publication or gradually put together a collection of sermons printed more than ten years after they were preached. Whatever the interval, these episodes remind us that editors, readers, and booksellers regarded some texts as untainted by time. Theme or genre mattered more than when a text had actually been written.[51]

Truth be told, the local book trade—the printing office set up in Cambridge in 1639 (strengthened in 1660 when a second printer and a second press arrived from England), followed by the transfer of a press to Boston in 1674 and the emergence of Boston-based bookselling as a profitable enterprise—lacked the means of printing substantial books until the ambitious John Foster, the second person to operate a printing office in Boston, began to do so. How he managed financially is unknown, for the necessary capital remained in short supply and any merchant who financed a substantial book was likely to lose on the deal, as the Boston merchant John Usher did when he paid for the printing of the 1672 Massachusetts laws, only to find that most copies remained unsold. Before 1660, the Cambridge printer Samuel Green limited himself to government-related publications, the annual almanac, a local translation of the Psalms, a few short catechisms, and not much else unless a subsidy was provided, as it was by the town of Dorchester for a sermon series by the town minister Richard Mather. By the 1690s the Boston trade had learned to spread the costs of printing a book among two or more printers. Another means of reducing the expense of reprinting important English books was to squeeze them into fewer pages by using a small size of type and shrinking the margins on the page.[52] By this time, too, the potential reading public was three or four times greater than what it had been in 1650. Even so, second printings were rare and the pace of sales was slow. As Hugh Amory has shown, some locally printed books remained "in print" (probably as unbound sheets) for a decade or more, and the broadside "Capital Laws" of 1642 may still have been available forty years later. Nor did local authors expect any return on their books other than a fistful of copies, most of which they gave away. Booksellers also imported books from England, though for any single title the quantities were usually quite small. The English bookseller who printed Cotton Mather's *The Christian Philosopher* in 1721 sent a mere hundred copies to Boston, apparently in line with what Mather thought the book would sell. These constraints explain why so much of what Mather published—and he published prodigiously—consisted of unbound pamphlet-length sermons, printed in perhaps two or three hundred copies and distributed as much by Mather or a sponsor as by the commercial trade.[53] If the slow-developing capacities of the local trade stood in the way of writers before 1660, even in 1700 they fell far short of what the London trade could accomplish.

The London trade had its own problems, which included overproduction, financial constraints, piracy, and attempts at regulation by the Crown or Parliament. For the colonists who sent their manuscripts to London, its advantages were two: the ability to print larger books, and the presence of booksellers who sympathized with Puritan politics and divinity, as happened especially during the 1640s and 1650s. The Protestant radicals who burst into view could count on Giles Calvert to publish much of what they wrote, and the orthodox colonists turned to Matthew Simmons and Andrew Crooke, among others. At century's end and on into the eighteenth century, booksellers who themselves were Nonconformists played a large role in Cotton Mather's career. In one respect, however, the local trade was better off than its imperial competitor and ally. There, a system of monopolies dating back to the late sixteenth century confined certain kinds of profitable books to a single printer or site (e.g., Oxford), and a system of partnerships or "congers" controlled others, such as broadside ballads and chapbooks. Moreover, the English trade relied on the principle of "rights to copy" that allowed a particular bookseller or printer to own, as it were, a manuscript. Trading these rights was a routine practice. So was piracy, or surreptitious printing of a book controlled by someone else.

None of these practices mattered to the colonists, for no guild or civil state acted either to create rights to copy or to enforce such rights, the one exception being the Massachusetts *Laws* of 1672, which the government entrusted exclusively to John Usher. The history of the First Folio of Shakespeare's plays is inexplicable except in terms of rights to copy, but no New England text had a similar history, for rights to copy and its obverse, piracy, though necessary means within the English trade of protecting (or illicitly appropriating) the commercial value of a book, were pointless on this side of the Atlantic. In a small way, therefore, the New England trade operated more freely than its English counterpart.

On both sides of the Atlantic the civil state intervened to control what was printed. A fuller account of why civil and religious authorities fretted about writers and the book trade follows in Chapter 5. Preliminary to that discussion, it is worth emphasizing that censorship—or better, licensing—curtailed but never eliminated the possibilities for evasion, which were several—underground or surreptitious printing, the circulation of handwritten copies, the practice of coded writing, and in New England, turning to printers who worked elsewhere, as Roger Williams and Samuel Gorton did when they carried their manuscripts to London to be printed. Because of these possibilities, censorship had some effect on *where* a book was printed and possibly on *how* a particular text was fashioned (or re-edited by someone), but little on the overall currency of writing and text-making.[54]

As in England, so among the colonists the practice of censorship would gradually shift from confrontation between writers and the civil state to something more like a process of negotiation, with juries less willing to convict those accused of libel and the civil state backing off from corporal punishment. This is what happened in 1700 when the organizers of a new church in Boston approached the only printer about publishing a defense of their controversial plan of organization, which Increase Mather had publicly (although anonymously) attacked in a printed book. Bartholomew Green, who had "Printed very privately" a "Manifesto" written by the organizers, responded like the businessman he was, discussing with them the number of "Copies and Price" and informing them that "Three Sheets of Paper might contain it," though he added that the job would have to wait until he had finished a project already in press. Thereafter, each side disputed why he changed his mind and declined to print the manuscript. In Green's version, he became uneasy "when they insisted upon doing it with Secrecy, [for] I considered that for ought I knew, Good men in the Country might be Offended at it." To cover himself, he decided to ask the advice of the lieutenant governor. In his defense he also pointed out that it was not "a new thing" for writers to "shew Copies to the Lieutenant Governour," specifying a book by Samuel Sewall. The organizers had their cake and ate it too: with their book safely printed in New York, they could twit Green and the Mathers, informing their readers in an opening "Advertisement" that "the Press in Boston is so much under aw of the Reverend Author" that they had to look elsewhere for a printer," and rubbing more salt into the Mathers' wounds by remarking that "it was a shame to so worthy a minister as Mr. [Solomon] Stoddard must send so far as England to have his Book printed, when young Mr. Mather had the press at his pleasure." Within a few years, however, Stoddard and the Brattle Street group were regular customers of Green and his successors.[55]

To return one more time to the question, what moved people to write, a final part of the answer is that some were encouraged to do so by friends and patrons. Early on, in the 1630s, the minister Hugh Peter was suggesting that John Cotton write a "new book of martyrs, to begin where the other had left off." In the mid-1640s, the ministers agreed to share the task of responding to English critics of the "Congregational Way," and in 1656, at a moment when the immigrant generation was worried about passing on its ideals and experiences to the next, the Commissioners of the United Colonies suggested that someone collect the "most remarkable passages of Gods Providence" among the colonists in order that future generations would "trewly understand the maine ends and aimes proposed in our Transmigration hither from our Dear Native Countrey and the great thinges that god hath heere done for theire fathers."[56] In this decade, too, the Massachusetts General Court asked John Norton to answer the slightly heterodox William Pynchon, and awarded him copies of his book for doing so. At the close of the 1660s, the Plymouth Colony government financed the publication of Morton's *New Englands Memoriall*, and by the 1670s, whoever preached the annual Massachusetts election sermon in May could expect that the General Court would order it printed. The same would happen with election sermons in Connecticut, where the government also commissioned two men in 1694 to reply to a critique of the colony.[57] After mid-century and especially toward the century's close, private societies, ministerial associations (the first to be founded was the Cambridge Association in 1690), congregations, and families were

commissioning catechisms, sermons and elegies or sponsoring a favorite minister's sermon series.[58] During these decades, an informal network of writers
and would-be writers gathered around Increase Mather and his son Cotton,
who shared the ministry of Second Church Boston. Encouraging each other
to write on behalf of practices like renewal of covenant and sometimes sharing manuscripts, this network also included people who participated in a
short-lived "philosophical society" that Increase helped to convene in 1683.[59]

Everyone who became a writer in seventeenth-century New England was
sensible of the circumstances, at once political, economic, and social, that
affected publication in either of the two technologies at hand. Everyone realized that what he or she wrote would pass into the hands of intermediaries
who did the work of producing the physical text and correcting the errata.
Everyone knew of the risk that a text would be refused a license or condemned in some other manner, as in being publicly burned. Yet the mundane
and material aspects of publishing co-existed with a high opinion of writing;
if the former could discourage, the latter could entice.

* * *

Text-making in early New England was heterogeneous and provisional, made
so by the politics that impinged on every act of writing and the possibility
that someone—printer, bookseller, copyist, proofreader, editor, writer—
would continue to make changes in a manuscript or the current version of a
printed book. For these reasons, a writer's voice could fluctuate within the
compass of a single text and, more certainly, from one act of writing to the
next. Yet the history of writing among the colonists must take account of a
particular understanding of author and reader that guided many of the people
who wrote.

As imagined by the colonists, the power of writing was closely associated
with a high opinion of authorship, which in turn was associated with the
three persons of the Trinity. The opening sentence of Cotton Mather's *Magnalia Christi Americana* (London, 1702) builds on these associations, initially
by associating Mather and his great book with Virgil's epic story of the
founding of Rome, the *Aeneid*. Thereafter, Mather shifted to a radically different understanding of authorship and writing: "I write the Wonders of the
Christian Religion, flying from the Depravations of Europe, to the American
Strand: And, assisted by the Holy Author of that Religion, I do, with all
Conscience of Truth, required therein by Him, who is the Truth it self,

Report the Wonderful Displays of His Infinite Power . . . wherewith His Divine Providence hath Irradiated an Indian Wilderness."[60] Representing God as the original author on whom all Christian writers depend for assistance, Mather pictures divine speech as "truth" that the godly writer is to reiterate, the end being to reveal—and of more importance, to participate in—the Almighty's "infinite Power." The *Magnalia* was also mundane, a product of negotiations and interventions at odds with the aura of epic, divine truth, and "infinite Power." Many of its readers would have realized that Mather had imported a host of official documents and texts by other writers into his book; Mather the author was also Mather the compiler and editor. Although he surely hoped that his writing had some of the qualities of the divine Word, any aura of this kind was contaminated by the everyday politics that shaped so much of the text. Mather as vehicle for the Spirit was also Mather the local partisan.

Leaving to another chapter the details of that partisanship and of how the *Magnalia* came to be, we recognize in Mather's opening evocation of God as author a perspective on authorship and writing of great importance to the colonists. Taking Scripture as their model, the colonists assumed that divine communication originated as speech (the Word) before it was written down. Divine speech was self-authenticating, its truth confirmed by the very power of the Word as witnessed in human history. The opening words of the *Magnalia* imply the possibility that human speech and writing can have the same qualities; Mather as author can speak the truth, and the truth will work astonishing effects. If God spoke through human authors, human authors could import God's own voice into what they wrote, as the poet-minister Michael Wigglesworth did in a handwritten poem where, to indicate the difference between divine and human speech, he enlarged the lines in which God speaks.[61] Given this association between the human and the divine, writing was less an "art" than a means of communicating "useful" truths that, by definition, were uniquely powerful.

Whatever the genre or material form that the godly favored, writing was always "practical," animated by the goal of speaking directly to the human situation. What made it practical was a premise of theology, that God had commissioned intermediaries—"ambassadors," in seventeenth-century parlance—to offer sinners the promise of salvation, a promise that, if acted on, could transform them into children of the kingdom. The purpose of writing was thus to bring about a singular form of experience, the "work of grace" that every sermon and sermon series outlined in detail and lay testimonies reiterated. The purpose of writing was also to celebrate the majesty of God and his "wonder-working providence," to borrow the title of Edward Johnson's history of New England. It served too as a means of devotion, recording the recurrent exercises of prayer and self-examination and modeling these exercises for others to emulate. At certain moments writing passed into prophecy, not in the sense of foretelling the future but of deploying Scripture to rebuke the wayward and rally the saints against their enemies. Prophecy looked ahead to the coming kingdom even as it simultaneously evoked the "first times" when early Christianity was uncorrupted. Always, godly writing proceeded from a heightened sense of difference: between truth and error, between saints or martyrs and those who persecuted them, between Christ and Satan, between "real" Christians and those who were mere hypocrites. Limning these differences, the godly writer summed readers to take sides.

A leitmotif of the vernacular tradition was plainness.[62] To write in the plain style was to do much more than avoid certain stylistic features practiced elsewhere. In the first instance, it was to look to Jesus as exemplar, Jesus the unlearned man who always used the "humble style," a language "easy and plain" for all who encountered it. Plainness shortened the distance between text (speaker) and audience. Plainness was also a matter of delivering the right message, and of wanting to be useful. As Increase Mather remarked of his father Richard, "His way of Preaching was plain, aiming to shoot his Arrows not over his peoples heads, but into their Hearts and Consciences." Always, the truth was plain in the sense of being self-evident (though denied by the wicked and sinful). Conflating plainness and truth, Samuel Willard, the minister of Third Church Boston, declared in 1700 that his purpose in preaching "was to accommodate it to the meanest hearer . . . and I hope these truths will relish never the worse to those that love truth for its own sake, because they are not garnished with florid language."[63]

But the most important aspect of godly authorship was its dependence on the Holy Spirit, with the faith of the writer serving as the Spirit's instrument. Without these, writing was hollow, ineffectual, mere show. Infused with the Spirit, writers could brush past the hierarchies that "the world" customarily associated with authorship. "It is true, I am a yong man and noe Scoller, according to that which the world counts Scollership," the young English radical John Lilburne declared in 1638 from the platform where he was about to undergo public punishment, "yet I have obtained mercie of the Lord to be faithfull, and hee by a divine providence hath brought me hither this day, and I speak to you in the name of the Lord, being assisted with the spirit and power of the God of Heaven and earth." Lilburne pressed on, his claims ever more emphatic. He had "desired [God] that he would direct and enable me to speake that which might be for his glory and the good of his people, And as I am a Souldier fighting under the banner of the great and mightie Captaine the Lord Jesus Christ, and as I looke for that Crowne of immortality . . . I dare not hold my peace, but speake unto you with boldnes in the might and strength of my God, the things which the Lord in mercy hath made knowne unto my Soule, come life come death."[64] Every colonial writer would have agreed with Lilburne that God acting through the Spirit empowered some to speak for him. So John Wilson II declared of his father, the John who immigrated to New England in the 1630s, in an introduction to a new printing (Boston, 1680) of *Song of Deliverance* (London, 1626) presenting to the "Christian Reader" "this heavenly Song, Endited by him, or rather the holy Spirit of God unto him many years agoe." And like Lilburne, the Connecticut minister James Fitch represented himself as "a poore instrument" to care for "our people and their posteritie," a "vaine and vile nothing" who nonetheless had been introduced to "the mysteries of the doctrine of Godlines" that he was sharing with readers in a printed book.[65]

Readers were always a presence in descriptions of godly writing, for every text in the vernacular tradition was, as Lilburne indicated, produced for "the good of [God's] people." In keeping with this rule, Wilson's son insisted on particularizing the benefits of his father's verse: "o how excellent was the matter contained in the same, being full of Direction, Correction, and Consolation, suiting much unto spiritual Edification. What Volumns hath he penned for the help of others in their several changes of condition . . . How was his heart full of good matter? He was another sweet singer of Israel, whoss heavenly Verses passed like to the handkerchief carryed from Paul to help and uphold disconsolate ones, and to heal their wracked Souls, by the effectual prisence of Gods holy Spirit." Here, as in many other prefaces, writers evoked the close connections between writing, reading and religious devotion, laying out a right way of reading that was mirrored in the very arrangement of a text and, in principle, in how devotion was performed. The printed word may have been mere ink on paper, but to a reader's "teachable heart" it was something else: "read it over with a teachable heart," Thomas Cobbet counseled readers of his treatise on the family, "and thou maiest find (I trust, through grace) some peculiar blessing superadded by the Lord, even upon this discourse also."[66] Like the transformations wrought by speech and writing, the wonders that reading could perform were visible evidence that author, manuscript, and print participated in the authority of the Holy Spirit.

Important in their own right for understanding the practices of text-making that is described in succeeding chapters, these representations of author and reader do not fit easily within the paradigm of indeterminacy that animates recent interpretations of the English Renaissance. Central to that paradigm is the argument that the workings of the book trade, together with the many other interventions that figured in the transmitting of texts, severely compromised the authority of the author. A text that was indeterminate was a text that had parted company with an author's intentions as embodied in a putative original. Useful as this mode of reasoning is for understanding the transmission of canonical texts in the seventeenth century, it ignores the possibility that authority had an entirely different meaning for anyone working within the framework of the Protestant vernacular tradition and, for that matter, any writer who eschewed the practices and values associated with canonicity. Almost to a person, the colonists would have insisted that the most important aspect of authority was whether writing or speech served the truth: did it bring home to the "teachable heart" the possibility of redemption, did it nurture the righteousness that bound a covenanted people together? Accuracy in transmission took second place to these goals, as did originality. To romantic writers of the early nineteenth century, originality meant being unique or singular; to writers within the vernacular tradition it signified the priority of the Word as source of uncontaminated truth and therefore model for authentic speech and writing.[67] To write well within the vernacular tradition was to subordinate one's self to the discipline of the Word and the authority of the Spirit. As two English ministers attested in a preface to John Davenport's *The Saints Anchor-Hold* (London, 1661), "the Text" had been "written by the finger of God" in his "heart . . . befor the Discourse was Penned by his own hand." [68] For the colonists, therefore, the practices and meanings associated with writing, and even more emphatically, with "literature," were different from, indeed in opposition to, the practices and meanings on which other writers of their day depended.

Notwithstanding the centrality of the vernacular tradition, the colonists employed other forms of writing, each with its own version of authority and authorship. Accuracy of a more literal kind was expected of official documents that were crucial to the functioning of civil or secular society: charters, proclamations, collections of laws, town and colony records, wills, depositions, deeds, and the like. The clerks who had the responsibility of preparing many of these documents took their task seriously; anyone who fudged was promptly punished.[69] Accuracy in certain kinds of printed documents also mattered, so much so that Edward Winslow arranged for a fresh printing of *A Platform of Discipline Gathered out of the word* (1653) to replace a badly done printing of 1652. Only on a few occasions were colonial writers able to correct the proofs of a book being printed in London, and when they could not, their response was often one of dismay. The passage from handwritten manuscript to printed page, or from one printed book to another, made for anxieties that Increase Mather tried to allay for the texts he incorporated into *The First Principles of New-England* (Cambridge, 1675): "if any should have Scruples about the truth thereof, they may easily in part satisfy themselves, by having recourse to the printed Books out of which these passages are faithfully excerp[t]ed. And as for those things which are (as most of the subsequent Collection is) taken from Manuscripts, I have by me the Original Scripts," which he offered to "shew . . . unto such . . . as shall hesitate touching the Fidelity of this publication."[70] Early on, factual accuracy mattered in how the conditions of life in the new world were described to prospective immigrants and in how the calendars in each yearly almanac were constructed. Another version of accuracy guided (albeit in tension with aesthetics) the translation of the Hebrew Psalms into English: "Gods altar needs not our pollishings." These examples bring home a simple truth: that text-making among the colonists and their English contemporaries cannot be divorced from intentionalities of several kinds, each of them linked to expectations of accuracy and authority.

Any history of text-making among the colonists must take seriously the distinctive features of the vernacular tradition and its consequences for the social history of writing and the transmission of texts. To this task I conjoin the purpose of exposing the anxieties that abound in prefaces and letters about the transmission of texts, and to detailing the processes of text-making that account for these anxieties. Despite the important ways in which the vernacular tradition resisted (or ignored) the uncertainties of provenance, attribution, and authority, the history of text-making in seventeenth-century New England cannot be understood apart from them.[71]

CHAPTER TWO

Not in Print yet Published

The Practice of Scribal Publication

JOHN WINTHROP may be the most cited of our seventeenth-century New England writers, evoked time and again because of his indispensable journal and evoked even more frequently for having declared of the new colony he was helping to found, "we shall be as a city upon a hill." A sentence that many of us can quote was, however, a sentence very few of the colonists would have encountered, for the text in which it appears, the "Modell of Christian Charitie," was never printed in the seventeenth century.[1] Although he shared his journal with a few friends, it became widely known after being printed for the first time in 1790. When he died in 1649, his name had yet to appear on the title page of any printed book or pamphlet, though his was one of several names appended to *The Humble Request* (1630), issued anonymously in London as the Winthrop fleet set sail for New England, and probably written by someone whose name was not listed.[2] Retrospectively, he has been credited with a book of documents and commentary relating to the Antinomian controversy of 1636–37, *A Short Story of the Rise, reign, and ruine of the Antinomians, Familists & Libertines*, printed in London in 1644 without any attribution on the title page. But this was not a book he wrote, or so I argue at a later point in this chapter.

Nonetheless, Winthrop was a published author once the meaning of publication is extended to encompass handwritten copies. Manuscript versions of the "Modell," together with some of his letters, were circulating in the 1630s and 1640s, and texts of his were still being distributed in handwritten copies in the early eighteenth century, for in 1714 the Boston-based magistrate Samuel Sewall asked a colonist then living in London to provide an English acquaintance with a copy of "Gov. Winthrop's Notes of the Election [of] 1637."[3] The earliest of Winthrop's writings to be published in this manner was probably a statement of reasons for immigrating to New England he drafted in 1629. The next in order was the "Modell," for an English friend of Winthrop's son John Jr., was soliciting the text in 1635, a request that is understandable only if it had previously been available in England. (Which is to say, Winthrop did not dash it off on board the *Arbella*.) Four years later, Roger Williams was thanking Winthrop for another text, a "relation" of the "monster birth" that Mary Dyer had tried to conceal; and, as reported in his journal, Winthrop arranged in 1643 for a political statement of his to be "published," that is, distributed and made public in handwritten copies.[4]

Winthrop may seem unusual for having published entirely in this manner. But once we seek out other texts that circulated in scribal copies or as authorial originals, his can be recognized as a common practice, so much so that in any history of text-making among the colonists, scribal publication deserves a central place.[5] A few examples must suffice; a fuller inventory follows.[6] Colonial governments resorted to the technology as a means of providing statute laws for local communities. Thus in 1649 the General Court of New Haven Colony was distributing the "Capitall and all other laws and orders made at the last Generall Court" to each town. Nine years later, the Plymouth Colony government ordered that "every township" be sent a handwritten copy of "a booke of the lawes of the Collonie."[7] Earlier, in 1641, the Massachusetts government had paid for nineteen manuscript copies of the "Body of Liberties," one for each town with a few left over for the magistrates.[8] After a small group of ministers drafted a "Model of Church and Civil Power" in 1634, and again in 1657 after a larger group had agreed on how to answer twenty-one questions about church membership, the respective documents circulated as handwritten copies, enough of the latter in Connecticut so that each church could have one.[9] A critic of the Salem witch hunt of 1692 shared his doubts in a handwritten letter, and Cotton Mather defended the charter of 1691 in "fables" he distributed in this manner.[10] Far from being unusual, scribal publication was an everyday event in seventeenth-century New England.

Winthrop and the many other colonists who employed this technology were not frustrated suitors of the trade in printed books. Like their English contemporaries, they recognized the quotidian utility of scribal publication and its advantages in particular situations. Not yet enclosed within modern—day assumptions about the "revolutionary" significance of printing and its eclipse of the manuscript tradition, the colonists were familiar with "books" that contained both printing *and* handwriting—for example, printed books ending in blank pages to be filled with handwritten information, or printed almanacs interleaved with blank pages so readers could make entries of their own devising, artifacts that in their materiality implied that printing was an extension of handwriting, not something radically different. In everyday experience, moreover, people encountered texts that passed back and forth between printing and handwriting, as often happened with elegies and proclamations and, less commonly, when someone filled out the missing pages in a printed book with handwritten text or preserved a poem by copying it into endpapers. But mainly the colonists experienced scribal publication on its own terms as the technology best suited for certain forms of writing or communication, a technology that also owed some of its significance to the complex meanings of "private" and "public."

Mingled though they were, and with printing understood as preferable in certain situations, the two technologies continued to function side by side throughout the seventeenth century. What, then, was utilitarian about scribal publication? We approach a sensible answer to this question if we bear in mind that the practice of writing in early New England was closely bound up with the practice of speaking, and remember as well that local printers never issued any of the thousands of sermons preached in the 1630s, 1640s, and 1650s except for Richard Mather's *Summe of Certain Sermons* (1652) and his *Farewel Exhortation* (1657). A greater share of sermons preached in the second half of the century were printed, but most were preserved, if preserved at all, in auditors' handwritten notes that lay colonists treated with as much care as they did any printed books they owned, binding them up and using them in meetings such as the one Anne Hutchinson convened in her Boston home in the mid-1630s to discuss the previous week's sermons.[11] Letters were always handwritten, their importance as a means of distributing information or responding to questions underscored by the frequency with which they were copied and recopied as they wound their way through a circuit of readers.[12] And, as this chapter demonstrates, handwriting was the technology of choice for other kinds of texts. Poetry was a major case in point, as were the texts that emerged from the workings of civil government—proclamations, letters, charters, patents, wills, legal forms, and bills of credit (or what would eventually become known as "paper money").[13] For all of these, manuscript reproduction was more expedient, and may have been regarded as more reliable, than relying on the local printer, and only in Massachusetts was such a person on hand until early in the eighteenth century.

Making copies by hand was utilitarian in another respect, a means of distributing a text that was meant for a select group of readers. Most of the poetry the colonists were writing was directed to families and friends. Cotton Mather intended his "Fables" only for a small circle of allies, and Richard Mather and John Davenport had a select readership in mind when they sent descriptions of an experiment in church government, the "Congregational Way," to England in the late 1630s. Making handwritten copies could also be a safer means of sharing a text that would frighten the authorities. John Stubbs's *Discoverie of a Gaping Gap* (1579) so angered Elizabeth I that she had the printed book condemned and Stubbs's right hand cut off. Yet it continued to circulate in handwritten copies, as did other printed texts the government suppressed.[14] Like the Lollards before them, the "Antinomian" underground in early seventeenth-century England relied on handwritten copies of certain texts.[15] Less agreeably to authors, handwritten copies were also an expedient means of sharing a text that may *not* have been intended for distribution. John Cotton repeatedly complained that unsanctioned copies were circulating of what he wrote, and some of Anne Bradstreet's poetry escaped from her control in this manner.

A fuller understanding of the versatility of scribal publication must wait on knowing more about the range of texts that the colonists were publishing. So too, we need to know more about the contexts in which the practice flourished. Much of this chapter is concerned with providing such information. Another purpose is to extend to scribal publication several of the questions that animate the rethinking of printed texts that proceeds apace in studies of the English Renaissance. What uncertainties of attribution and authenticity arose within the realm of scribal publication? Who prepared manuscript copies or arranged for their transmission, and what role did these intermediaries play in the shaping of texts? Did scribal publication function as a means of articulating illicit or controversial opinions that otherwise would have been censored or suppressed?[16] And how should we understand the major writers who confined themselves to this technology, as Winthrop and his great contemporary William Bradford did?

* * *

These questions return us to the commerce, culture, and materiality of scribal publication. Before the "invention" of printing in the mid-fifteenth century, handwriting was the only means of making copies and transmitting texts. In 1400 English booksellers stocked and sold manuscript books of different sizes, subjects, and material qualities just as, a century later, they were selling various kinds of printed books. So too, at the beginning of that century the professional scrivener or clerk was playing the role that printers would eventually assume. But by the time of the great migration to New England, the commercial trade in books had become, almost universally, a trade in printed matter. Only a few categories of handwritten texts, such as newsletters and political "separates," had any commercial value in England, and fewer still would have a cash value in New England, a rare example being the newsletters that the Boston postmaster John Campbell was preparing at the debut of the eighteenth century.[17] Once this transition had occurred, the most important provocation or context for handwritten texts may have been the "scribal community" of readers (or users) that shared in the production and distribution of manuscript copies.[18] A social context of this kind is almost a defining feature of scribal publication—almost but not quite, because many printed texts were also associated with patrons or specific groups of readers. But the connections between text and social context were much more immediate in the world of handwritten texts.

Any text that existed in one or more handwritten copies can be considered published. This definition encompasses a text in an author's handwriting that he shared with others as well as what Harold Love has named "user" publication, the making of copies (perhaps no more than one) by someone else. Love has also called attention to "entrepreneurial" publishing of scribal texts in seventeenth-century England, newsletters being an obvious example; and to this tripartite scheme we can add (as he would do himself) the civil government and, for New England, congregations and synods, as producer-publishers.[19] Any inventory must include texts that, at some point in the seventeenth century, passed into print, together with handwritten copies of texts that initially were printed and those that were preserved in commonplace books or other sites of record-keeping, for as Love and others have pointed out, private record-keeping of a kind we might classify as "antiquarian" was a practice charged with political significance.[20]

Making handwritten copies was slow going and expensive if done by scriveners, as frequently happened in England. No one in early New England made this task easier by using a writing machine of the kind that, more than a century later, Thomas Jefferson would employ, and it was uncommon for anyone who took notes on sermons or political debates to employ short-hand.[21] Clerks and secretaries labored on behalf of colony and county govern-ments preparing copies of statute laws, legal forms, proclamations, and the like, but we know next to nothing of how these men were trained or their work practices. A professional scrivener was plying his trade in Boston in the late 1630s and early 1640s, the Boston minister John Cotton relied on young men living in his household to make copies of his letters, and on two occa-sions John Higginson, a young minister-to-be, was employed to make copies of manuscripts and keep track of public debates.[22]

As for costs and quantities, the little specific information we have is entirely for texts that a civil government wanted to distribute. En route to preparing the "Body of Liberties" that was formally adopted in 1641, the Massachusetts government asked Thomas Lechford, a Boston-based scriv-ener, to prepare "12 Coppies of the said Lawes" and related texts so that discussion of them could take place in each town. For another set of five, Lechford charged the government twelve shillings sixpence, and for copies of the freeman's oath, sixpence a piece.[23] As more towns were founded and as county courts were organized, a larger quantity of the annual sessions laws was undoubtedly required. Any enumeration must be speculative, especially in reckoning with copies made for their own use by individuals of letters and broadside verse that came their way. The letter of spiritual counsel that Jo-seph Eliot wrote his brother in 1664 seems to have circulated in this manner, for the five handwritten copies that the antiquarian Thomas Prince had seen in the early eighteenth century were almost certainly copies of a copy, and but a fraction of the total that probably had been made in the course of seventy years. Any calculations of quantity must also take into account the work that a text was supposed to do. John Cotton wanted a letter he wrote Samuel Skelton in 1630 to circulate as widely as possible, as indeed it seems to have done,[24] just as the Massachusetts General Court wanted every adult in the colony to know what laws were in force. But for many other texts, the intended audience was far smaller—for example, a son or daughter or every-one in a family.

The distribution of handwritten texts varied with the genre of the text itself, the writer's social world, and the political context. In England, hand-written copies tended to circulate within coteries or connections defined by patronage, education, aspirations as a writer and reader of literature, or some common interest, usually political or religious.[25] Within these milieu a text could circulate widely, as happened, for example, with an apologia written by the Jesuit Edmund Campion shortly after he arrived in England in 1580, whereof "many copies were taken . . . in a small time" from the single copy Campion had entrusted to a "friend."[26] The social world of the colonists was unlike the English in two key respects. No religious or political underground of the kind that formed around English Catholics and radical Protestants existed on this side of the Atlantic, and no coterie patronized the writing of poetry or other literary genres. Something of this sort would emerge in colonial cities, including Boston, in the early eighteenth century, but in the seventeenth century there were no equivalents of the patrons and collectors who, in England, appreciated and preserved the poetry of Sidney, Donne, and many others. This said, the continuities are many, for handwritten texts usually circulated within networks of friends and relatives, clergy and church members, office holders in colony and town governments, college students, and transatlantic religious connections such as Quakers and Nonconformists.

These ways of distributing a text were not as constrained as, at first glance, they might seem to be. A small number of copies or even a single exemplar could reach a significant audience. John Cotton's account of the distribution of a letter of his is paradigmatic: "Little did I think, that a private letter of mine written to a very friend, should ever have been divulged abroad. But it seemeth some got copies of it; and in process of time, one copy multiplied another."[27] Nathaniel Briscoe's "book against" the taxing of non-church members for the support of the ministry "occasioned much stir in" Watertown, where he lived, though in all likelihood he or an ally made but one or two copies. When Winthrop responded in 1643 to popular protests against the government's welcoming of the French Catholic adventurer Charles La Tour, his handwritten defense "satisfied many." And when Cotton addressed the congregation of the Salem church in 1636, he remarked that "many" of them had copies or knew of a letter he had written in 1630 to the congregation's founding minister.[28] Copied and recopied, passed from hand to hand, mentioned in conversations and the stuff of rumor, texts had a currency that exceeded the specific number of copies.

Thanks to letters and diaries, a few of these networks emerge from the shadows of time. The international correspondence of Increase Mather, whose base was Boston but who lived in London between 1687 and 1691, reveals him in his capacity as compiler of "wonder" stories he solicited for the book that became *An Essay for the Recording of Illustrious Providences* (Boston, 1684); several years earlier, he had relied on local connections for manuscripts he incorporated into the histories he wrote of warfare with the Indians and his defense of a controversial policy concerning access to baptism, *The First Principles of New-England* (Cambridge, 1675).[29] Another network formed around the Boston merchant and office-holder Samuel Sewall. Through his household passed poetry, theological statements, extracts from Winthrop's manuscript journal, copies of letters containing news of various kinds, proclamations, and essays on contested issues in politics and religion. Friendships accounted for some of this influx, as when the Northampton minister Solomon Stoddard sent him manuscripts "with license for me to do with them what I pleased." Meanwhile Sewall was sharing verse of his own composition with friends in Connecticut and Massachusetts and recirculating the verse of others, some of which he preserved in a notebook.[30] Still·other networks spanned the Atlantic: in the 1630s, with supporters and sympathizers of the Massachusetts Bay Company; in that decade and for the remainder of the century with like-minded Nonconformists in England; and by the 1690s, with "natural philosophers" gathered around the Royal Society.[31] After 1660, and especially after 1675, the ever thickening presence of Crown-appointed officials brought into being another network that relied on manuscript copies of instructions from London and reports of affairs in New England such as Edward Randolph's "An answer to severall heads of enquiry concerning the present state of New- England" (1676).[32]

Families must also figure in the story, and especially parents. Two of Anne Bradstreet's children, a daughter and son, made copies of her "Meditations," a text she dedicated to her son Simon.[33] For many years Joseph Tompson of Billerica, Massachusetts, copied poems about members of his family into a notebook that he also filled with expressions of his own piety and other kinds of memorials.[34] We cannot trace the passage of Thomas Shepard's "autobiography" (as it was classified in the twentieth century) from his study into the hands of his son Thomas II (Fig. 1) and quite possibly into those of English friends as well, but pass it did, and Cotton Mather would glance at the manuscript in preparing the life of Shepard that appears in the *Magnalia Christi Americana* (London, 1702).[35] Sarah Whipple Goodhue of Ipswich, Massachusetts, addressed her "Monitory and Valedictory Writing," composed during the course of a pregnancy that ended in her death in 1681, to her husband and children.[36] Official or unofficial, family-based or flowing through local and international networks, scribal publication was remarkably commonplace.

But it is possible to be more specific about how this technology was used.

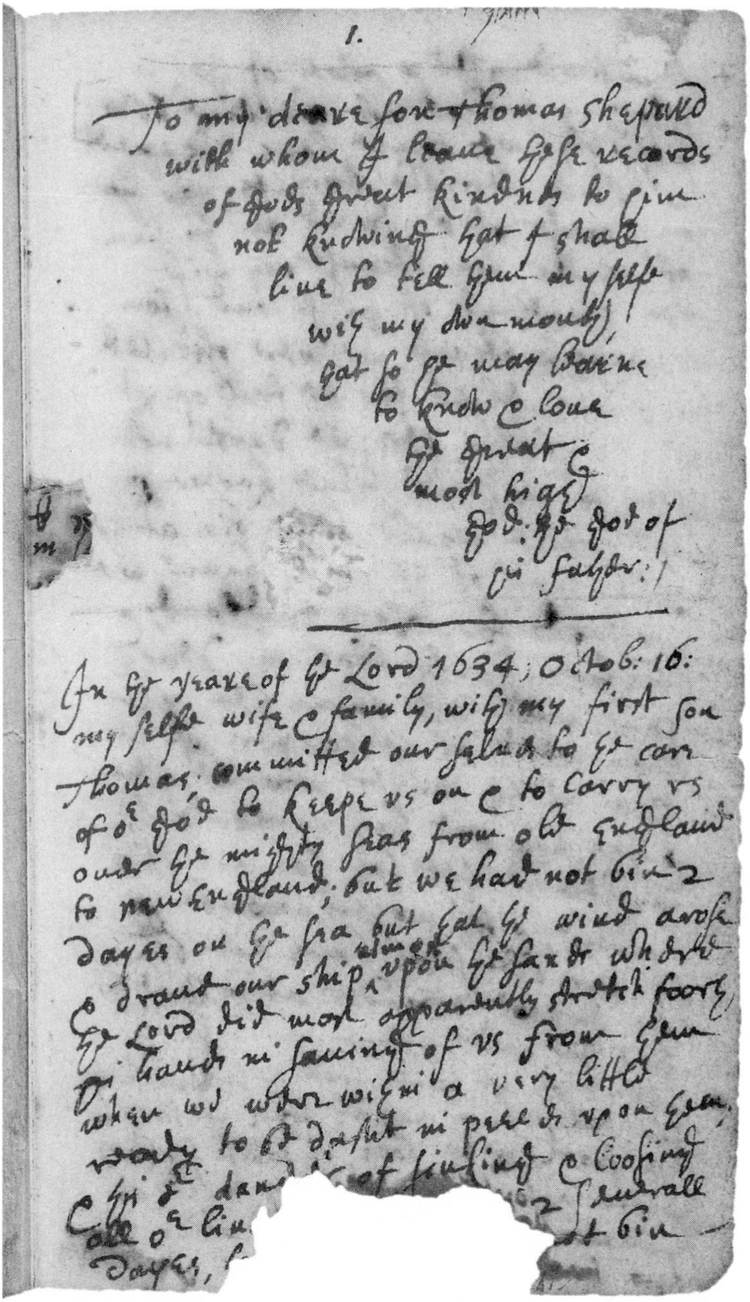
1.

To my deare sonn Thomas Shepard
with whom I leave these records
of Gods great kindnes to him
not knowing that I shall
live to tell them my selfe
with my own mouth
that so he may learne
to know & love
the great &
most high
God: the God of
his father:

In the yeare of the Lord 1634; Octob: 16:
my selfe wife & family, with my first son
Thomas committed our selves to the care
of our God to keepe us on & to carry us
over the mighty seas from old England
to new England; but we had not bin 2
dayes on the sea but that the wind arose
& draue our ship upon the sands where
the Lord did most apparently stretch forth
his hands in saving of us from them
when we were within a very little
ready to be dasht in peeces upon them,
this our danger of sinking & loosing
all our lives ... 2 severall
dayes, ... bin

Figure 1. Thomas Shepard creates a legacy for his son Thomas. "To my dear son Thomas Shepard with whom I leave these records of Gods great kindness to him." Thomas Shepard, Autobiography, bMS Am 1671 (1), Houghton Library, Harvard College Library.

To follow the trail of manuscript publication is to realize, early on, its utility as a vehicle for information about the colonization of New England, and in moments of political and religious controversy. Once the Great Migration began, letters acquired a distinctive significance as the means of conveying to English friends what was happening in the new world and transmitting the reactions of those who stayed at home. Recalling, late in life, the 1630s, the immigrant Joshua Scottow remembered that "a Letter then from New-England, and for a considerable time after, was Venerated as a Sacred Script, or as the Writing of some Holy Prophet, 'twas carried many Miles, where divers came to hear it."[37] Several such letters circulated widely: the minister Francis Higginson's "true relation of the last voyage to New England" (1629), which was read in England by John Winthrop and was being requested by an English correspondent of the Winthrops in 1635; Thomas Dudley's sobering letter to the Lady Bridget, Countess of Lincoln (early 1631), printed in Boston in 1694 from one of the surviving copies; the minister Thomas Weld's letter (1632) to his former parishioners in Terling, Essex, extolling the spiritual and cultural freedom the colonists were experiencing, so widely known that it was copied and preserved by the London joiner Nehemiah Wallington in one of his notebooks; and Anthony Thacher's account of a shipwreck off Pemaquid Point in 1635 and the hazards endured by its survivors, also copied by Wallington in London but surviving as well in the Mather family papers and elsewhere.[38] Letters between the Plymouth colonists and their friends and allies in England and the Netherlands were so important to William Bradford that he preserved them in a letter-book.[39] Immigration accomplished, a few of the colonists undertook to explore the hinterland of New England. Darby Field did so in 1642, traveling as far as the White Mountains, where he climbed the future Mt. Washington, a journey recounted in a "relation at his return" with a sequel, a "more exact version" that Winthrop read.[40]

Immediately, too, people in England were demanding information about the experiments in church government the colonists were undertaking, experiments that had the taint of "Separatism," the much criticized alternative to orthodox Puritanism. Such suspicions led the English minister John White to write in 1629 "The Planters Plea," printed a year later in London after being distributed in manuscript copies. A letter John Cotton sent from England in 1630 to the Salem minister Samuel Skelton protesting his Separatist-like actions circulated widely in manuscript, as demonstrated by the provenance of the copies that survive. The real audience for Cotton's letter was not Skelton but the community of Puritans in England as well as the London merchants and East Anglia gentry who were financing the Massachusetts Bay Company; his was a letter he licensed others to copy, for it was part of a larger campaign to overcome the impression that the immigrants of 1630 were secretly Separatist-minded. In far away Yorkshire, the minister Richard Mather, soon to become an immigrant himself, received a copy of the letter, and another came into the hands of the resolutely anti-Separatist English minister Richard Bernard. By the 1640s yet another copy reached the Scottish Presbyterian Robert Baillie, who, contrary to Cotton's hopes, employed it as evidence that Cotton's own ecclesiology, the "Congregational" or "New England Way," sprang from Separatist stock. As already noted, this well traveled letter circulated on this side of the Atlantic; William Coddington of Rhode Island reported to Cotton in 1641 that he too possessed a copy.[41]

The refashioning of church and state in New England prompted the circulation of many other texts. This trail of publications begins with the earliest effort by the ministers in Massachusetts to clarify the relationship between church and state, "A Model of Church and Civil Power" (1634), reproduced only in handwritten copies, one of which Roger Williams incorporated into *The Bloudy Tenent, of Persecution, for cause of Conscience, discussed* (London, 1644). Similarly, a letter John Cotton wrote in early 1636 to an English minister and another he sent to Williams were transmitted in manuscript until printed in London in 1641 and 1643, respectively.[42] Other texts of these early years remained unpublished, like Richard Mather's "Some Objections against Imposition in Ordination" of 1635. When Mather replied in 1639 to two sets of queries from English ministers, the first a list of thirty-two questions, the second a set of arguments about church covenants, he did so expecting the manuscripts "to be dispersed for the satisfying of all questionists out of desire of the truth." Some years later, his son Nathaniel, then in England, described his father's treatise on covenants as written "for his private use in his own Study." Nathaniel was responding to its being printed in London contrary to Richard Mather's expectations, he "never intending, nor indeed consenting to its publication, nor so much as knowing unto this day how the copy of it came abroad into those hands by whom it was made public."[43] One such intermediary was the future minister of Sudbury, Edmund Browne, who sent a copy of "our churches apology" to an English correspondent.[44] None of the ministers in New England expected the "notes" taken at a 1643 meeting of clergy to be published, but the Scottish Presbyterian Samuel Rutherford did so delightedly in 1644, using a manuscript copy that somehow reached him.[45]

Local controversies were thus a matrix for scribal publication, especially when those controversies had an international significance. When a manuscript relating to these debates began to circulate, no one could control that process, and some abetted it. This lesson learned from the early 1640s, the ministers in New England had a change of heart that we can date to July 1645, when, as reported by John Winthrop, a group that met in Cambridge decided that "writeings" which some of them had prepared "in Answeare" to critics of various persuasions should be "sent over into England to be printed." The one "answer" Winthrop specified was a manuscript Thomas Hooker of Hartford had brought with him, hoping to have it reviewed by his colleagues; a year after his death in 1647 it was published in London as *A Survey of the Summe of Church-Discipline*.[46] So were several others, including Cotton's *The Way of the Congregational Churches Cleared* (London, 1648), and John Norton's *Answer* (London, 1648), both of them attempts to reach a wider audience via printed texts. For the first time, too, the Cambridge printer was given a relevant manuscript to publish, *A Platform of Church Discipline* (1649).

For religious controversies that originated in the colonies, however, scribal publication persisted as a feasible technology. The most significant of these local events was the Antinomian dispute of 1636–38. Erupting before the printing office in Cambridge was up and running, it spawned a slew of texts, all of them published in handwritten copies at the time. Its story follows in detail. The flavor of that controversy lingered on in Dorchester, where the young minister Jonathan Burr was voicing theological opinions in the late 1630s at odds with those of his senior colleague Richard Mather. Under pressure to conform, Burr prepared a statement of his views that "was published." The tensions that beset the Hartford church in the 1650s, when a group of lay people protested the policies of Samuel Stone, the minister, were played out in handwritten texts, as was the intensely political founding in 1669 of Third Church Boston by a group of lay people who withdrew from First Church. Of the many other schisms and debates that arose before 1700 out of efforts to alter the principles of church membership and church government, all but one was confined to manuscript publication.[47] The exception to this rule was the synod of 1662; its story is told in Chapter 5.

To follow the trail of secular or political controversies and the texts that emerged from them would carry us from Israel Stoughton's "book against the Magistrates" of early 1635 (a text we know about because his London-based brother's papers were seized by the government) to Richard Saltonstall's "book . . . wherein the institution of the standing council was pretended to be a sinful innovation" (1642) and, beyond 1660, to a host of texts prompted by the efforts of the English government to enclose the New England colonies within the English empire.[48] That process would also affect how the colonists wrote about King Philip's War, and even more so, the making of texts in the aftermath of an insurrection in Boston of April 1689 that overturned the regime of the royal governor of Massachusetts, Edmund Andros. Both sides—the colonists who returned to power and the administrators associated with Andros—spelled out their arguments against the other in texts that circulated in manuscript before being printed. Thus John Palmer, who had come from England to work with Andros in administering the Dominion of New England, wrote an "Impartial Account" that, as he pointed out in the London-printed edition, circulated in Boston anonymously "in Manuscript, by stealth, branded with the hard Name of a Treasonable and Seditious Libel."[49] But a fuller reckoning with text-making in the context of the imperial situation is reserved for Chapter 5.

Another genre that commonly circulated in manuscript copies before passing into print, as some did after 1695, were stories of religious experience and letters of spiritual counsel. The English precedents include letters that John Foxe incorporated into the *Book of Martyrs* and, in the seventeenth century, the Scottish minister Samuel Rutherford's much-circulated letters of advice.[50] As a young minister in England, Thomas Hooker was called on to heal Joan Drake, an English woman who thought that she had sinned against the Holy Spirit. Almost certainly, the narrative of her "ecstatic conversion" passed within Puritan circles in manuscript before being printed in 1647.[51] The earliest stories of this kind in New England date from 1636 and early 1637. Someone who witnessed the death of Thomas Shepard's wife in February 1636, a few days after she was admitted to membership in the newly organized Cambridge church, recorded her ecstasy at being enclosed within the covenant. Many years later, in 1713, Cotton Mather incorporated the manuscript into one of his briefer sermons, preached at the founding of a new congregation.[52] When Jonathan Mitchell was a student at Harvard College, he advised a brother on how to overcome his spiritual depression. Twenty years later, Mitchell's executors added a copy of his letter of advice to a series of sermons they had prepared for the printer. In the mid-1660s another young minister, Joseph Eliot, wrote *his* brother a letter of counsel that seems to have been copied repeatedly for the next half century until the antiquarian Thomas Prince added it to a new edition of *Mr. Mitchel's Letter to His Brother.*[53] Someone in the family of Mary Clarke Bonner, who died in Cambridge in 1697, wrote down what she was saying to those who gathered around her bed; one copy survives of her shifts of mood—the "Joy" she felt at hearing Christ speak to her, the terror of Satan coming "upon me Like a Lyon."[54]

Spiritual biographies complemented these testimonies of experience. Three of John Cotton's colleagues, John Norton, John Davenport, and John Wilson, honored him with biographies, but Norton's was the only one to be printed; the other two, although known at the time or later, have not survived.[55] Increase incorporated two manuscripts of his father's into *The Life and Death of . . . Richard Mather* (Cambridge, 1670), and Cotton Mather stuffed *Early Piety, Exemplified* (London, 1689), a biography of his older brother Nathaniel, who died in 1688, with extracts from Nathaniel's diary and other spiritual writings that the family, and possibly others, had read over. Mather's *Early Religion, Urged* (Boston, 1694) contained spiritual writings that pious young men and women, or their parents, had written, such as the "Large Paper of Admonitions" that someone cited only as "Nash" "Left behind him, in the Hands of his Young Friends," and the "Account of his Experiences" written by a young man of Taunton.[56] By this time, too, manuscript narratives were circulating of pious children who had died prematurely. Mather redacted several of these for *A Token for the Children of New England* (Boston, 1700), a book he transferred into the *Magnalia*. But "A Sorrowful Memoriall of my dear Sister Sarah Tompson who entred into Glory 15. J 1679: Aetatis sue 43," remained unpublished, incorporated into a family memorial assembled by one of the Tompsons of Braintree that contains Sarah's "relation," verse by her brother Benjamin, and extracts from an English Nonconformist's "Useful Questions whereby a Christian may every day Examine himself."[57]

For the most part, the many people who wrote verse did so assuming that their poems would circulate in handwritten copies. John Wilson, the minister of First Church Boston, may have been the most prolific poet among the immigrants of the 1630s. A London bookseller had already printed his *Song of Deliverance* (1626), a versification of recent English history. When this book was reprinted in Boston in 1680, his son John Wilson II reminded readers of the "Volums" his father had "penned for the help of others in their several changes of condition, which if they were all compiled together, would questionless make a large Folio." Except for a few commendatory poems, none of this verse was printed.[58] After Thomas Dudley died, a scrap of verse was discovered in his clothes—or so the story went, for the verse itself was widely known though not printed until Cotton Mather included it in the *Magnalia*. Edmund Weld, a Harvard College graduate who practiced his ministry in Ireland, wrote a "dialogue" on death that his widow sent to relatives in New England; it survived in manuscript and was printed by an antiquarian in the early nineteenth century.[59] Philip Walker described some of the early battles of King Philip's War in a verse narrative, "Captain Perse & his coragios Company." Toward the end of the century, an uncle of Benjamin Franklin, himself named Benjamin (1650–1727), passed his spare time versifying the Psalms and composing "anagrams, crosses, ladders, and other devices," together with verse addressed to young Benjamin and others in the Franklin family.[60]

The poetry that flowed through the household of Samuel Sewall reached him both as printed broadsides and as manuscripts, and he used both of these means for sharing the verse he enjoyed writing. His family mattered intensely to Sewall, so it must have pleased him that his cousin Daniel Gookin II wrote "A Few Shadie Meditations occasioned by the Death" of Sewall's father-in-law John Hull. Sewall's network of versifiers included friends and Harvard College classmates, one of them the poet-minister Edward Taylor. Poems by two friends survive in Sewall's commonplace book, copied, it seems likely, from printed versions; and a letter of 1724 reveals him forwarding several texts, printed and handwritten: "Mr. N. Hobart's Verses," his own "Merrimak River 2 copies" (a printed text) and "Judge Lynd's Poem 2 copies," undoubtedly another printed broadside.[61] For Sewall and several others, a commonplace book served as a convenient site for preserving verse, but for John Eliot the Roxbury church records did just as well; and other poems survived because they were written on the flyleaves of printed books.[62]

The passage of manuscripts in and out of Sewall's household is a reminder that scribal publication was ideally suited to a practice that remains alive and well today, trying out a text on someone else before making it widely available. Sewall did this with his speculations on the end times, subsequently printed as *Phaenomena quaedam Apocalyptica* (Boston, 1697), asking William Stoughton to advise him on a draft. In 1646 the lay writer Thomas Stoughton was nervous about sharing a treatise on when the Sabbath began with a few ministers, but did so wanting their approval. Many other manuscripts passed from hand to hand for this reason—Cotton Mather's sketch of the life of Thomas Dudley (see Chapter 3), Thomas Lechford's treatise on prophecy, and Thomas Hooker's initial draft of what became *A Survey of the*

Summe of Church-Discipline, to cite but three examples.[63] One well-documented exchange dates from mid-1629, when John Winthrop sent a draft of "General Observations for the Plantation of New England" to other persons involved with the Massachusetts Bay Company and incorporated some of their responses into subsequent versions.[64] The decade-long debate (1678–88) carried on in handwritten texts between the near-neighbors Solomon Stoddard of Northampton and Edward Taylor of Westfield was provoked by the two ministers' sharply different conceptions of church membership and the Lord's Supper; Stoddard was the more "evasive," declining at one point to "write a particular answer to all" the objections Taylor was making to his views, but willing to transmit a fresh copy of a document dating from the Reforming Synod of 1679.[65] Traces remain of many other manuscripts that friend or foe was asked to read, a practice that deserves a large place in any history of intellectual life among the colonists.

The practice of copying poetry into blank paper books had its twin in the practice of preserving prose texts in the same manner. To characterize these compilations of prose as diaries is misleading,[66] for some mix entries about everyday affairs with copies of sermons, letters, and other documents. Joseph Green preserved letters of spiritual counsel in a blank paper book that dates from the beginning of his ministry in troubled Salem Village. Matthew Grant, who served the town and church of Windsor, Connecticut, as clerk for much of the seventeenth century, kept a "diary" (a retrospective designation) that he filled with the texts of sermons by Thomas Hooker and other local ministers, extracts from books of spiritual counsel (with no indication of source), and a partial transcription of one of the documents of the Antinomian controversy, all written out in his remarkably clear hand with no sign of corrections.[67] The amplitude of the sermon texts in Grant's notebook suggests that some ministers, or else a very skillful auditor, prepared extensive versions of workaday preaching and allowed these manuscripts to circulate. (The sermons recorded in shorthand by Henry Wolcott of Windsor are much shorter.) Other manuscript sermons must have been circulating, some exchanged among the clergy or passed around by lay men and women. One trace of this practice is the summary of a John Cotton sermon that Thomas Shepard entered into a manuscript book he was keeping, probably a copy of a copy.[68]

Poetry passed back and forth between manuscript and print. But in the case of the verse or prose statements known as libels, scribal publication was the *only* possibility and anonymity a defining feature. Narrowly construed, a libel was a commentary on affairs of state that the authorities found offensive. Broadly construed, it encompassed the petty confrontations or acts of defamation that troubled every local community. To some members of the Chelmsford, Massachusetts church, "a paper without any hand to it" growing out of a confrontation between two men had "the sense of a libel"; as was often the case, the identity of the writer was not really secret, but "said" to be someone who was named. Joseph Rowlandson, the future husband of Mary, pinned a libel protesting a local injustice to the door of the Ipswich, Massachusetts meeting house in 1651, an action that got him suspended from Harvard.[69] John Slater of Concord composed two obscene "libels writ in papers"—prompted, it seems, by St. Valentine's Day—that he nailed to a post in front of the meeting house in 1664. A middle-aged Malden housewife wrote "a kind of rhyme" commenting on Michael Wigglesworth, the town minister, a few years after Wigglesworth had married his much younger servant maid.[70] At times, however, libels took on a political edge. During King Philip's War, a handwritten placard signed "A.B.C.D." was posted in Boston denouncing two of the magistrates as "traitors to their king and countrey."[71] A much-disliked royal official, Edward Randolph, found himself mocked in "Randolph's Welcome Back Again" (1679/80), an anonymous poem that circulated only in manuscript.[72] A few years later Randolph was complaining of another anti-royalist prose libel, "disper'sd in Boston," that portrayed the "horrid Conspiracy" (the anti-Charles II Rye House plot of 1683) as "but a sham plot &c. [and declared] That the Governor Magistrates and Ministers were grievous Backsliders and betrayers of their Libertyes and Country &c." Rumor had it that the author was a "young hott headed Minister," but in this instance as in most others (Rowlandson was an exception) the anonymity of the genre could not be penetrated.[73] Many more such texts were produced in the seventeenth century; none were printed, in contrast to what was happening in England.[74]

Though textbooks and other classroom-related documents at Harvard had none of the qualities of libels, they too were reproduced only in handwritten copies. The faculty at Harvard did not expect students to purchase the books they were using to learn languages, logic, and the sciences. As Thomas and Lucia Knoles have pointed out in their study of student-fashioned manuscripts, "For almost the first hundred years of Harvard's existence, many of the texts used for instruction in the college were manuscripts, transmitted in manuscript only." This rule holds, they point out, even when one or another of these books existed in a printed version. This practice explains why so many copies survive of Hebrew grammars, textbooks in logic, and a survey of physics compiled by Charles Morton, an English minister who wrote a series of such texts, none of them ever printed, for an academy he founded in Restoration England. After Morton immigrated to Massachusetts in the 1680s, his "Compendium Physicae" became the standard work of its kind in the Harvard curriculum as it also did at newly founded Yale; at least thirteen student-made copies have been identified.[75] Not until the 1730s did Boston booksellers begin to publish grammars and the like. The scribal culture of Harvard College also encompassed the college laws each entering student was required to copy. The college authorities rejected Samuel Sewall's offer to have the laws printed, preferring, it seems, the benefits of a more personal technology.[76] Meanwhile, master's students in the college were making copies of a summary of theology written by Samuel Stone. One copy of Stone's "The Whole Body of Divinity in a Catecheticall way" (undated, but probably completed in the 1650s) survives in a notebook that also preserves extensive notes on sermons being preached in Hartford and nearby towns; a second, in the handwriting of Samuel Willard and signed by him, "Finis Deo Soli Honor, et Gloria. Finisd September 13. 1697. by (or per) S. Willard," may have been prepared in the hope of getting the manuscript published. Willard himself wrote a "Brief Directions . . . for the Study of Divinity" that was "dispersed in a few private Manuscripts" until printed in 1735.[77]

One other kind of text that circulated primarily in manuscript was the opinions, political and religious, of people who had a quarrel to pick with the Puritan system. By the 1640s, the religious radical Samuel Gorton and his allies were distributing manifestoes, and Baptists became active by the 1650s, the same decade that saw the first Quakers arrive in New England and William Harris of Rhode Island inveigh "against all earthly powers, parliaments, laws, charters, magistrates, prisons, rates, yea, against all kings and princes" in "writings or Books" that irritated even Roger Williams, who ordered him arrested. Gershom Bulkeley, who retired from the ministry of Wethersfield, Connecticut, in 1677 but continued to practice medicine in the town, detested the chartered government of Connecticut and said so forcefully in "Will and Doom, Or the Miseries of Connecticut by and under an Usurped and Arbitrary Power" (c. 1692); the only copy that seems to have survived wound up in the archives of the English government. Earlier, in 1689, Bulkeley had become the first New England writer to benefit from the presence in Philadelphia of a printing office run by William Bradford, who published a letter of his to the colony's leaders, *The People's Right to Election*, and in 1694, after Bradford had moved his shop to New York, he printed another of Bulkeley's critiques of local privilege, *Seasonable Considerations for the Good People of Connecticut.*[78] But for critics on either end of the political spectrum, the possibilities for going into print either in New England or New York were few.

Partial and incomplete though it is, this inventory underscores how persistent, yet also episodic, the practice of scribal publication was among the colonists. Its visibility would be even greater if more documents had survived the vicissitudes of time—and the appetite of "mice or rats," a threat the elderly minister Samuel Stowe specified in describing a mechanism he had devised for protecting a work of history he wrote in the 1690s: "Those my Chronilogicall Decads have rings or loops by which they may be fastened together or hang'd up, to preserve from mice or rats."[79] Some manuscripts found their way into print in compendia such as the *Magnalia* or in works of controversy such as Samuel Gorton's *Simplicities Defense* (London, 1646) and Edward Winslow's *Hypocrisie Unmasked* (London, 1646). Despite the many losses, substantial archives accumulated in the households of Increase Mather and his son Cotton. Increase inherited the papers of John Davenport of New Haven and probably the papers of John Cotton, whose widow had married his father, and put these materials to use in writing *The Life and Death of . . . Richard Mather* and assembling *The First Principles of New-England.* As Cotton Mather was writing the *Magnalia*, he quoted from dozens of manuscripts that dated from the early years—letters of his step-grandfather and John Winthrop, a manuscript of Winthop's "Considerations" of 1629, some autobiographical remarks by William Bradford, and the deathbed testimony of Edward Hopkins, to name but a few. Cotton was also indebted to documents William Hubbard had acquired as he was writing his "Generall History of New England."[80] Early in the eighteenth century Thomas Prince began collecting printed books and manuscripts,[81] and in the mid-eighteenth century, Thomas Hutchinson, a public servant and politician (and great-great-grandson of Anne Hutchinson) who became lieutenant governor of Massachusetts in 1758, assembled what was probably the most comprehensive of all these collections, a trove that included correspondence of Hooker, Cotton, Davenport and most of the Mather family archive, loaned to him by Samuel Mather, Cotton's son. It is telling of the depth of this archive that, when his fellow antiquarian Ezra Stiles of Newport told him that a manuscript of John Wheelwright's fast-day sermon of 1637 had come into his hands, Hutchinson replied dryly that he already owned a contempo-

rary copy.[82] The citations and appendices in the first two volumes of Hutchinson's *The History of the Colony and Province of Massachusetts-Bay* (Boston,
1764, 1767) are another demonstration of its richness—a richness brutally
disrupted when a Boston mob bent on protesting the Stamp Act sacked
Hutchinson's house and, as he remarked in the preface to the second volume
of the *History*, turned to "scattering and destroying all my furniture, books,
papers, &c." Though he was thankful that some papers were recovered, "the
most valuable materials were lost." Even so, Hutchinson was able to print the
"Examination" of his great-great-grandmother Hutchinson as an appendix to
volume 2 and to publish others in *A Collection of Original Papers Relative to
the History of the Colony of Massachusetts Bay* (Boston, 1769).

* * *

Every handwritten text was problematic. Some of the anxieties that readers
and writers expressed about printed texts, like the well-rehearsed complaint
that booksellers were a pack of thieves motivated only by self-interest, did
not apply to handwritten copies, none of which, in New England, had any
commercial value. Yet every handwritten text shared three problems with
those that were printed: did it have an obvious provenance, how closely did
the text coincide with a putative original, and was it properly attributed? In
two other respects, the anxieties provoked by scribal publication were distinctive: were such texts "private," not "public," and, in the absence of any
rules for licensing handwritten copies, were they a means of voicing illicit or
subversive opinions?

The distinction between writings deemed "private" and those considered
suitable for "public" viewing was immensely significant for handwritten
texts, all of which were situated in close proximity to representations and
practices associated with the category of the private.[83] The power of this
category resonates in John Cotton's dismay that Roger Williams, then in
London, had published in print a letter of his: "The letter, and so the error
contained in it, (if it was an error) it was private, and so private, that I know
no man that hath a coppy of it, no not my selfe who penned it (for ought I
could find) but himselfe onely."[84] The distinction resonates as well in Anne
Hutchinson's insistence that her criticism of several ministers as "legall" was
voiced in a conversation and could not be used as evidence against her, and
in the preface to Mary Rowlandson's *The Sovereignty & Goodness of God*,
where she was described as a woman of "modesty" who "would not thrust"

her text "into the Press" had not others been "so much affected . . . as to judge it worthy of publick view."[85] Already, these few examples suggest that the distinction between private and public functioned in several different ways. For Cotton, a private text was one he intended to share with specific readers (the recipient of a letter) or, in the case of sermons, a specific audience; as someone said of one of his sermon series, "it was not intended, when first delivered, for any more publike use, then of his owne private Auditorie."[86] For the anonymous author of the preface to *The Sovereignty & Goodness of God*, private and public were gendered categories, the assumption being that women's speech and writing were properly confined to a domestic space. Hutchinson may have had in mind the passage in Matthew 18 describing how to proceed in a situation of church discipline, the first step being a "private" encounter between two people.[87]

The meanings of private and public were associated, as well, with the competing technologies of handwritten copies and those that were printed; to have a text printed was to make it distinctively public. So Cotton pointed out in protesting the publication of his letter: "when I heard of its being put in print, it was to me unwelcome news, as knowing the truth and weight of Plinies speech, aliud est scribere, aliud omnibus [it is one thing to write for one, another for all]." Nathaniel Mather made the same assumption about printing when he defended his role in having a manuscript printed on the grounds that a text which otherwise was "hid in a private hand or two" would better serve the truth by appearing in a "publick and common light."[88] Yet printed texts could still be coded as private if a writer or patron paid the printer's bill for a text that was essentially meant for a small group of readers—as it were, a private press run in our modern sense of the term. John Eliot represented a text of his in exactly this manner, declaring in the preface to *The Communion of Churches* (Cambridge, 1665) that it was printed only to serve a "private" audience. Texts that were handed down within families must also have been regarded as private; unlike her verse, Anne Bradstreet's meditations were not exposed to the general reader until the late nineteenth century. To Joseph Green, who came as a young man to minister to the troubled church in Salem Village (Danvers), the notebook in which he recorded sermons, letters of religious counsel, and comments on his own spiritual state was singularly private, so much so that in one of its entries he noted his intention to "have commited this book to the flames" before he died; should he fail to do so, he gave "leave to my nearest relation to look over it; but I give a strict charge to him not to expose it to the view of any; And it is my will that this book be viewed by none unless by one person which is nearest related unto me."[89]

Another powerful context for the meaning of private was its association with secrecy. Long before the colonists arrived in New England, scribal publication had proved its usefulness as a means of commenting on and criticizing the policies of the English government. Anyone who did so in print ran the risk of severe punishment of the kind inflicted on Stubbs for publishing in printed form a critique of the proposal that Elizabeth I marry Francis, Duke of Anjou. When Philip Sidney protested the same affair of state in a manuscript, nothing happened to him, and the people who made handwritten copies of Stubbs's book also escaped punishment.[90] The safety of handwritten texts was relative, not absolute, for the civil state could seize and expose handwritten texts, as sometimes happened with letters in New England. Yet when King and Parliament became at odds in the 1620s and critics of the Crown such as William Prynne emerged in the 1630s, scribal publication flourished as a vehicle of dissent.[91] Much, too, that was not explicitly oppositional, though certainly not in keeping with the government's own view of things, circulated in manuscript—for example, Thomas Hooker's sermon of 1629, "The Danger of Desertion," a despairing analysis of religion in England, a paper of October 1629 containing "Arguments for the Plantation of New England" drawn up by some of the organizers of the Massachusetts Bay Company, and texts associated with the Antinomian underground of the 1620s and 1630s.[92]

For English writers, the private aspects of scribal publication could also make it a haven for any writer who shrank from the "stigma of print." Among the colonists it was not the commercial aspects of print that made it less appealing but the near-certain possibility that having something printed would "expose" a writer to "censure" if not ridicule.[93] A broader reluctance was also at work, a strong preference for a mode of communication that was less disruptive of social peace. The goal of preserving that peace was among the most explicit priorities of the colonists. It may have been conventional to declare that truth was one and that all lovers of the truth should live together in unity and peace, but this wisdom was immensely significant in New England, embodied in church covenants, with their injunctions that the covenanted Christian "walk in . . . love, humility, wisdom, [and] peaceableness," and reiterated in countless sermons, as when John Davenport remarked in an "Epistle to the Reader" in Increase Mather's *The Mystery of Israel's Salvation* (London, 1669) that happiness depended on "Gods people" being truly in agreement on "Divine truth," a happiness he contrasted with the "misery" that followed from allowing "differences in apprehension [to] cause . . . distances and animosities," differences that in turn "weaken the hearts and hands of Saints in the work of the Lord, and strengthen adversaries in their malicious and subtil designs and enterprises against the truth."[94] The same ethos explains certain actions of the civil state, as when the deputies in the General Court decided not to "publish" a protest, the reason being, as recorded by Winthrop, the "apprehension, that it would cause a public breach throughout the country; and, if it should come to that, the people would fall into factions."[95]

This ethos invited acts of trespass. Despite the respect for texts deemed private, the boundary between private and public was constantly being violated. The civil state in New England intervened again and again to intercept and publicize handwritten letters or other "writings," as it did in 1647 when it seized the letters that Robert Child and a few others had entrusted to a ship about to leave for England, fearing that his accusations of unfair treatment would turn Parliament against the colonists. The leaders of Massachusetts relished, too, the "publishing" of letters written by Samuel Gorton by having them read to a crowd.[96] If governments trespassed, so did individuals. Roger Williams arranged for a John Cotton letter to be printed, and the Scottish Presbyterian Robert Baillie did the same for another. Cotton Mather intentionally exploited the ambiguities of private and public in 1718 when he advised Lord Barrington, whose brother had recently been appointed royal governor of Massachusetts, "if there should be any occasion for it [Mather's effusive account of the colonists' respect for George I], you may expose this letter wherever it may be serviceable."[97] Even among the leaders of Massachusetts, privacy could not be taken for granted if someone wanted a document to be shared. So it happened with a letter Richard Saltonstall and other notables of Ipswich sent John Winthrop in 1643 protesting his support for La Tour. After it arrived, Winthrop noted, no doubt correctly, that "it was directed to my selfe first, but came to me through many hands (and so it seemes to have been intended by you, being sent unsealed)."[98] That letters were always and everywhere vulnerable to exposure explains why, after Winthrop reached New England, a few of his overseas correspondents resorted to anonymity and cipher.[99] As these episodes demonstrate, the line between the private and public was always negotiable. Yet the difference between the two would play a major role in the publishing history of the Antinomian controversy of the 1630s and others that succeeded it.

As with printed texts, every handwritten copy was situated somewhere between the authority of a putative original and the variations introduced by the process of making copies.[100] Some copyists were astonishingly careless, as Cotton Mather was for many of the poems and prose he incorporated into the *Magnalia* from manuscripts; the speed at which he worked almost certainly kept him from checking his quotations against a copy text.[101] His father also edited with a certain abandon, rewriting some of the stories of "remarkable providences" he solicited for *An Essay for the Recording of Illustrious Providences* and, in at least one instance, William Morse's description of a possessed house, interpolating what seems to be his own language. When Mather inserted John Mason's narrative of the Pequot War into *A Relation Of the Troubles which have hapned in New-England* (Boston, 1677), he made significant changes to the text as well.[102] For some texts, exactitude mattered and people cared about their accuracy, but for others, the differences were never cause for anxiety, like the minor variations between copies of the Massachusetts charter of 1629 or those in copies (printed and handwritten) of the Mayflower Compact. Writing from England to Governor Leverett in the 1670s, the minister John Collins remarked that "The enclosed coppy of the letter is, as far as I remember, just as wee wrote it."[103] In contrast to Collins, John Cotton renounced the printed text of his letter of 1635 to a prisoner in Newgate, specifying two errors of transcription and implying there were others, and he was dismayed by the errors in the printed version of his handwritten answers to a set of questions his New England colleagues had given him in 1636.[104]

Where exactitude really did matter was in documents originating within civil government or having legal or economic consequences. Such texts were encompassed within a system of material signs that warranted their authenticity—a wax seal, a clerk's signature with the words "vera copia" (meaning, in principle, that the copy had been compared with an exemplar), the signatures of witnesses, a distinctive quality of paper or a special "hand." So important were these notations of authenticity that the Massachusetts magistrate Thomas Danforth carefully reproduced them in a notebook he compiled in the mid-1660s of political texts, writing "seal" in a circle to indicate where and when this mark appeared. Though Bradford did not go to the same lengths in his letter book, he copied the names of all the signatories to an agreement forged between the colonists and the English "adventurers" in 1626, noting that "So the thing was fully concluded, and the bargain fairly engrossed on parchment, under their hands and seals, as legally and formally done, as by the learnedest lawyers could be devised."[105] Accuracy mattered, too, in certain situations of high tension. When Boston First Church invited John Davenport of New Haven to become its minister, a minority in the congregation withdrew, knowing that Davenport opposed the policy of membership they favored. In the dispute that broke out between the two groups, a key text became a letter sent by the New Haven church to Boston First Church. Davenport had already moved to Boston. With his consent, someone fiddled with the letter, copying only a small part in order to make it seem that New Haven had consented to his departure. Once word of the distortions began to spread, a special meeting of ministers in the Boston area condemned what Davenport and others had done.[106] As it did in this instance, so in others, a political goal (the determination of Davenport and First Church to hold the line against changes in church membership) could disrupt the normal workings of authenticity.

These disputes remind us that, for most handwritten texts, the marks of attribution and provenance that routinely appeared in printed texts (where, to be sure, they were sometimes falsified) were missing. No title page framed Winthrop's "Charitie" discourse, and nowhere on the manuscript was he or the copyist identified or the provenance of the copy noted. Mather attributed Mason's narrative to John Allyn, the secretary of the Connecticut General Assembly, who sent the manuscript (possibly a copy) to him. In this instance as in many others, authors' names were missing from handwritten texts, as they were, for example, from all of Bradford's manuscripts. Letters were the exception, a handwritten text that routinely contained dates and someone's signature, information usually reproduced when copies were made of them. But with verse, the writer's name was absent or indicated only by initials. Hence the misattributions that happened in the seventeenth century as poetry was being copied. When the immigrant clergy replied in the 1630s to the questions sent them by English Puritans, the manuscript responses made no indication of authorship; and when two of these were printed in London in 1643 several years after reaching England, the bookseller assigned them to the "elders" of New England as a whole. Two years later in a printed book, John Cotton specified an attribution.[107] Cotton Mather began to set matters straight at the end of the century and Thomas Prince in the early eighteenth, Prince when he identified John Mason as the author of the narrative Increase Mather had assigned to Allyn, and Cotton when he recognized that a manuscript attributed to John Cotton when it was printed in Cambridge in 1663 was really the work of John Davenport.[108] In most situations, the warrant that a handwritten text was adequately attributed and reasonably authentic seems to have been provenance and handwriting: who was transmitting it and in whose hand was it written? Manuscripts may have been much like oral gossip or rumor. When the diarist Samuel Sewall recorded the rumors that reached him orally, he invariably noted the name of the bearer of these stories, his means of weighing the truth of these reports.

A different way of approaching the questions of authenticity and attribution is to ask if New England writers worried about losing control of their prose or poetry as it circulated in handwritten copies. The answer is yes in some instances, and no in others. Letters seem to have aroused the most concern, in part because (as John Cotton insisted) most of them were distinctively "private." They were also easily altered and, at an extreme, could be counterfeited, something that happened to Increase and Cotton Mather.[109] A harder question to answer is whether any local writer attempted to curtail the variations in a text by preparing a fresh or better version, as happened with a handful of printed texts. If the answer is no, as seems to be the case, it would be in keeping with the colonists' indifference to the game of canonization. Indifference had its limits: it mattered that some kinds of documents be verified as "true" and that private writings be shielded from "publicity." Otherwise, the colonial writer tolerated a process of transmission that necessarily fell short of reproducing an original with exactness.

* * *

The event that must occupy the largest place in any reckoning with scribal publication is the Antinomian controversy. It originated in two separate but associated critiques of how religion—true religion—was being taught and practiced among the colonists. John Cotton, who arrived in Boston in 1633 and immediately became co-minister with John Wilson of the town church, was complaining in his sermons of the mid-1630s that the colonists were relying on "duties" or "sanctification" for assurance of salvation, a practice he regarded as contradicting the priority of divine grace and the Holy Spirit. Meanwhile, Anne Hutchinson, an educated woman in his congregation who arrived from England in 1634, was warning in private meetings that "trusting to common gifts and graces, without any . . . witnesse of the Spirit" was akin to relying on a "Covenant of works." Cotton welcomed her message, affirming a decade after the controversy had ended that "all this was well . . . and suited with the publike Ministery, which had gone along in the same way."[110]

The two had an ally in the minister John Wheelwright and another in Henry Vane, a young English aristocrat who was elected governor of Massachusetts in May 1636. Some of the "legall" ministers (as Hutchinson was terming them) met with Wheelwright and Cotton in October "to the end they might know the certainty of these things," and talked with Hutchinson in December about her complaints. By early November John Winthrop was so troubled by Wheelwright's preaching that he "wrote his mind fully" on two points in dispute, a text he shared with John Cotton. Later that month or in December, Winthrop, John Wilson, and "divers others" were disputing "the indwelling of the person of the Holy Ghost in a believer" with Vane and some members of the Boston congregation, a debate carried on "in writing, for the peace sake of the church, which all were tender of"; about this time, too, the congregation sent a summary of its thinking to the Cambridge congregation. In November or early December, Cotton was handed a list of sixteen questions drafted by a group of ministers and dealing with "all the points, wherein they suspected [he] did differ from them." "Pressed" to provide a "direct answer," Cotton did so shortly thereafter.[111]

Consensus within the Boston congregation and the colony as a whole was tested in December when Cotton and many lay members complained of John Wilson's objections to having Wheelwright join them as a minister, and tested anew in January 1637 when Wheelwright declared in a fast-day sermon that "the whole country [was divided] in two ranks; some . . . under a Covenant of Grace, and these were friends to Christ; others under a Covenant of Workes . . . those . . . were . . . enemies to Christ."[112] Nor were the ministers moving any closer to agreement. Though Cotton's answers to the sixteen questions "cleared . . . some doubts," on others he "gave not satisfaction," a judgment that prompted some of his colleagues to write a "Reply" to which Cotton responded with a "Rejoynder."[113] In March, a session of the General Court became the next site of text-making once the Court arraigned Wheelwright on the charge of sedition, a step to which his allies responded with a "remonstrance or petition." Called to account by the Court and his colleagues, Wheelwright distributed fresh copies of the fast-day sermon and "set forth a small tractate about the principal doctrine of his sermon"; to this, some of the ministers produced an "answer," with John Cotton weighing in as well. Twenty years later, Wheelwright would allege that the "answer" of the ministers was "conceal[ed]" from him until "one of the Magistrates . . . did procure a copy to be transcribed secretly in al haste, and sent it unto me."[114] The next six months saw the political defeat of the "Antinomians" and, among the ministers, fresh efforts to detach Cotton from his allies and bring him around to their point of view. At the General Court election in May, Winthrop replaced Vane as governor, at some point in the summer Cotton wrote answers to a list of five questions, in September the ministers met for three weeks as a "synod" (lay people were also present) to work through their differences, and in November the Massachusetts General Court fined, exiled, or otherwise punished Wheelwright, Hutchinson, and some of their supporters. For Hutchinson, the final blow was her church trial of March 1638, which ended in her excommunication.

During these tense months of argument, protest, and negotiation, *every* text emerging from the controversy—sermons such as Wheelwright's, exchanges between the clergy, Winthrop's musings, the findings of the synod, petitions, apologies, and records of debate within the General Court—was reproduced and distributed only in manuscript. From start to finish (summer 1636 to early spring 1638), the controversy unfolded within the limitations and possibilities of scribal publication. And "publish" is the operative verb, for we have it on Winthrop's authority that in December 1636 or January 1637, "many copies" were made of Cotton's answers to the sixteen questions and "dispersed about." Some months later Winthrop was noting that "diverse writings were published," the magistrates who in 1637 wrote "A briefe Apologie in defence" of the punishment of Wheelwright made their statement "publike"—"publish" or made "public" always meaning, in this context, distributed in handwritten copies—and the person or persons who wrote an "Answer" protesting a law of 1637 restricting who could settle in the colony "published" this text, as undoubtedly happened with the two documents defending the statute.[115] But the principal evidence of scribal publication is the number of copies that survive or that contemporaries reported having seen. Ignoring the letters that were exchanged and the many sermons being preached, some of which (especially Cotton's) were being shared, as many as twenty-five different texts were circulating by the early months of 1638.

How were these texts being produced and distributed in the mid-1630s? For John Wheelwright's fast-day sermon of January, the answer is that he (or someone helping him) wrote out copies and gave one or more to the General Court; of these, two full-length versions survive.[116] The debate in March 1637 within the General Court as to how he should be punished was not recorded in the official records of the Court or in Winthrop's journal, but from another text, the "briefe Apologie," we learn that "As for such passages as fell by occasion, and are too large to be here inserted, such as desire to know them, may receive satisfaction from three or foure of Boston . . . who tooke all by Characters (we doubt not) will give a true report thereof." William Coddington of Boston may have done so surreptitiously, for he was almost certainly the magistrate who gave Wheelwright this information. Coddington was also cited by Samuel Groom as the source of a manuscript account of the proceedings, now lost, that Groom quoted in *A Glasse for the People of New England* (London? 1676).[117] As already noted, Winthrop referred to the "briefe Apologie" as "publike," and so, it seems, were other texts originating with Wheelwright and his supporters, for a loyal supporter wrote Winthrop from Maine in mid-April to inform him "That all the late differences between mr. Wheelwright and your selves in Church and Court are in writing at Richmunds Ile [in Maine] where Turlany shewed him six sheets of paper full written about them."[118] By this time, "many copies" of the sixteen questions were circulating, and by mid-summer, Cotton's answers to the five questions were being reproduced.[119] The synod that met in Cambridge compiled "A Catalogue of such erroneous opinions as were found to have beene brought into New England," a text prepared by someone hired to make a record of the synod's deliberations; copies of this text were known in the eighteenth century.[120]

At the November session of the General Court, the magistrates, deputies, and ministers confronted Anne Hutchinson, questioning her for two days about the legitimacy of the private meetings at her home, her role as a spiritual teacher, and what she had been saying about the "legall" ministers. Out of this give-and-take came the text that her great-great-grandson owned and would print in the late eighteenth century, the "Examination" that concludes with her telling of a "voice" that enabled her to recognize which ministers to believe. The trail of texts associated with Hutchinson extended into the early spring of 1638 when the Boston church, now purged of her strongest supporters, called her to account for theological errors. Two different ministers who had interviewed her during the winter months, Shepard of Cambridge and Weld of Roxbury, had prepared independent lists of "Things . . . layd to" her "Charge," lists that may have been combined into another that totaled sixteen. At some point during the winter Hutchinson "wrote down her answers" to some set of "Articles," a document that may be the same as the written "recantation" she "presented . . . before the whole church." This document does not survive, but the list of the sixteen questions does, though as printed in the *Short Story* it has swelled to twenty-nine, of which "a coppy . . . had been sent to her divers dayes before" the trial began.[121]

As the controversy was winding down, it yielded one of its oddest textual artifacts, a manuscript description of the deformed fetus born to the "Antinomian" Mary Dyer in October 1637 and exhumed on Winthrop's orders in the early spring of 1638. One version of this description was printed in London in 1642 as *Newes from New-England: of a most strange and prodigious Birth.* The London bookseller attributed the text to "a gentleman of good worth now resident in London." Well before this date, manuscript descriptions that were almost certainly Winthrop's doing had been circulating in England and New England. Thus in April 1638 William Bradford thanked him for a copy, and two others reached friends and enemies in England, one of these a brief manuscript that concludes, "I saw the Monster and doe affirme this relation to be true. John Wenthropp gent. Of the Massachusett."[122]

None of these texts could have been printed in Massachusetts, for the simple reason that the Cambridge printing shop was not set up until 1639; but whether any should be printed in England, as several eventually were, was already a troubling and divisive question in 1637. Divisive, because the losers in the controversy were angered by the distortions in the manuscript record, and because the winners realized that tales of disarray would play into the hands of their enemies in England. As some of the colonists would make explicit, the publishing history of the controversy cannot be separated from a long-persisting ambivalence about the benefits and possibilities of the private and the public. But that some documents would make their way to England and come into the hands of intermediaries who arranged for them to be printed was, in retrospect, inevitable.

Initially the magistrates and ministers in Massachusetts may have *wanted* some documents to reach their English allies, though only in the form of manuscript copies. So Thomas Hooker of Hartford argued in April 1637 in a letter to Thomas Shepard in Cambridge, at a time when the principal texts in circulation were exchanges that began with the sixteen questions handed to John Cotton. Though Hooker feared the damage being done in England by word of mouth, he was realistic about any efforts to preserve secrecy. Would "naked" publication serve the colonists better and be more convincing than rumor, he wondered? "My present thoughts run thus," he wrote Shepard: "That such conclusions which are most extra, most erroneous, and cross to the common current,[123] send them over to the godly learned to judge in our own country, and return their apprehensions. I suppose the issue will be more uncontroulable. If any should suggest this was the way to make the clamour too great and loud, and to bring a prejudice upon the plantations, I should soon answer, there is nothing done in corners here but it is openly there related and in such notorious cases, which cannot be kept secret, the most plain and naked relation ever causeth the truth most to appear."[124] Who acted on this advice cannot be determined, but someone did, for copies of some of the more theological documents were in English hands by the end of 1637.[125]

Hooker was right to worry about secrecy, for in 1644 the London press began to spill the beans. The English reading public first learned of the wider controversy from a book that was published in January 1644 and, with significant additions, reprinted a few months later, *A Short Story of the Rise, reign, and ruin of the Antinomians, Familists & Libertines, that infected the Churches of New-England,* to use the title of the revised edition. Shortly thereafter, another bookseller printed *Sixteene Questions of Serious and Necessary Consequence, Propounded unto Mr. John Cotton of Boston, in New-England.* Two years later, yet another bookseller printed the text containing the five questions of the summer of 1637, with Cotton's answers, *A Conference Mr. John Cotton Held in Boston With the Elders of New-England.* With this the printing history of texts that defined the controversy ended, though the *Sixteen Questions* and *A Conference* (each under a different title) would be reprinted and John Wheelwright would publish his *Apology* in 1658. Half a century later, in 1698, the *Short Story* would be reprinted a fourth time in the context of another phase of theological dispute among Nonconformists in England.

Each of the printed texts that arose directly from the controversy is problematic, for each is encircled with questions of authenticity, attribution, and publicity (in the sense of making these texts public), questions that return us to the handwritten manuscripts of the 1630s. By early 1638 five major sets of texts existed.[126] The earliest to be assembled contained the discussions prompted by the sixteen questions: the questions themselves, Cotton's answers, the ministers' reply, Cotton's rejoinder, and the five questions (preceded, it seems, by a list of three) of mid-1637. A second encompassed the texts associated with Wheelwright's fast-day sermon and a third, the findings of the synod of September 1637. A fourth consisted of documents that emerged from the proceedings of the General Court during the sessions it held in 1637, including, possibly, another "Remonstrance."[127] A final set comprised the texts associated with Anne Hutchinson and the public inquiries of late 1637 and early 1638 in which she participated. At least half a dozen other texts also existed in manuscript copies, including three efforts by John Winthrop to resolve the theological issues that he was advised to suppress and a collection of extracts "gather[ed] out of" Cotton's "Sermons to the people."[128]

The question of authenticity was being raised as early as December 1636 by the "Church at Boston" when the congregation realized that a list of five "propositions . . . given in writing" to the congregation in Cambridge (then still known as Newtown) had suddenly grown to fifteen, all of them "things which were not spoken by us" but "forge[d]" by someone in Cambridge.[129] In March 1637, John Wheelwright gave the Court a "true copy" of his sermon even as his friends were protesting that the magistrates and ministers who were voting his censure were relying on "broken Notes" "taken by others." Wheelwright also complained that his theology had been distorted.[130] Another text that circulated in two quite different versions was the "Examination" of Anne Hutchinson. Hutchinson printed one of these, but a much shortened text (which contains language that is absent from his version) was printed in the *Short Story*. It ignored almost all of the second day's proceedings, when the ministers who wanted to testify against Mrs. Hutchinson were put on the spot by her insistence that they were abusing "private" remarks. She also disputed the accuracy of the notes a minister had taken of her remarks to the group that met with her in December 1636.[131] Thanks to the existence of multiple copies, other texts reveal the lapses that occurred as someone was making handwritten copies and as compositors in a printing shop were setting type from a manuscript. The printed version of the *Sixteen Questions* differed from manuscript versions in diction and punctuation, and occasionally lacked phrases and sentences; a misleading "not" appears in one sentence, and in other places "justification" was transposed into "sanctification" and "concealeth" into "consenteth," changes that may have been the doing of a copyist or of the London-based compositor. Someone knew of these corruptions, for an amended copy of a 1647 reprinting, entitled *Severall Questions of Serious and necessary Consequence*, survives with changes entered in a hand that a nineteenth-century antiquarian regarded as John Cotton's (Fig. 2).[132] Similar errata litter the 1646 printing of Cotton's responses to three other questions, *A Conference Mr. John Cotton Held at Boston With the Elders of New-England*, as a comparison of manuscript copies with the printed version reveals.[133] Far more challenging to analyze, though certainly affected by self-censorship, is John Winthrop's journal, for his entries about the con-

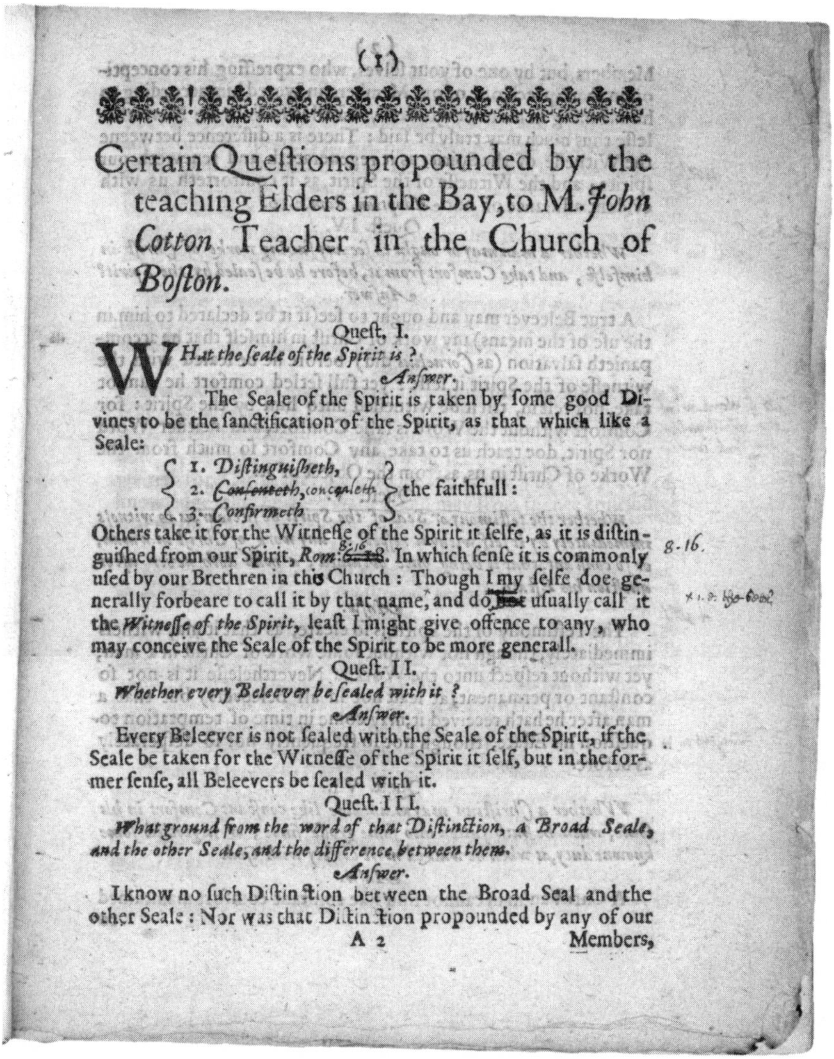

❀❀❀❀!❀❀❀❀❀❀❀❀❀❀❀❀❀❀

Certain Questions propounded by the teaching Elders in the Bay, to M. *John Cotton* Teacher in the Church of *Boston.*

WHat the ſeale of the Spirit is ?

Anſwer.

The Seale of the Spirit is taken by ſome good **Di**vines to be the ſanctification of the Spirit, as that which like a Seale:

{ 1. Diſtinguiſheth,
2. ~~Confenteth~~, concealeth } the faithfull :
3. Confirmeth

Others take it for the Witneſſe of the Spirit it ſelfe, as it is diſtinguiſhed from our Spirit, *Rom:* 8:16. In which ſenſe it is commonly uſed by our Brethren in this Church : Though I my ſelfe doe generally forbeare to call it by that name, and doe ~~not~~ uſually call it the *Witneſſe of the Spirit,* leaſt I might give offence to any, who may conceive the Seale of the Spirit to be more generall.

8-16.

× 1. P. bjo-ſoaz.

Whether every Beleever be ſealed with it ?

Anſwer.

Every Beleever is not ſealed with the Seale of the Spirit, if the Seale be taken for the Witneſſe of the Spirit it ſelf, but in the former ſenſe, all Beleevers be ſealed with it.

What ground from the word of that Diſtinction, a Broad Seale, and the other Seale, and the difference between them.

Anſwer.

I know no ſuch Diſtinction between the Broad Seal and the other Seale : Nor was that Diſtinction propounded by any of our

Members,

Figure 2. Correcting the mistakes in a printed text against a manuscript "original." *Severall Questions of Serious and necessary Consequence* (London, 1647), opening page, possibly in John Cotton's handwriting. Courtesy of the Massachusetts Historical Society.

troversy were inserted retrospectively, as evidenced by a vagueness about dates, sequences, and events and, more surprisingly, a silence about matters as significant as Wheelwright's sermon.[134]

This trail of texts that were abridged, self-censored, or inaccurately copied and printed concludes with an imprint that is still something of a mystery. In 1645 an unnamed London printer/bookseller published a book entitled *Mercurius Americanus, Mr. Welds his Antitype, or Massachusetts great Apologie examined, Being Observations upon a Paper styled, A short story of the Risse, Reign, and Ruine . . . wherein some parties therein concerned are vindicated, and the truth generally cleared.* It was no such book, nor was "John Wheelwright junior," the author's name as given on the title page, the actual author. A satirical essay that transposes the controversy into the realm of the absurd, the *Mercurious Americanus* may be linked with a literary tradition previously exemplified by Thomas Morton's *New English Canaan.* But we learn nothing from it of what happened in Massachusetts.[135]

How was the *Short Story* related to this stream of texts? If we take at face value Hooker and Winthrop's comments of mid winter and early spring (1637) reporting or encouraging the distribution of a few texts, it seems likely that the magistrates and ministers intended to send the sixteen questions, Cotton's answers to them, and perhaps some of his sermons or of Wheelwright's, to a coterie of readers in England. For the moment at least, the policy of the winning party was to avoid the publicity of print. In all likelihood, no one on the winning side was bothered by the London 1642 imprint that reported Mary Dyer's monster birth, a story that could be advantageous. But the *Short Story* was a different matter. Thomas Hooker, who expressed his dismay about the book in a letter to Shepard in the mid-1640s, blamed its appearance on the colonists' enemies among the English and Scottish Presbyterians: "I cannot be persuaded but these men had a secret hand to provoke Mr. Welde to set forth his 'Short Story' touching occasions here in Mr. Vane his reign," adding that he blamed them as well for two other imprints of 1643 that originally circulated in handwritten copies.[136] What seems certain is that for many of the colonists, the publication of the *Short Story* was an unwelcome surprise, a book that transposed what had been private into something dangerously public.

What were the sources of the *Short Story,* how was it put together, and what made the book dangerous? Materially, the book was the London bookseller Ralph Smith's attempt to dispose of unsold sheets that remained from *Antinomians and Familists Condemned By the Synod of Elders in New England:*

with the Proceedings of the Magistrates against them, And their Apology for the same; Together with a memorable example of God's Judgements upon some of those persons so proceeded against, published in January 1644. Neither this version nor the *Short Story* specify an author or had the apparatus of errata, preface, and dedication. The second began, however, with a "To the Reader" by someone who declared that, having encountered the January version "newly come forth of the Presse," he asked the bookseller if he could "perfect it, by laying downe the order and sense of this story, (which in the Book is omitted)," and by offering "some additions to the conclusion." The author of these new sections identified himself as "T.W.," and, at the close of the introduction, as "T. Welde." Thomas Weld had immigrated to Massachusetts in 1632 and resumed his ministry in newly founded Roxbury before returning to England in 1641 at the behest of the Massachusetts government, which needed agents to represent its interests. Weld said nothing about the sources of the *Short Story*; he made no attribution and offered no assurances of authenticity. Well aware that many in Parliament and the Westminster Assembly regarded the colonists as far too radical, he wrote with two goals in mind, to give English readers some context for what they would encounter in the *Short Story*, and to blame Anne Hutchinson and John Wheelwright for the turmoil of 1636 and 1637. Not once did Weld mention John Cotton or Henry Vane, who by 1644 had become a leading figure in Parliament.

What was in the book that Weld attempted to improve by his additions? The *Short Story* contains four texts carried over from the printing of January: a "Catalogue of such erroneous opinions . . . condemned by an Assembly of the Churches," that is, a list of eighty-two errors, each followed by a "confutation," drawn up by the assembly of ministers that met in September, together with nine "unsavoury speeches" the synod seems also to have identified (pp. 1–20); the "proceedings of the Generall Court holden . . . October 2. 1637. Against Mr. Wheelwright and other erroneous and seditious persons" (pp. 21–43), including a shortened version of the "Examination" of Mrs. Hutchinson; an account of Mary Dyer's monstrous birth, headed, "At Boston in New England, upon the 17. day of October" (pp. 44–45); and "A brief Apologie in defence of the generall proceedings of the Court . . . against Mr. J. Wheelwright" (pp. 46–59). Two of these texts were authorless—the first the doing of a group of ministers, the "Apologie" the work of "some of the magistrates"[137]—leaving only the "monster birth" story and the narrative of the Court's proceedings as texts that possibly can be attributed to someone, though whoever wrote out the second had at his elbow a transcription of what was said and done during the proceedings of the Court. Weld added an account of Hutchinson's church trial, a list of twenty-nine "opinions" he attributed to her, news of her death in 1643, and a great deal of invective.

How did the first of these authorless documents come into being? To this question a long-overlooked letter provides a fresh answer. In August 1643, John Higginson, who came to New England in 1629 at the age of thirteen, wrote the Massachusetts General Court requesting payment for his services in 1637. He began by recalling what he was hired to do: "I was employed by the Magistrates and Ministers of the Bay At the Synod held at Cambridge 1637: to take in short hand all that then Passed, At the end of it I was desired to draw up a copie of all the Materiall Passages, that it might be printed for Publicke use, which so farre as it did belong to me, after the Expence of much time and paines on my Part was done." The "Expence of time" had been considerable, for it was not until May 1639 that Higginson gave the General Court his manuscript account.

What happened after he did so is critical to an understanding of the scribal history of the controversy, for the Court "ordered that the Ministers should have the viewing of it: and then that it should be printed and that I should have the benefit of the printing of it for my paines It being then conceived it would amount to about a hundred pounds[.] And so it was returned to me again by the Court with a charge that I should so order it that it should be faithfullie printed[.]" This was an extraordinary bargain— extraordinary to the point of being fantastic, for it was absurd to assume in 1639 that the Cambridge printer, then just barely under way, could have sold enough copies to earn Higginson one hundred pounds, and no less absurd to suppose that a London bookseller would have risked this amount on the documents. That there was more at work than simply a commercial transaction was indicated, however, in the stipulation (as reported by Higginson) "that no damage might arise from it either to the cause or the Countrey, and then that I should have the profit of it."

The dunning letter of 1643 suggests the sequel—no printed book, no payment as yet to the clerk who had spent so much time preparing the text, and the reason for inaction: "being thus ordered by the Court I left it for a time in the hands of the ministers who had the viewing of it &c. After which I had the occasion to under stand the Judgment of divers concerning the publication of it, and I found that so some were for it, yet others were against it conceiving it might possibly be an occasion of further disputes and differences both in this Country and other parts of the world; whereupon I found a Scruple arise in my spirit so that I durst not have a hand in the publishing of it, fearing what might be the consequence of it." All this transpired by May 1641, when Higginson first petitioned the Court to release him of responsibility for the manuscript and pay him something. But debate was not yet ended. "It was then considered of mutually by the Magistrates and Ministers, and it was resolved (upon the grounds before mentioned) that it should not be printed." With printing no longer a possibility, Higginson had been "Promised" a cash payment of fifty pounds when the colony treasurer could afford to make it, a figure the copyist may have regarded as what the manuscript would sell for, presumably within the London trade.[138]

Here, then, is one mystery solved, the source of the first of the texts in the *Short Story*. It is virtually certain that Higginson prepared the narrative that underlies the "proceedings of the Generall Court" either as copyist or, more likely, as the record-keeper for the Court during the November session, for the labor of writing up the eighty-two errors and nine speeches seems completely inadequate to warrant his earning a hundred pounds even if he were being paid for making several copies—and he was being assisted during the proceedings of the synod by the young minister Giles Firmin, who many years later declared that he was on hand to help "another young Man [Higginson] write for the Elders at Night." Whether Higginson's doing or someone else's, there came into being "a Book or manuscript in which is all their Proceedings."[139]

Should the *Short Story* be attributed to Weld, to Winthrop, to both of them, or to no one at all? The attribution to Winthrop that began to pass as common knowledge in the nineteenth century deeply bothered James Savage, a Boston lawyer-antiquarian who spent many evenings in the 1820s transcribing the three manuscript volumes of John Winthrop's journal from the originals. In the footnotes to his edition (1825) of the journal and again in the second edition of 1853 as well as in his multivolume *Genealogical Dictionary* under the entry for Thomas Weld, Savage insisted that, although Winthrop had probably written the thirteen page "briefe Apologie," the rest was Weld's doing. Savage regarded Weld as a liar who attempted to conceal his authorship by arranging for a second printing of the *Short Story*—the version entitled *Antinomians and Familists*—shorn of his introduction and conclusion. Deeming him an "Inquisitor" for his role in the controversy, Savage spurned the minister's own explanation of how he came upon the text, insisting in one of his notes to Winthrop's journal that "this is altogether a pretense on the part of the virolent pamphleteer" and supporting his interpretation by a close bibliographical analysis of the typeface and other material features of the first two printings. As other antiquarians promptly demonstrated, however, the bibliographical evidence confirmed the sequence of printings as Weld had described it.[140]

The only sensible approach to the *Short Story* is to set aside this agitation about authorship and to treat it as an example both of social authorship and of texts that have no author in any meaningful sense. In all likelihood, Winthrop played a part in creating the abridgment of the Court's proceedings. That he did this on his own, at a time when he was sharing so much with Thomas Shepard and others, is quite unlikely. Although Winthrop may have intervened to group these documents together, the random character of the collection suggests that it was the unintentional fruit of Higginson's labors as clerk, with additions by others. Hence the rawness of *Antinomians and Familists* that Weld undertook to remedy with his preface and conclusion, a rawness appropriate to a collection of texts assembled by circumstance, not design, a collection, moreover, that the ministers and magistrates had decided not to reproduce in print. Any attribution of the text to Winthrop must rely on the shakiest of evidence, the statements (always generalized) made by critics such as Robert Baillie. But John Wheelwright, who had a large stake in how and why the controversy was publicized, never named Winthrop in his *Apology*, complaining instead that "the Author of the short story, who is [Greek word for anonymous], conceales his name against natures light, and hath born notable false witness against me . . . and his other witness is Mr. Thomas Weld, both of them being parties in the cause."[141]

Shorn of the smoke and fury of antiquarian battles about authorship, the *Short Story* has a significant place in the history of scribal publication among the colonists. Higginson's letter and Hooker's misgivings demonstrate that the scribal history of the controversy was deeply affected by anxieties about what should be kept private and what made public, even if, as Hooker was suggesting in 1637, going public was confined to manuscript copies. As so often happened to English writers and would happen again among the colonists, any coding of such copies as private became an invitation to make them public, as Ralph Smith did by having them printed in London in 1644. One other aspect of these texts is how they held back information from contemporary readers—the printed version of Hutchinson's examination, which curtailed her responses to the ministers and magistrates, the *Short Story* as a whole, from which, as Weld acknowledged, some documents were omitted, and Winthrop's journal, with its artful reconstruction of events.

Threads of secrecy, self-censorship, and deceptive copy-making thus wound their way through the documents of the controversy.

Some colonists knew of the covert aspects of the controversy—the magistrates, deputies, and ministers, for sure, but others too, for documents that came into the hands of former Antinomians and other dissidents would continue to emerge in the course of the century. In later years, scribal publication served some of these dissidents well, and especially the Quakers who, twenty years after the Massachusetts government shut down Hutchinson and the "Antinomians," began to arrive in New England bearing with them the prophetic message of a movement that arose in England in the early 1650s. Other dissidents had already turned to writing as the means of making their views known. Roger Williams, who questioned several of the colonists' policies and was expelled from Massachusetts for doing so in December 1635, was sharing a "treatise" in 1633 with the civil leaders of two colonies, Massachusetts and Plymouth.[142] Samuel Gorton, who gathered a small group of religious radicals around him at the beginning of the 1640s, prepared a "Writing" that his group posted on a tree in Providence, Rhode Island; the same text was also distributed in handwritten copies, as were letters by Randall Holden, a leading "Gortonist." About the same time the group "sent a writing" to the General Court, "four sheets of paper, full of reproaches" against the government and churches.[143] After 1650, the few Baptists began to circulate manuscripts among themselves, as Obadiah Holmes did with his "Confession," which concluded with a list of persons who should receive copies: "This for Mr. John Angher, and my brother Robert Holmes, and brother-in-law and sisters, with Mary Honly, and to them that love and fear the Lord."[144]

But these episodes were far exceeded by the text-making of the lay men and women who responded in the 1650s to the message of George Fox and James Naylor that all true Christians had Christ within themselves, an indwelling "light" that eclipsed the authority of church, ministry, and learning. The near world-wide journeys these early Quakers undertook were prompted by Fox's imperative that everyone awakened by this message should spread the "light" to others: "Let all nations hear the sound by word or writing. Spare no place, spare no tongue nor pen, but be obedient to the Lord God . . . The ministers of the Spirit must minister to the spirit that is . . . in every one, that with the Spirit of Christ people may be led out of captivity up to God, the Father of spirits."[145]

Acting on this imperative, Mary Fisher and Ann Austin sailed in 1655 from England to the West Indies, where they lingered for several months.

Arriving in Boston in July 1656, they had their baggage searched and the books it contained confiscated—almost certainly, unbound pamphlets that Quakers in England were beginning to print and distribute—for the government regarded the two as agents of "mutiny, sedition, and rebellion" embodying the same "Enthusiasme" that, a century earlier, had turned all things upside down in the German city of Munster.[146] The punishments imposed on the two women as they moved from place to place did little to deter other missionaries. Eight more reached Boston in early August 1656 and many others would follow, all knowing that beatings, imprisonment, and loss of property awaited them. By mid-1659 some knew that if they returned again to Massachusetts after having been banned from the colony, the civil state would order them executed. Thus it happened that four died on the scaffold in 1659–60: William Robinson, Marmaduke Stevenson, William Leddra, and Mary Dyer.

As soon as these people reached New England, they began to publicize their message in speech and writing. The printed books they brought with them were easily confiscated, but the missionaries were also carrying "Pen, Ink, and Paper." At moments of liberty and even in prison they used these means to make multiple copies of "letters" protesting their innocence, proclaiming the "light," and warning the magistrates and ministers of God's judgments on those who persecuted true Christians, as Mary Prince did in a letter informing Governor John Endicott that she spoke "as a prophetesse of the Lord . . . guided by the infallible Spirit of the Lord."[147] Copies of some of these letters and descriptions of the colonists' aggressive response were carried back to England, where some were quickly incorporated into a printed book, Humphrey Norton's *New Englands Ensign* (1659). Other texts, such as Christopher Holder and John Copeland's "paper on Truth and Scriptures," passed into the hands of converts or sympathizers, including two residents of Salem, Massachusetts, and others in Rhode Island, where a copy was recovered by a nineteenth-century Quaker historian. From prison, too, Holder and Copeland sent out letters describing the "true peace and rest" they were experiencing amidst their "sufferings," a theme reiterated on both sides of the Atlantic.[148]

Everyone who followed Holder and Copeland to Massachusetts underwent the same severe beatings and imprisonment, but the flow of letters seems only to have increased. William Robinson managed to prepare a "Paper to the Court" describing how the voice of the Lord told him to give up his life; signing it "Written in the Common Goal, the 19th of the 8th month 1659." His "Paper" would reach London and, two years later, pass into print in George Bishop's *New England Judg'ed* (1661), which had an "Appendix . . . being Certain Writings, (never yet Printed,) of those Persons which were there Executed." For some of the texts by John Rous, Stevenson, Mary Dyer, and William Leddra in the appendix, we learn of an intermediary: "This . . . [a Leddra letter] was copied by W. Coddington of Rhode-Island." That the former Antinomian William Coddington would participate in reproducing and distributing such texts was in keeping with his prominence within the Quaker community. The singular importance of handwritten texts to Quakers on both sides of the Atlantic (even as the movement was sponsoring an extraordinary quantity of printed texts) is suggested by the practice of preserving spiritual testimonies within a family; a letter written by Christopher Holder and dated 1676 survived in this fashion, carefully tended among the papers of a Massachusetts family that converted to Quakerism.[149]

Important in its own right, Quaker practice also reminds us that, depending on the wishes of writers and their intermediaries, scribal publication could serve either to conceal or reveal the conflicts taking place in New England. Quaker missionaries craved publicity for their message—entering a Boston meetinghouse and disrobing, handing out copies of their letters, declaiming in a court room. The majority in 1637 wanted none of this, sensing that the less said, the better. The irony may be that the Quakers gained but a tiny number of adherents in New England and orthodoxy persisted.

* * *

The utility of scribal publication is exemplified in the lives of two poets, Benjamin Tompson and Edward Taylor, and two who wrote in a variety of genres, though remembered as historians, William Bradford of Plymouth and John Winthrop of Massachusetts. Case studies of these writers follow; Winthrop's continues in Chapter 5.

Harvard College students wrote verse, as did old men who never had formal literary training. Accessible to almost everyone, verse lent itself to themes and stories that fell within the scope of the Protestant vernacular tradition, such as the workings of divine providence that the lay man John Dane recalled in his autobiographical verse and prose. The same theme informed William Bradford's 431-line poem on "Som observations of Gods merciful dealing with us in this wilderness, and his gracious protection over us these many years."[150] Many wrote elegies commemorating someone they had known or wanted honored, as John Cotton did for Thomas Hooker (d. 1647) and two of his own children. The Harvard students who, each year, prepared the annual almanac that was printed in Cambridge added verse to its few pages on the seasons or similar subjects. Only a small portion of this poetry was printed in the seventeenth century, the rest of it circulating in handwritten copies preserved as much by chance as by intention—on the fly leaf of a book, in a journal or family archive, in a copy made long afterward by a chain of transmission that cannot be reconstructed. Some verse found its way into Mather's *Magnalia* in versions that strayed from any putative original, for Mather's memory was unreliable and he was a careless copyist.[151] As with those he reprinted, so with many others the transmission of hand-written copies or their transfer into print introduced changes in diction and accidentals. Yet with the exception of Edward Taylor and possibly Bradford, no poet in seventeenth-century New England attempted to fix his manuscript verse in anything like a final version. Verse that circulated in this manner was vulnerable not only to destruction and errant copying but also to misattribu-tion, for most of it was signed only with initials or not signed at all. Thus it happened that Joseph Tompson credited his brother Benjamin with a poem written by Samuel Danforth, and that modern scholars cannot decide which of the several possibilities for "E. C." wrote the poems signed with these initials.[152]

Benjamin Tompson (1642–1714), a schoolteacher and Harvard College graduate, wrote so much verse, and was so widely known for doing so, that his gravestone in Braintree, where his father had been minister, contained the words, "the Renouned Poet of N: Engl."[153] Tompson moved back and forth between print and scribal publication for the elegies that were his principal genre; two story poems recounting King Philip's War were printed in 1676. He belongs in this chapter because of the close connections between the elegies and the families or individuals who commissioned (or received) such verse, nearly always in the form of handwritten copies. The surest evidence of these connections is how Tompson's verse was preserved. He made no efforts himself to collect or pass on his elegies, but others did: John Leverett II copied a poem on his father John into a commonplace book; Deacon Hobart of Salem Village made a copy of a poem honoring his father, the minister Peter Hobart; and one of the Winthrops preserved an elegy on the six-year-old granddaughter of Samuel Sewall, Rebecca Sewall, perhaps because the Winthrops had already been patrons of Tompson. Still other verse survived in Samuel Sewall's commonplace book (possibly based on printed broadsides), in mid-eighteenth-century manuscript copies, and on flyleaves of printed books. But the convergence of poetry writing, scribal publication, and local patronage is best demonstrated by the history of the verse Tompson wrote to honor members of his family. The earliest of his poems, an elegy written not long after the death in 1666 of his father William Tompson, the minister in Braintree, Massachusetts, was preserved by Benjamin's great-nephew Samuel in a copy that dates from the early eighteenth century.[154] Eventually Benjamin would commemorate four other members of his family in verse, most of it copied into a journal his brother Joseph assembled.[155]

Tompson was singularly aware of writing for patrons even when he could not have expected anything in return. Alone among the colonists, he honored two Englishmen of aristocratic background, offering consolation to the London merchant Sir Humphrey Davie on the death of his son Edmund Davie (who died c. 1681 after graduating from Harvard College in 1674), and addressing the elder Davie as "my Honoured Patron." In late 1699 he celebrated the first visit to Boston by Richard Coote, Lord Bellomont, who had been appointed royal governor in 1697, describing himself as a writer of "rural" verse and evoking the colonists' "loyal Hearts." Bellomont may not have been interested in the poem but others were, for a copy was preserved in the papers of a mid-eighteenth-century country minister. Meanwhile, some verse was passing back and forth between manuscript and printed versions, with changes to suit. "The Grammarians Funeral," written in 1678 or 1679 to commemorate a Boston schoolmaster, remained in manuscript until it was printed in 1708 in honor of a different person, "The late and famous School-Master of Boston," Ezekiel Cheever. By this time, too, Tompson had written commendatory verse for books by two of his contemporaries, William Hubbard and Cotton Mather, who incorporated the elegy on William Tompson into the *Magnalia*.[156]

None of this verse was signed with Tompson's full name, and most was anonymous, though his patrons surely knew he was the author. Meanwhile, the printers who were publishing his story poems and broadside verse were doing so with their customary casualness. When fighting broke out in the late fall of 1675 between the colonists and the Native Americans, Tompson wrote a narrative poem on its beginnings and the early battles that John Foster, who had just set up shop in Boston, quickly printed as *New Englands Crisis*, with Tompson identified only as "a Well wisher to his Countrey" and, in keeping with this anonymity, voicing authorial humility: "I never thought this Babe / of my weak Phantasie / worthy of an Imprima/ tur; but being an Abortive, / it was beg'd in these perplexing / Times to be cherished by the / Charity of others." An expanded version, retitled *New Englands Tears* and with Tompson identified merely as "an Inhabitant of Boston in New England" writing "to his Friend in London," seems to intermingle his revisions of the earlier poem with many other changes made by the London bookseller or printer (or putative "friend"). At some point in the early eighteenth century a Boston printer published the elegy on Rebecca Sewall in the form of a composite, possibly the printer's doing, of the two versions Tompson himself had written.[157] That so few printed broadsides of this kind survive reminds us, once again, of the superior utility of scribal publication for elegies and of the crucial role that patrons, but especially Tompson's family, played in preserving his verse.

The minister-poet Edward Taylor (1642–1729), who came from England to Massachusetts in 1668 and graduated from Harvard College in 1671, kept his poetry to himself, and two extensive poem-series, "Gods Determinations touching his Elect" and the "Preparatory Meditations," may have had no contemporary readers. Yet the material history of this verse strongly suggests that Taylor wanted to preserve it in final, "fair copy" versions to entrust to his family. Though he never used the word itself, he created a legacy similar in kind to Anne Bradstreet's prose "Meditations" and Thomas Shepard's autobiography. As Thomas L. Davis has pointed out, by the early 1680s he had prepared an "impeccably clean fair copy" of "Gods Determinations." Later on, at two different moments he transcribed the "Preparatory Meditations" and other verse, all of it in what he probably regarded as a final state, into a leather bound book to which he gave the title "Poetical Works."[158] This attentiveness to legibility and permanence can only mean that he was counting on the poetry being preserved, and preserved to be read. The same material qualities also imply publication. So Thomas and Virginia Davis have noted: "The fastidious way he transcribed the poems, neatly drawing borders, column lines, headnotes, and so on, his careful preservation of the manuscripts, and—quite late in life—going back over all of the poems and writing (usually, vertically in the margin) phrases which were unclear in the texts, suggest a conscious expectation of a future audience."[159]

For Taylor as for so many others, reticence and privacy were relative, not absolute, conditions of writing. Every so often he made his talents known, as when he sent Samuel Sewall, his Harvard classmate and lifelong friend, the poem, "Upon Wedlock, & Death of Children." Sewall passed it along to Cotton Mather, who incorporated two stanzas, identified as written by "E.T." of Westfield, into a sermon of spiritual consolation, *Right Thoughts in Sad Hours* (London, 1689), a book he dedicated to Sewall, who had recently lost a child. Another occasional poem, an elegy commemorating the Westfield church deacon David Dewey, who died in 1712, was included in a short pamphlet printed in 1713 that contained a collection of Dewey's prose meditations, three "Exhortations, Pen'd and Left . . . as a Legacy to His Children," and Taylor's poem, which concludes with the salutation "Sic flevit maestus amicus, E.T."[160] As a young man in England and again during his years in Cambridge, Taylor had written other occasional verse that almost certainly was reproduced in handwritten copies—an elegy on a former lieutenant governor of Massachusetts, for example, and another commemorating the second president of Harvard. In some of this verse he employed the themes and structural effects of the jeremiad, breaking into a mode of public address: "To New England," "To Connecticut," and a third that begins, "Alas poor Farmington."[161] Moreover, Taylor wrote on themes that, in the context of the times, were considered central to public life. A series of poems he entitled the "Metrical History of Christianity" has an explicitly political subject matter, the meaning—rehearsed in election sermon after election sermon—of New England as example to other Christian communities or nations. Taylor was exceptional in holding back so much of his poetry from circulation. But to think of him as unpublished is to ignore the poems that appeared in print or were distributed in handwritten copies and, above all, to ignore his assumption that he had written a body of verse his family would guard and someday put to good use.

When William Bradford died in 1657, nothing of his had been printed under his name on either side of the Atlantic, though he had probably written one section of the anonymous *A Relation, or Journal, of the Beginning and Proceedings of the English Plantation settled at Plymouth* (London, 1622). Yet Bradford was a prolific writer of prose and poetry. In his will of 1657 he singled out the verse he had been composing in the 1650s, "commend[ing]" to his executors "some small bookes written by my owne hand to bee improved as you shall see meet. In special I com[m]end to you a little booke with a blacke cover, wherein there is a word to Plymouth a word to Boston, and a word to New England, with sundry useful verses."[162] He said nothing of the prose texts that also existed in manuscript, three in the form of "Dialogues" or conferences with the "Young Men" of Plymouth[163] and a manuscript he entitled "Of Plimmoth Plantation," annals of Plymouth Colony prefaced by chapters that recounted the origins of his Separatist community in England, its life in the Netherlands, and the passage across the Atlantic in 1620. Together with the "dialogues," this manuscript was part of an archive that also included a letter-book and originals or copies of letters he or other officials of the colony had received or sent during his many years of service in the colony government, most of the time as governor. Some of these letters were preserved in "Of Plimmoth Plantation," which had chapters that approximated a compilation of documents.[164]

The only verse to be printed under his name appeared posthumously, a thirty-four-line "Epitaphium Meum," probably written near the time of Bradford's death, that his nephew Nathaniel Morton incorporated into *New Englands Memoriall* (Cambridge, 1669), a history of Plymouth based in part on Bradford's annals. The "little book with black covers" does not survive, but in 1657, the year Bradford died, John Willett, a neighbor still in his teens, copied the three texts specified in Bradford's will, together with three others (the "sundry verse"), into a notebook (Fig. 3).[165] Why someone of Willett's limited skills undertook the work of copying is a mystery, for he had no feeling for poetic diction and punctuation. His deficiencies can be specified because a version of one poem, "Som observations of Gods mercifull dealing wt us in this Wildernes, And his Gracious protection ouer us these many years," survives in Bradford's own hand. Willett's transcription ignored the arrangement of that poem in stanzas, introduced "accidental variants in almost every line" (omitting, for example, Bradford's elisions and the mid-line punctuation that he used to indicate rhythm), contained misreadings of a great many words, and dropped entire lines as well as words. Thus in line 419 Bradford's "fate" became "state," in line 202 "Many men of worth, for" became Willett's "many worth of," and in line 429 Bradford's "let these few lines you move" became "let these few ayes you move."[166] Bad as they may be, Willett's are the only versions of most of the verse.

The task of preserving and transmitting Bradford's prose manuscripts fell mainly to Morton, an experienced clerk who for many years was secretary of Plymouth Colony and keeper of the Plymouth Church records. Morton copied one of the dialogues, the first, into those records, almost certainly as a means of perpetuating the ties between the colony's most "ancient church" and Bradford's history-telling. The same impulse led him to enter on the church records "a few poems made by a frind on the deplored death of Mr John Robinson the worthy Pastour of the Church of God att Leyden" that

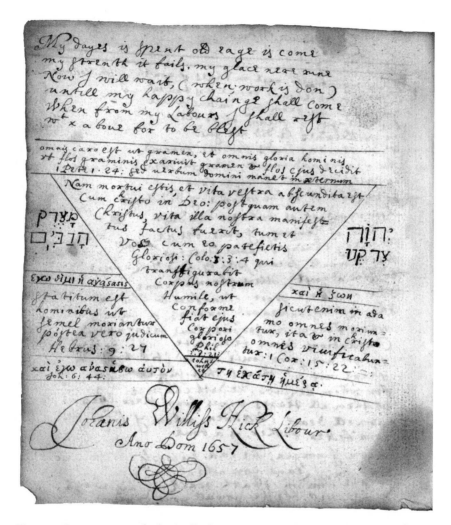

Figure 3. Opening page of John Willett's transcription in 1657 of William Bradford poems. Courtesy of the Massachusetts Historical Society

modern historians regard as probably by Bradford,[167] though Morton never specified him as their author. Morton resumed his labors as copyist with the history of Plymouth colony, transcribing a significant part of it into the church records and incorporating some of the text into *New Englands Memoriall*, "wherein the greatest part of my intelligence hath been borrowed from my much honoured Uncle, Mr. William Bradford, and such Manuscripts as he left in his Study."[168] The uncertainties of textual authority that surround several of these texts extend to questions of attribution. Modern arguments that Bradford wrote the verses on Robinson rest on no authority other than his sympathetic portrait of Robinson in "Of Plimmoth Plantation." The *Relation* of 1622 was collectively authored, with Edward Winslow in the lead and clearly the person responsible for two or more of its sections; it is plausible, however, that Bradford wrote another of them.[169] The longest poem in the Willett notebook, "On the Various Heresies in Old and New England with an Appeal to the Presbyterians," though sometimes attributed to Bradford on the grounds of being included in the "little book with black covers," is probably not his but the doing of an English writer, for the narrator speaks repeatedly of being "here in England" and gestures toward rapprochement with English Presbyterians at a time when English Independents (or Congregationalists) were riding high. It seems likely, therefore, that the "little book with black covers" was a miscellany, a compilation of verse by Bradford but also by others he did not identify.[170]

Bradford wrote with a strong sense of audience, most immediately the "young men" of Plymouth he addressed so explicitly in the dialogues. "Of Plimmoth Plantation" also had its seventeenth-century readers—more of them, perhaps, than of the manuscript poetry. Increase Mather, who consulted the text in the mid-1670s, was certainly reading the original, a manuscript that survives to this day despite being carried back to England when British troops evacuated Boston and vanishing for nearly three-quarters of a century, for he cited it as "a large Manuscript of Governour Bradfords (written with his own hand)," in *A Relation of the Troubles* (Boston, 1677). His colleague and rival William Hubbard also drew on the manuscript in writing his "Generall History of New England." As did Morton, these two readers encountered a manuscript with a neatly written title on the first page of text, followed by lines that set off the brief introductory paragraph from "Chap. 1," also marked off by lines, as were succeeding chapters. Had Bradford prepared the text to be printed? Its material qualities contradict any such argument, for the heading "Of Plimmoth Plantation" is not part of a separate title page. The one other prose manuscript of his that survives, the third "Dialogue," has something much closer to a title page, with more elaborate penmanship, but lacks the fuller apparatus—found for example in Daniel Gookin's "Indian Converts"—that signal a printer's fair copy. Just as telling is that Bradford did not treat the manuscript history as finished, but returned to it at several moments in the 1640s, using the blank side of the pages to interpolate some of the passages that have become famous, like his lament that people were breaking away from the original area of settlement. In its final form, Bradford's manuscript could not have served a printer well: no table of contents, no expansive title, no catchwords or running heads, no author's name indicated.[171]

At long last, we return to John Winthrop. For him the practices of writing and publication unfolded in a context that warranted caution if not secrecy. Hence his preference while in England for scribal publication. Dismayed by the policies of Charles I, he relied on a network of friends and correspondents to keep him informed of current events. He may have shared some of the letters he received with others who were of the same persuasion, but he learned, early on, to be careful in how he expressed himself, for he knew that criticism of the Crown could be construed as sedition. Once he made the decision in 1629 to immigrate to New England, writing became a means of persuading others to participate in the Massachusetts Bay Company. The first text of his to be distributed in any quantity, though only in handwritten copies, were the "Considerations" he shared in draft with other members of the company. After reaching New England and beginning to exercise his authority as governor, writing became an important means of governance. On this side of the Atlantic as in England, he never turned to a printer but continued to employ handwritten copies when he was asserting his position on issues being debated in the Massachusetts General Court or addressing a wider audience. A fully public figure, in practice he preferred a medium of publication he regarded as significantly private. Only once did he intentionally turn to a printer, though the decision to publish the *Humble Request* (London, 1630) may have been made by others. At the very same moment he was sharing the "Modell of Christian Charitie" in handwritten copies, and as soon as he reached New England he sent back a handwritten description of the voyage, "replete with daily descriptions of the weather and of information about the course," asking that "copies . . . be distributed to members of his family and friends."[172]

Scribal publication also served his purposes when he decided to narrate the ups and downs of his spiritual history. The books of "practical divinity" he read and the many sermons he listened to provided both an outline and the details of appropriate experience and practices: the self-examination that would persuade him of his utter worthlessness, the faith to rely on the "promise" that, despite his sinful state, saving grace would still be granted; and, thereafter, the "duties" of a righteous life, or as Thomas Hooker was wont to say, the routines of "evangelical obedience." But as forecast in the model, the heart and will were easily distracted or deceived. Near the end of 1636, having been "awakened" by John Cotton's critique of "duties" as a sign of grace and the initial stirrings of the Antinomian controversy, he put pen to paper narrating what he remembered of his spiritual journey from childhood to the present moment, a text he shared with others, for the one copy that survives was the doing of the Cambridge schoolmaster (and soon to become president of Harvard) Henry Dunster, who transcribed it into a notebook.[173] About the same time (December 1636?), he tried his hand at a different kind of writing, a reasoned defense of the proposition that "a man is justified by fayth, and not before he beleeveth." He did so hoping to calm the tempest that Anne Hutchinson and John Cotton were arousing with their critique of this very theme. But when he shared the manuscript with Thomas Shepard in nearby Cambridge, the young minister counseled him that the text could add fuel to the fires that were burning. "Its a great scruple in my thoughts," Shepard wrote in 1637, "whether it will be most safe for you to enter into the conflict with your pen . . . it being an easy thing for a subtill adversary to take advantages at woords." Leaving the decision to Winthrop to "forbeare wrighting for a while," he urged him not to "send these papers as they are" to others. As best we can tell, Winthrop heeded Shepard's advice and put the manuscript away.[174]

The experience renewed his sense of the perils of writing in the midst of "subtil" enemies. But the Antinomian controversy also pulled him in another direction. When he heard in April 1638 that one of Anne Hutchinson's supporters had given birth to a deformed (and no longer living) foetus, he ordered it exhumed and publicized, triumphantly, a description he almost certainly wrote.

Silence, self-censorship, and (at best) scribal publication figure as well in how he approached the journal-history he had begun to keep in 1630. The longest of his manuscripts by far, it occupied him intermittently for the rest of his life. Generally speaking, the entries record events that happened weeks or months before he wrote them out, intervals that became much longer after 1644. By the mid-forties, too, he was incorporating official or semi-official documents into the history, or leaving spaces for doing so.[175] A framework of meaning that accounts for many of the entries was the lore of wonders, itself a version of the doctrine of divine providence. As Bradford would do in his narrative of Plymouth colony history, Winthrop wanted to preserve evidence in the form of wonders or remarkable providences that God was on the side of the colonists and would sustain them against their enemies.[176] It seems certain he intended his ever-increasing accumulation of wonders to be shared with others. From the start, however, the journal was something else, a running narrative of political and religious events seen through the eyes of someone who served at the highest levels of civil government as the colony's leaders figured out a system of civil government and collaborated with the ministers as they fashioned the "Congregational Way." Keeping a record of these discussions and events meant keeping a record of controversies, for at every step of the way his views on the nature of state and church, and his practices as governor or magistrate, were viewed with suspicion by others in the colony. Inevitably, the journal-history became a partisan document leavened with behind-the-scenes information, the anxieties of governance, and pointed criticism of ministers, magistrates, and lay people who disappointed him.

That these very qualities of the journal made others anxious is apparent from a letter Shepard sent Winthrop in 1640 commending him for attempting a history of New England but warning that, unless Winthrop were careful in selecting what he recorded, the book "may prejudice us in regard of the state of England if" some "secret hid things" were "divulged." Knowing that the journal was available for others to read—Shepard himself had probably been among its readers—he advised that, "if there be any secret hid things which may be prouoking; it may be left to the judgement of others how far it will be fit to divulge them when the coppy is privately examined."[177] Yet again, therefore, Winthrop was being reminded that writing was precarious even (or especially) in the mode of a handwritten journal. Another contemporary reader was less anxious. Robert Child, the soon to be "Remonstrant" of 1646, wrote in 1645 to an English friend that "Mr. Winthrop the elder every day writes particular passages of the country in a great book which he freely communicates to any and saves me a labour in this kind, who intended the same busines."[178] The sense of ease in this report is deceptive, for Winthrop remained guarded in what he wrote down, refusing, for example, to tell the story of sometime governor Richard Bellingham's hasty marriage. The real measure of his self-censoring lies in how he shaped the entries he wrote in retrospect, a practice he followed throughout his life but especially in the 1640s.

Another side of Winthrop's life as a writer is represented by the texts he wrote in response to political controversies during the 1640s. The story of these texts, a story inexplicable except in the context of Winthrop's anxieties about the danger of "public" debate, belongs within a larger narrative of the practice of criticism that follows in Chapter 5. For now, the story of Winthrop and Bradford as writers who relied on scribal publication returns us to the larger argument of this chapter, that this system served many of the colonists well. Why it did so has something to do with a deep preference for consensus that the more public medium of printing could jeopardize. For Tompson and Taylor as poets, the technology was well-matched with the forms of sociability that account for their elegies, and it suited the needs of anyone constructing a legacy for future generations, as many colonists did—the Tompsons, Anne Bradstreet, Thomas Shepard, and John Dane, among others. Politics provided another context, for the local printers were unwilling to publish statements of dissent until the closing years of the century.

As these case studies remind us, the practice of making handwritten copies was utilitarian in its own right. So was printing, and for some handwritten texts, being printed was how they survived or reached a wider audience. For texts that every household was expected to own or know, like catechisms and the laws in force, printing was displacing scribal publication by the 1660s. In the 1730s the Boston book trade began to publish some of the schoolbooks that students at Harvard and Yale had been copying, by the turn of the century printed broadsides were becoming a vehicle for poetry, and after 1704 handwritten newsletters gave way to printed newspapers. Always, too, certain manuscripts lent themselves to being printed, perhaps because this is what an author had wanted or, more likely, because of another person's intervention. The antiquarian minister Thomas Prince was responsible for the printing of Joseph Eliot's letter of spiritual counsel and John Mason's narrative of the Pequot War, and Cotton Mather was probably behind the sudden appearance in the early eighteenth century of manuscripts dating from the 1630s and 1640s, including John Cotton's Salem sermon and a treatise on the power of the keys by Richard Mather (Boston, 1712). Such moments of transition remind us that scribal publication was never a tightly closed system but always and everywhere contingent on circumstance, intention, and codes of meaning.

CHAPTER THREE

Social Authorship and the Making
of Printed Texts

JOHN COTTON WAS SHOCKED. When someone in the late summer of 1642 showed him a newly arrived copy of a London printed book that had his name on the title page, he learned for the first time that John Humfrey, a former member of his Boston congregation, had arranged for sermons he had preached in Boston to be printed in London. And printed, Cotton realized, using sermon notes taken as he was preaching. So Humfrey acknowledged in his preface. Cotton learned too that, although he would earn nothing from the book, Humfrey was being well rewarded. An entry in John Winthrop's journal records Cotton's reaction: "Now came over a book of Mr. Cotton's sermons upon the seven vials. Mr. Humfrey had gotten the notes from some who had took them by characters, and printed them in London, he had 300 copies for it, which was a great wrong to Mr. Cotton, and he was much grieved at it, for it had been fit he should have perused and corrected the copy before it had been printed." Wanting control over what he wrote or preached, Cotton had been denied that control by a London bookseller and the anonymous note-taker, with Humfrey acting as go-between.[1]

But Cotton may have been less surprised than Winthrop shows him being, for he surely knew that London printers and booksellers routinely accepted sermon notes as copy text for a printed book, and did so without consulting the author. During the 1630s, most of Thomas Hooker's sermon series had been published in this manner, as was the first printing of Thomas Shepard's *The Sincere Convert* (1641). Shepard, who did not review the printer's copy, complained in a letter to an English friend that it was a "ragged child," a "collection of notes in a dark town in England, which one procuring of me, published without my will or privity. I scarce know what it contains; nor do I like to see it, considering the many typographical errors, most absurd, and the confession of him that published it, that it comes out mutilated and altered from what was first written."[2] Unusual though these complaints may seem, many English writers could have testified to the same experience. If misery loves company, Cotton and Shepard had plenty of it.[3]

Every story of this kind tells of people (some named, some unnamed) who intervened to bring a book into being, some deciding the material format, others choosing the copy text or tidying up a manuscript, and still others supplying a preface, correcting errors in the proof sheets, or paying the printers' bill. To take these intermediaries seriously is to understand the making of printed texts as a process of collaboration. William Shakespeare participated in one form of collaboration when he helped write *Pericles*. After his death, the editors who compiled the First Folio of 1623 became his partners by selecting which versions of his plays they judged most "authentic."[4] No one in New England wrote plays, but the three or four ministers who made a fresh translation of the book of Psalms into English, *The Whole Booke of Psalmes*, were partners in writing just as Shakespeare was with George Wilkins and John Fletcher. Other modes of collaboration figured in the making of Cotton's printed sermons and the publishing of Anne Bradstreet's poetry. All of these interventions carry us beyond the figure of the solitary author and the author-controlled text to a wider field of practices and meanings that, for the colonial writer as for his English counterpart, is evoked by the phrase "social authorship."[5]

Everyone who participated in the making of a text was caught up in a contradiction from which there seemed no escape: should the presence of an author be emphasized and the role of intermediaries downplayed or concealed, or should this role be honestly acknowledged when doing so could make readers question the authority of a text? John Humfrey felt this contradiction as much as anyone in his day. In his preface to the "Christian Reader" he declared that *The Powring Out of the Seven Vials* consisted of words "taken from [Cotton's] owne mouth," though admitting immediately thereafter that Cotton had not "styled over his owne notions" (i.e., reviewed the text). Nor had he "intended [the sermons], when first delivered, for any more publike use, then of his own private Auditorie."[6] A friend who professed to respect a writer's own words and acknowledged that person's preference for privacy was actually violating both. Yet we would misread the workings of social authorship in the seventeenth century if we questioned the authority of every printed text. Accuracy or authenticity mattered not only to writers, but to everyone who participated in text-making. Had there been no such expectation, Humfrey would not have acted to reassure readers of *The Powring Out of the Seven Vials* that they were encountering Cotton's actual preaching. Collaboration must be understood not as an either/or that produced good texts and bad, but as a middle ground on which writers, patrons, printers, and other intermediaries worked their way through a complex system of meanings and practices.

We enter this field of practices and meanings at the point when a writer's original or someone else's transcription was transformed into "fair copy." Then, in turn, comes the making of preliminaries or front matter, all those parts of a book that precede what we customarily think of as the "text"—title pages, tables of contents, prefaces, dedications, and errata (which were often placed at the end). The wording of title pages and the information in prefaces about provenance lead us to the people who, well-meaning or not, intervened along the way, especially the printers and booksellers who transformed manuscripts into printed books, broadsides, and pamphlets. Not until the 1670s did the printers in Cambridge and, by 1675, their Boston successors, publish manuscripts of any length. Even when they began to do so, some of the colonists continued to rely on the London trade as the first-generation immigrants had done almost without exception. The story of the colonial writer and the world of print thus encompasses practices and people on both sides of the Atlantic.

* * *

An initial hurdle, and a real one, was preparing copy for the press. Then as now, printers wanted copy text that was legible, a "fair copy," as such versions were named.[7] So did readers of handwritten versions, as Thomas Lechford, a professional scrivener in Massachusetts, recognized in 1639/40 when he was asked by some of the ministers to show them a commentary he had written on the prophetic books of the Bible. Lechford replied that the manuscript "was not yet ready for theire view; I must faire write it."[8] For manuscripts directed to a printer the stakes were higher: the less legible a manuscript, the greater the likelihood of compositors' mis-readings. Hence the apology by the London intermediaries for John Cotton's *Way of the*

Churches (1645), "If all things in this Treatise, as now printed, doe not answer punctually word for word, to the first written Copie, let the reverend Authour, and the candid Reader pardon us, because wee had not the fairest Copie, nor knew wee, till the Book was near done, that there was a better to be had, nor to this day yet ever saw it."[9] The prefatory notice to the "Gentle Reader" in James Noyes's *Moses and Aaron*, published posthumously in London in 1661, included the warning that "thou mayest not expect this work should be so perfect and correct, as if the Author had been living to put it out himself," the reason being that "the original copy" had vanished in a shipwreck. In its place the printer had relied on a copy "not written by the Author, but by an unlearned Scribe," a practice that had enlarged the quantity of errata.[10]

The task of preparing sermons for the press was especially fraught. More often than not, the colonists continued the long-standing practice of preaching from "short Notes" that were "written [out] after the minister had Preached them," as the English minister Anthony Tuckney remarked in a preface to a sermon series of John Cotton's. As two of his ministerial colleagues pointed out, Samuel Whiting's *A Discourse of the Last Judgement* (Cambridge, 1664) was based on "the heads of what was prepared for his preaching," a deficiency they tried to turn into an advantage by remarking that the reader will find "much in a little room."[11] When the copy text consisted of notes someone in the congregation had taken during the service, the possibilities for error were many. John Davenport, the founding minister of the New Haven church, worried about a sermon series of his for this very reason. Hearing that the notes taken on his weekly lectures by a parishioner named Mark Pierce were filled with "greate mistakes" and disturbed because other "imperfect copies" of his sermons had already passed into print, Davenport entrusted his own manuscript notes to Pierce to aid him in preparing a copy text. Pierce was candid about the limitations of his note taking, telling Davenport that no matter how "diligently" he "wrote," "his head and pen could not carry away some materiall expressions." To Davenport's relief, Pierce welcomed having the minister's version "to perfect his owne by them."[12] Facing the same difficulties, Increase Mather felt he had overcome the problem by relying on a woman in his congregation of "rare dexterity" to capture his preaching; her notes, he remarked in 1719, were more accurate and substantial than any he had previously depended on.[13]

These anxieties about notes as copy text—and, in this instance, a disorderly archive to boot—were unusually explicit in the making of the first book in the format of folio to be printed in New England, the sermon series Samuel Willard initiated in the 1680s on the Westminster Confession and sustained until shortly before his death in 1708. Joseph Sewall and Thomas Prince, who followed Willard in the ministry of Boston Third Church, decided some years later that the lectures should be published. As they reported in the preface to *A Compleat Body of Divinity* (Boston, 1726), they found themselves struggling to make sense of a mass of manuscripts, only some of which were "Originals" in Willard's own hand. "Others were but Transcripts from them," and not very good transcripts at that, for they contained "several small Mistakes, both in the Scriptures cited and in diverse Words and Pointings, and sundry obscure places so very difficult to read." In both copy and original, moreover, the citations of Scripture did not include the actual passage. Reasoning that Willard had preferred to quote these from memory, though doubting "he recited them all," the editors had been "oblig'd . . . to search the Scriptures . . . and to use our best Discretion both in selecting those we tho't most proper" and in fixing the length of the quotation. Once this mixture of original and copy had been put in good enough order to send to the printer, other difficulties arose. Because of the "vastness of the Composure" the editors had to farm out the task of preparing the manuscript and proofreading the printed sheets "into the hands of many." When *A Compleat Body of Divinity* was finally available for sale, the two editors acknowledged in their preface that what had "come forth" was lacking "that beautiful *Symmetry* which it wou'd have done in the hands of the Author, or of any one accurate Person that had Corrected the whole."[14]

Fair copy in hand, decisions followed about what kinds of preliminaries should be added. How would the title be worded, and should quotations from Scripture or other sources amplify the themes it suggested? Would the printer and bookseller add their names and specify the place and year of printing, or would this information be omitted or fictitious? Would someone provide commendatory verse? Would there be a preface that opened with a dedication to friend, patron, or community? Authors' names, too, could appear in a variety of ways—the real name, printed with or without other marks of identification, a pseudonym, initials, or no name at all, the bibliographer's "anon."

Writers could decide some of these questions, or at least attempt to do so. Little evidence survives of these attempts, in part because so few fair copy manuscripts can be compared with printed versions. Mather may have asked the printer John Foster to insert the Massachusetts General Court's commission to the "Reforming Synod" of 1679 on the title page of the report he wrote of its findings, *The Necessity of Reformation* (Boston, 1679), and as manuscripts that survive indicate, he drafted titles for three other books. When Daniel Gookin's scribe was preparing the fair copy version of "Indians converted," he wrote out an unusually substantial title page (Fig. 4) that specified the contents and quoted several passages of Scripture. The inventive titles of Cotton Mather's books were surely his doing, as were the great variety of quotations that adorned them.[15] Otherwise, much of what appeared on a title page was the doing of booksellers and printers who chose the decorative ornaments, decided the wording of the colophon, and called attention to a theme or topic with their choice of type size. When a title page announced that the book was "extremely useful" to a particular kind of reader, the bookseller was probably responsible for this trick of advertising, and it was a trade practice to insert brief summaries of what the book was about.

Naming the writer was the least certain feature of a seventeenth-century title page, and not because so many texts were controversial. No name appeared on quarto editions of Shakespeare's plays until 1598, and not until 1608 did someone in the trade assume that his name would help sell a playbook, though some printings remained unattributed as late as 1622. As Marcy L. North has pointed out, within the English trade "more than 800 known authors were published anonymously between 1475 and 1640," a figure that does not include the use of pseudonyms. Nor was 1640 a moment of transition, for anonymity persisted well into the eighteenth century and would have a new significance in the nineteenth. A practice used this widely was a "flexible convention" that, for certain writers, was "an act of self-protection," for others, "an act of modesty," and for some texts, "an accident of text transmission." Anonymity could heighten a reader's interest in knowing the identity of the author and, in doing so, emphasize authorial presence; alternatively, it could help foreground the presence of others, sometimes named, sometimes not, who had participated in the making of the text. Anonymity was paradoxical in its relationship to the marketplace, serving both to reduce a writer's renown and to underscore someone's importance, as the initials "T. H." may have done for Thomas Hooker at a moment when his books were coming into favor. But of most importance, the absence of a name from a title page was not always intended to conceal someone's identity. Secrecy and anonymity were never one and the same.[16]

New England writers were well aware of the political significance of

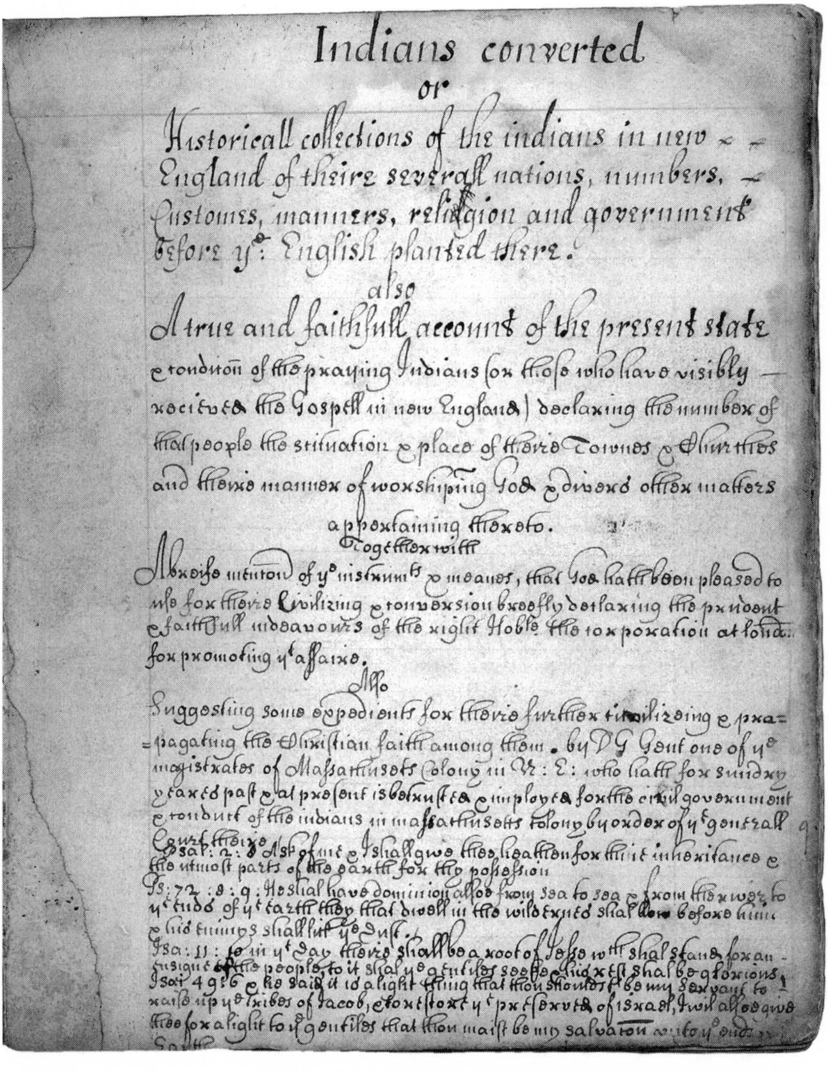

Indians converted

or

Historicall collections of the indians in new
England of theire severall nations, numbers,
Customes, manners, religion and government
before y^e English planted there.

also

A true and faithfull account of the present state
& condition of the praying Indians (or those who have visibly
received the Gospell in new England) declaring the number of
that people the situation & place of theire Townes & Churches
and theire manner of worshiping God, & divers other matters
appertaining thereto.

Together with

A breife intent of y^e instrum^{ts} & meanes, that god hath been pleased to
use for theire Civilizing & conversion breefly declaring the prudent
& faithfull indeavours of the right Noble the corporation at lond:
for promoting y^e affaire.

Also

Suggesting some expedients for theire further civilizing & pra-
=pagating the Christian faith among them. by DG Gent one of y^e
magistrates of Massachusets Colony in N: E: who hath for sundry
yeares past & al present is betrusted & imployed for the civil government
& conduct of the indians in massachusets Colony by order of y^e generall
Court theire

Psal: 2: 8 Aske of me & I shall give thee heathen for thine inheritance &
the utmost parts of the earth for the possession

Ps: 72: 8: 9: He shall have dominion also from sea to sea & from the river to
ye ends of ye earth they that dwell in the wildernes shall bow before him
& his enimys shall lick ye dust

Isa: 11: 10 in ye day there shall be a root of Jesse wch shal stand for an
ensigne of the people to it shal ye gentiles seeke & his rest shal be glorious
Isai 49: 6 he said it is a light thing that thou shouldst be my servant to
raise up ye tribes of Jacob, & to restore ye preserved of Israel, I will also give
thee for a light to ye gentiles that thou maist be my salvation unto ye end
&c.

Figure 4. Fair copy, but never printed: title page of Daniel Gookin's "Indians
Converted." Courtesy of the Massachusetts Historical Society.

anonymity, for Protestant radicals and their Catholic counterparts in Tudor-Stuart England frequently concealed their names in order to protect themselves from being caught and punished. A daring Puritan manifesto, the *Admonition to the Parliament* of 1572, was unsigned, and the two or three men who wrote the "Marprelate" tracts that an underground press began to print in 1588 signed themselves "Martin Mar-prelate," with false colophons thrown in for good measure.[17] Closer in time and cultural space to the colonists were the books William Brewster printed in Leiden during his years within a refugee Separatist community. For his first two imprints, one of them by the academic intellectual William Ames, himself a refugee, Brewster named himself as printer and specified the author. Soon he was venturing into more dangerous waters by printing the Scotch Presbyterian David Calderwood's diatribe against episcopacy, a book from which he prudently omitted both his own name and Calderwood's. Closer still in time were the anonymous or pseudonymous books and pamphlets of the 1630s and 1640s critical of the Stuarts and the Church of England—three by John Milton, for example, in which he protested the validity of bishops.

Yet on home ground there was little reason for any colonial writer to worry about the consequences of publishing under his own name, and not until the early 1660s, when the nature of church membership was being intensely debated, and again in the mid-1680s, when civil authority passed into the hands of an anti-Puritan royal governor, did anyone do so for political reasons. The Springfield magistrate and lay theologian William Pynchon may have wished in retrospect that his name was not on the title page of *The Meritorious Price of Our Redemption* (London, 1650), for the Massachusetts General Court demanded that he "give full satisfaction both here and by some second writing, to be printed and dispensed in England." But by 1652 Pynchon had returned to England, where he continued to publish his less than wholly orthodox opinions.[18] Before and after him, other dissidents put their own names on what they published through the English book trade, as Roger Williams and Samuel Gorton were doing in the mid-1640s, though Parliament would condemn one of Williams's books.

Where anonymity was conventional, not political, was in situations of collective authorship and for certain genres. It was in keeping, too, with the assumption that the truth-speaking writer remove himself from the marketplace of print. Robert Cushman, who visited Plymouth in 1622, explained in a preface to *A Sermon preached at Plimmoth* (London, 1622) that he had "not set downe my name, partly because I seek no name, and principally, because

I would have nothing esteemed by names." Collective authorship explains why the ministers who fashioned *The Whole Booke of Psalmes* did not identify themselves, and its anonymity persisted throughout the seventeenth-century re-printings in England and New England. Nor did the writers and compiler (probably Hugh Peter) of *New Englands First Fruits* (London, 1643), a description of the first commencement at Harvard College and a brief account of missionary outreach to the Native Americans, indicate their presence, or those of *Church-Government and Church-Covenant Discussed* (London, 1643), a collection of responses to inquiries from English Puritans about the "Congregational Way," which purported to speak for all of the ministers in New England. Another reason for this last text's anonymity may have been that these tracts originated as "private" responses to queries that reached the colonists from England, private in the sense of circulating in manuscript to a small group of people. Verse in almanacs was invariably "of Incerti Authoris," and before the 1660s and sometimes afterwards the almanacs written by Harvard College tutors were usually anonymous or signed with initials.

For many books and broadside verse, anonymity was temporary, contradicted by other evidence within the printed text itself or by someone's determination to spill the beans. Cotton would promptly indicate how little the ministers' anonymity of 1643 mattered when, a little later, he identified Richard Mather as the author of one of the texts included in *Church-Government and Church-Covenant Discussed*.[19] A poem in the almanac of 1670 signed "Incerti Authoris" was attributed ten years later by a reader to "Mr. [Charles] Chauncy President." Anne Bradstreet's name was not on the title page of *The Tenth Muse lately Sprung Up in America* (London, 1650), but the title page identified the author as a woman and, not far into the cluster of commendatory verse by several colonists, she was identified first as "A.B." and three times as "Anne Bradstreet," in one instance as "Wife of the Worshipfull Simon Bradstreet Esq." Once past the paratext of poems, the book opened with a poem of hers dedicating the verse "To her most Honoured Father Thomas Dudley Esq.," and signed "Anne Bradstreet" (Fig. 5). The first printing of Mary Rowlandson's captivity narrative, *The Sovereignty & Goodness of God* (Boston, 1682), was anonymous, but not her identity as its author. The Indian raid on Lancaster, Massachusetts that began her captivity had been widely publicized by word of mouth, and another burst of publicity accompanied the campaign to raise the funds to random her. In the opening pages she mentioned her husband's absence in Boston, and a sermon her husband Joseph Rowlandson preached in 1678, after the family had resettled

In praiſe of the Author,

Miſtris *Anne Bradſtreet*, Vertue's
true and lively Patterne, Wife of
the Worſhipfull *Simon Bradſtreet* Eſquire.

At preſent reſiding in the Occi-
dentall parts of the World, in
America, alias

N O V-A N G L I A.

VVHat Golden ſplendent S T A R is
this, ſo bright,
One thouſand miles thrice told, both day
and night,

(From

Figure 5. "Anon" but not anonymous. Anne Bradstreet's authorship acknowledged
in commendatory verse. *The Tenth Muse Lately Sprung Up in America* (London, 1650).
Courtesy of the Massachusetts Historical Society.

in Wethersfield, accompanied Mary's narrative. She would also thank by name some of the family's benefactors. Any doubts would have been resolved by the London printing of 1682, which had her name on the title page. The one contributor to the book who, to this day, remains unidentified was the "Per Amicam" who signed the preface.

The men who collaborated with Rowlandson and Bradstreet in bringing their manuscripts into print may have not wanted to put a woman's name on the title page, for women were always and everywhere encompassed within the rule of "modesty" that, in principle, kept them from speaking in public.[20] But as the title pages of Cotton Mather's immense corpus indicate, gender was a secondary factor in decisions about anonymity. Year in and year out, Mather omitted his name from two thirds of his hundreds of publications, usually as a sign—possibly not persuasive—of his humility. (Increase Mather preferred anonymity at the beginning of his literary career and Cotton's brother Samuel of Witney, England, put his name on only two of ten imprints in the early eighteenth century.) Simultaneously, Cotton or his collaborators filled his books with allusions to his authorship. On three different occasions in the 1690s, Boston booksellers advertised lists of his imprints, some of them previously anonymous, as by "Mr. Mather." In others, like the spiritual biography *Early Piety Exemplified* (London, 1689), he placed his name at the end of the text and either he or the London printer put it on the title pages of the three re-paginated sermons that followed. Now and then, he signed a preface but left his name off a title page. And, as in the case of Rowlandson, circumstances would have sufficed to identify his hand in other publications. Robert Calef, one of Mather's most irritating critics in the 1690s, played the part of a bibliographer by noting his authorship of the anonymous *Pietas in Patriam* (London, 1697), but Mather would drop any pretence to anonymity by including the book within the *Magnalia*.[21] Increase would do something similar in his election sermon of 1693, announcing at a moment when he thought it would help him politically that he was the author of several pamphlets published anonymously in 1689 and 1690.[22] In the cozy world of Boston publishing, secrecy and anonymity were rarely aligned. That Samuel Sewall wrote the anonymous *The Selling of Joseph A Memorial* (1700) was known to John Saffin, who responded with *A Brief and Candid Answer to a late Printed Sheet* (1701), with his name attached. But the "S.S." in another text that sometimes is attributed to Sewall, the anonymous *Early Piety, Exemplified in Elizabeth Butcher of Boston* (Boston, 1718), with a preface by his son Joseph, may be another person's doing.

Always, anonymity and pseudonymity were stylistic mannerisms that some writers employed to amuse themselves and their readers, as Edmund Spenser did in *The Shepheardes Calendar*. The New England minister Nathaniel Ward was having fun when he transmuted his name into Theodore de la Guard in *The Simple Cobler of Aggawamm* (London, 1647), and whoever wrote *Mercurious Americanus* was equally playful with the name "John Wheelwright Jr."[23] Yet at moments of political or cultural crisis, anonymity and pseudonymity regained their importance as the means of concealing a writer's presence. The tense situation of Nonconformists in early 1680s England and Ireland explains why Increase Mather's brother Nathaniel, a minister in Dublin, asked him to omit his name and "the land where it was preached" from sermons of his being published in Boston.[24] Most of the colonists who participated in the controversies that surrounded the overthrow of royal government in Massachusetts in 1689 and the Salem witch-hunt of 1692 did so anonymously.[25] But these events and their textual history must be deferred to another chapter.

Title page decided, the next phase of book making was to insert a preface. Very brief texts—for example, the sermons of forty pages or less that Cotton Mather published in abundance—rarely contained a preface, but they were a near-universal feature of much longer books. Within the vernacular tradition, the convention was to begin a preface with the phrase "Christian Reader" or "To the Reader." Often, however, those words were preceded by a dedication. Adding a dedication to the paratext had long been the custom among English writers, who inserted words of praise and gratitude into ninety per cent of the books that were published in the early seventeenth century. For the most part the people honored in these dedications were members of the aristocracy, favorites of the Crown, bishops of the Church, and the reigning monarch or his children; of the hundreds of dedications listed in Franklin B. Williams's *Index of Dedications*, the most common are to Elizabeth I and her Stuart successors, James I and Charles I.[26] Dedications also flourished within coteries of sympathetic readers and writers where friendship sometimes overlapped with patronage and literary taste. In the closing years of Elizabeth's reign and on into the seventeenth century, Mary Sidney, the Countess of Pembroke, was famously the central figure in such a coterie. Yet the aspiring writers who honored the Countess received next to nothing in return, and the Stuart kings were scarcely more generous.[27] A practice that yielded so little was nonetheless the means of sustaining a useful fiction, that the writer was a gentleman addressing what he wrote to the high-born few. Dedications set the writer's voice apart from the rough-and-tumble marketplace of print.

The very different politics of writing among the colonists was visible in how the colonists employed the practice—or failed to employ it. No New England writer before 1660 honored anyone associated with the Stuarts or the state church,[28] and no dedications of any kind appeared in the many printed books by Cotton, Hooker, and Shepard, with two exceptions; Cotton dedicated *Of the Holinesse of Church-Members* (London, 1650) to his former parish of Boston, Lincolnshire and Shepard honored his English friend William Greenhill in *The Sound Believer* (London, 1645).[29] The high valorizing of the "Christian reader" in the Protestant vernacular tradition was one reason for this silence, a valorizing evident in Peter Bulkeley's *The Gospel Covenant* (London, 1646), dedicated in part to his Concord, Massachusetts congregation, and in Richard Mather's *Farewel Exhortation* (Cambridge, 1657), which he addressed to his Dorchester church both to honor his special relationship with the townspeople and to thank them for paying the printer's bill. Others followed suit. Jonathan Mitchell dedicated Shepard's posthumously published *The Parable of the Ten Virgins* (London, 1660), to the Cambridge congregation Shepard had served and Mitchell inherited, John Norton singled out Ipswich, which he served as minister before moving to Boston First Church, in *The Orthodox Evangelist* (Cambridge, 1657), Increase Mather his late father's Dorchester congregation in *Renewal of Covenant* (Boston, 1677), and his own, Boston Second Church, in two collections of sermons printed in 1674 and 1684. Posthumously, Eleazar Mather (with Increase as intermediary) honored his congregation in Northampton in *A Serious Exhortation* (Boston, 1671). Meanwhile, a few ministers were acknowledging well-placed friends or family in England, as Edward Holyoke did in *The Doctrine of Life* (London, 1658) and Ephraim Huit in *The whole Prophecie of Daniel Explained* (London, 1643).

Yet the colonists also recognized the political benefits of flattering Englishmen in high office or well placed politically, never, of course, recognizing Charles I or anyone in his circle, but doing so for aristocrats and gentry associated with the Puritan program. The primary dedication in Bulkeley's *The Gospel-Covenant* was to Oliver St. John and his father; identified as the King's solicitor, St. John was in fact a longtime ally of critics of the king and, through his wife, related to Oliver Cromwell. Edward Winslow was the most emphatically political writer of the mid-1640s, turning out two books in short order that rebutted Samuel Gorton, English critics of the colonists' disdain for toleration, and the protesters associated with Dr. Robert Child.[30] Thanks to being in England as he did so, Winslow was attuned to shifting allegiances in the English government and currents of popular opinion. He dedicated the first printing of *Hypocrisie Unmasked* (1646) to the Earl of Warwick, who headed the Parliamentary committee for colonial relations, and to both houses of Parliament. But Warwick had fallen out of favor by the time Winslow arranged for a second printing, from which he omitted the dedication of 1646 and the original title, adding one that linked his defense of New England orthodoxy to a hot issue in English politics, *The Danger of Tolerating Levellers In a Civill State* (London, 1649). Gorton could play this politics himself, first in *Simplicities Defence against Seven-Headed Policy* (London, 1646), a book filled with accusations that the colonies were spurning the authority of Parliament and dedicated, like Winslow's retort, to the Earl of Warwick in recognition of his "spirit of tendernesse and compassion against the oppressed," then in *An Antidote Against the Common Plague Of the World* (London, 1657), dedicated to Oliver Cromwell as an instrument of God's will.

Cromwell would reappear in one of the dedications of the "Eliot tracts," the pamphlet-length books publicizing the missionary outreach to Native Americans. These books were political from beginning to end, as close as the colonial leadership and its London allies came to manufacturing books in response to public criticism. Ostensibly their purpose was to refute Gorton and other critics who complained that the colonists were neglecting the Indians. A second purpose was to acknowledge the services of a charitable corporation, the New England Company, dedicated to soliciting the funds needed to support the missionary enterprise and a third, to defend the colonists against accusations of intolerance at a moment when some English Congregationalists and their gentry or aristocratic allies were beginning to favor liberty of conscience. The company had much to do with the making of the tracts, and for several Edward Winslow played the role of editor. When he returned to England in late 1646 he brought with him the manuscript of what became the first in the series, *The Day-breaking, if not the sun-rising of the Gospell with the Indians in New-England* (London, 1647), and may have solicited the ministers who signed the dedication in the second of the series, *The Clear Sun-shine of the Gospel* (London, 1648). In all likelihood he recommended to them that they rehearse the history of the colonists' sufferings in England under Charles I and Archbishop Laud, to the end of representing the immigrants as victims, not persecutors. Here as in the rest of the series, some of which he or Henry Whitfield compiled from letters, the tracts employed celebratory language on the title page, followed by commendations of John Eliot and statements endorsing the truth of what the pamphlets were reporting. Dedications followed suit. The earliest honored the New England Company. Four contained an address to Parliament and one to Oliver Cromwell, a fulsome expression in *Tears of Repentance* (London, 1651) of John Eliot's sympathy for Cromwell's expectations of the end times.[31]

The apparatus of the Eliot tracts turned them into something akin to state-sponsored publications. So were other texts, as registered by their dedications. At the behest of the Massachusetts government, John Norton wrote *A Discussion of that great point of Divinity* (London, 1653) in response to Pynchon's *Meritorious Price*, and took on religious radicals in *The Heart of New England Rent* (Cambridge, 1660), in both of them acknowledging the government. William Hubbard was responding to critics of the Massachusetts government. among them his literary rival Increase Mather, when he dedicated his election sermon of 1676 to Governor John Leverett and "the rest of the Honourable Council of Magistrates," noting as he did so that "in this critical age" sermons such as his, a plea that people "live quietly and peaceably" under the care of the magistrates, merited "the shadow and protection of some Worthies" to spare the writer from "malevolence."[32] When the Restoration of Charles II in 1660 brought a new kind of politics into play, it too was registered in dedications. Thomas Parker, the minister in Newbury, Massachusetts who had never liked the "Congregational Way," signaled a broader disaffection by dedicating the late James Noyes's *Moses and Aaron* to Charles II. The first locally-printed dedication to the king came from Roger Williams, who honored Charles in his anti-Quaker *George Fox Digg'd Out of his Burrowes* (Boston, 1676), two years after Daniel Gookin had written a fulsome dedication to the Prince of Wales in the manuscript of "Indians converted." Dedications to royal governors would figure in sermons and poems of the 1690s, as in Benjamin Tompson's poem honoring William Bellomont's entrance into Boston.

The "To the Reader" (or, characteristically, "Christian Reader") that stood by itself or followed a dedication had other tasks to perform. The earliest of the Cambridge imprints, *The Whole Booke of Psalmes*, contained an anonymous preface justifying the project of translation and, indirectly, apologizing for the roughness of the verse, that was John Cotton's doing. He collaborated with his colleague John Wilson in providing a preface for Richard Mather's *The Summe of Certain Sermons*, the first collection of its kind to

be printed in New England, something Shepard had already done for Bulkeley's London-printed *Gospel Covenant*. During these early decades, manuscripts that came into the hands of the London trade habitually appeared in
book form with prefaces by someone living nearby. More often than not, the
men who provided these prefaces were already well known to the English
reading public. William Greenhill, who introduced three of Thomas Shepard's books, may have known Shepard during the years the two were preaching in England, but by the mid-1640s he had been thrust into prominence as
preacher to Parliament. Daniel Featley, a moderate Anglican who co-signed
the preface to Samuel Newman's massive *A Large and Complete Concordance
to the Bible in English* (London, 1643), had almost certainly been solicited by
a bookseller who knew that Featley had lent his name to an earlier concordance. By the 1670s, the books being printed in Cambridge and Boston were
beginning to contain prefaces written by local allies, invariably other ministers if the writer were one too.

In the early years of controversy back and forth across the Atlantic, prefaces were emphatically political. Few were as rhetorical or defensive as
Thomas Weld's in *A Short Story*, but the burden of defending the colonists
in an Atlantic context can be felt in many of them. The larger task that
prefaces undertook was to specify and resolve a series of contradictions. For
collections of sermons in the tradition of the "practical divinity," the central
contradiction was the inescapable difference between what the human hand
had written—the "letter," as it were—and divine truth as conveyed by Word
and Holy Spirit. The work of a preface was to elide this difference by representing any printed sermons as preached in "the demonstration of the Spirit"
(1 Cor. 2:4). Another, more easily negotiated contradiction concerned the
motives of the writer and bookseller: was the text a marketplace commodity
or a gesture of self-sacrificing service? Throughout the seventeenth century
the front matter in some London-printed godly books gestured toward the
marketplace, as when William Greenhill declared of Shepard's *Sincere Convert*, "Is it not a good purchase? Can you bestow your pains, or lay out your
money better?" Yet Shepard's English friends also insisted that the point of
buying the book was to learn more about "the great and glorious truths of
the Gospel," and someone as obsessed with marketplace success as Cotton
Mather was would persistently declare in his diary that the sole reason he
published, and did so incessantly, was to advance "soul-searching . . .
truths."[33]

The most-reiterated theme in the prefaces served both to counteract the accusation of self-interest and to associate the writer with Christ. This was the trope of humility that, as Mark Twain remarked of certain jokes the hero of *A Connecticut Yankee in King Arthur's Court* encountered during his unexpected return to the early Middle Ages, was already a venerable antique by the time it made its way into New England texts.[34] Age had not dimmed its appeal. As the first wave of colonists was embarking for Salem in 1629, a well known Puritan minister was describing a collection of his sermons as "unworthy . . . to bee brought into publike view." Thomas Shepard's version of the trope was to insist that he would have "more readily committed to the fire then to the light" his sermons on the Sabbath, which happened only because "some have so far compelled me" to publish what "my heart had opposed." In 1652 Richard Mather was insisting that he "had no thoughts" that his sermons on justification "should ever have been further published in this way that now thou seest" and that he had agreed to publication only after "sundry Godly Christians and Brethren having heard them delivered in preaching . . . came to mee with a serious and solemn request that I would further and fulfill their earnest desires in this thing." By his own account, Mather had continued to plead his inadequacy until he came to recognize God's role in the affair: "Against which motion though I alledged many objections, yet they still continued to desire as formerly. Whereupon at the last, considering with my self that God who hath the hearts of all men in his hands, might in moving their hearts . . . have some farther intent therin for his own glory and the good of some or other of his servants, then I at the first did apprehend, or could perceive[.]" Thirty years later, Samuel Willard was no less self-effacing, describing himself in the preface to *Mercy Magnified* (Boston, 1684) as "deeply sensible of my own insufficiency to Display these Mysteries: all the account which I can give of the publishing this imperfect thing, is knowing it the desire and duty of those that fear God." Like Mather before him, Willard attributed publication to the "many Souls" who "have desired they might have the further advantage of their being made publick."[35]

From Shepard in the 1640s to Willard in the mid-1680s and Cotton Mather well into the next century, this convention found its way into preface after preface. The layman Thomas Wheeler declared in his preface to a description of a battle during King Philip's War that he wrote it "not at first intending that it should by my means be brought to publick view: but several persons having seen it . . . they perswaded me, and urged it as a Duty . . . to put it forth in print, that many may thereby be provoked to give God the glory." James Allen, who gave the election sermon of 1679, insisted that only

"the earnest desire of many that it might be published for their further benefit" moved him to consent to publication. Used and re-used, this figure of
speech was occasionally supplemented by another, the voice of the dying
author who, lingering between this world and the next, spoke (or so the trope
implied) with even greater authority. At a moment when he was still relatively
unpublished and troubled with sickness, Increase Mather represented himself
in this manner in *Wo to Drunkards* (Cambridge, 1673), though his prediction
that these were probably his last words was soon belied by a torrent of publications.[36]

Were we to take all of these protestations at face value, we would wonder
how it happened that Willard, Shepard, and Increase Mather published so
much. But the trope of humility has to be understood as part of a wider field
of signs and practices, all of them—dedications, title pages, anonymity—
employed as means of establishing the power of writing and the authority of
an author. Authority flowed from compounding presence and absence: the
godly writer who was formidably present because of his piety and because he
claims to speak as Christ's representative to a people who otherwise will only
know darkness, death, and damnation, was also the writer whose name was
sometimes absent from a title page, who insisted that nothing of his had any
merit, and who feared being "Exposed" by the publicity of print. And as
recounted again and again in prefaces, authority involved two other circumstances, the reader and the provenance of the text. As much as any other
evidence, the right kind of reading certified the authority of a text. As construed in these prefaces, reading was a technology of devotional practice that
presumed repetition and rumination—returning again and again to a text, or
parts of it—the better to absorb and employ the printed word as a means of
self-discovery. No pleasure awaited some readers who practiced this technology, for the point of reading in this manner was to be awakened to the
dreadful plight of the sinner. For others who were already awakened, reading
was a means of rehearsing and re-enacting the ever-necessary process of repentance. For still others, reading as devotional practice was a means of remembering in dark times the wonders of divine providence and God's loving
care of his saints. Always, the benefits of godly reading called for spiritual
preparation of a kind the text itself was designed to create and sustain. As
with any spiritual exercise, reading worked only if the "heart" were alive or
"sincere," not "dead" or merely "formal." "Reader," Jonathan Mitchell declared in his preface to Shepard's *The Parable of the Ten Virgins Opened and
Applied*, "if thou bringest with thee a serious and humble heart, desirous to

have thy soul searched to the quick, the sores whereof lanced, thy spiritual work and way directed, and the interest of thy eternal peace furthered . . . then mayest thou here find that that will suit thee." "Reader," declared the "Per Amicam" who signed the preface to Rowlandson's *Sovereignty & Goodness of God*, "if thou gettest no good by such a Declaration as this, the fault must needs be thine own. Read therefore, Peruse, Ponder, and from hence lay up something from the experience of another, against thine own turn comes."[37] Like the transformative consequences of preaching, the wonders that reading could perform were visible evidence that author, print, and Holy Spirit were as one.

But the reader's experience could never fully allay the question of authenticity: did a text contain the actual words that someone had written or spoken or was it something else, a product of interventions that made everything about it potentially uncertain, from title page and attribution to the words that followed? For London-printed books, especially, these questions demanded a response. Thus it happened that prefaces were filled with information on how a text had come into being, stories of provenance that demonstrate again the place of social authorship in the world of the colonial writer.

* * *

Every printed book owed its material form to practices and expectations about fair copy, anonymity, dedications, and prefaces. Every printed book owed some of its authority, and every author his or her voice, to the same signs and frameworks of meaning. But the story of text-making among the colonists must also encompass the intermediaries who participated in transmitting a text to a printer and what happened in a printer's shop where manuscript was set in type. A starting point for understanding these intermediaries is how they spoke about their work in the prefaces they wrote to introduce a book. They may have done so in order to resolve any questions of attribution and authenticity, but like so many other features of a printed book the information in these prefaces was artfully dispensed, intended both to conceal and reveal the circumstances that entered into book-making. Fuller studies of several major writers follow in Chapter 4. Here, the purpose is to describe the practices and politics of those who took in hand the making of a book, be it as friend or foe, printer or proof corrector.

When Thomas Shepard reached New England in 1635 he had yet to publish anything in England. Despite his doubts about *The Sincere Convert* (1641), the first of the books published under his name, it was reprinted more times in the seventeenth century, and in more places, than any other book by a seventeenth-century colonist. By the end of the 1630s he was writing a spiritual autobiography he addressed to his son Thomas. A few years later, agitated by the upsurge of religious radicalism in England and still on guard against any vestiges of "Antinomianism" in New England, he was defending the importance of the "law" and warning that "subjection to Christ" was an essential part of Christian practice. By the mid-1640s he was collaborating with John Allin of Dedham on a response to Presbyterian critiques of the "Congregational Way," and as many other ministers in the colonies were doing, preparing a catechism for his Cambridge congregation. In his will (1649) he left his "books, manuscripts and papers" to his eldest son Thomas, still only in his teens but already being trained for the ministry. Out of this archive came five books, the earliest in 1652, the second in 1660, a third, on infant baptism, in 1663, the fourth a sermon against drinking (1668),[38] and the fifth (a publishing artifact of the revivals of the 1740s) in 1747. Of the larger mass of manuscripts but one of book length survives, the autobiography, finally printed in 1832.[39]

The Sincere Convert was a London bookseller's doing, and a book Shepard virtually disowned. It did not help that in 1645 a second bookseller advertised a new London printing as "corrected by the author" when the principal changes to the text were improvements in punctuation and spelling, changes best explained as the doing of a more careful copyeditor who, here and there, realized that periods should be replaced with question marks and modified the arrangement of phrases within a sentence to make the flow of words more logical. Another printing of the same year retained these corrections, but its reason for being may have been a more pleasing visual structure—larger type, better separation of questions, answers, uses, and the like—and accurate pagination, composed by someone who consistently dropped the extra e's that compositors of previous printings had used.[40]

Once burned, and aware, no doubt, of what was happening with his father-in-law Hooker's sermon series, Shepard prepared the manuscript that became *The Sound Believer* (1645) and sent it to an English friend, the prominent Congregationalist William Greenhill, to transmit to the London trade. He also tried to control the text of *Theses Sabbaticae*, a defense of the Sunday Sabbath coupled with a critique of "licentiousness," published in London in 1650. Yet it had an unusual history Shepard himself narrated in a preface.

Beginning with advice to the reader on how to make his way through the arguments—the book contained three series of theses or propositions, each numbered—Shepard reported that the text originated as sermons "preached in my ordinary course" on Sundays in Cambridge. What happened next was "a more larger discussing" of the topic among the Harvard College students who, each Sunday, attended his services. For their benefit, and probably for classroom use, Shepard had "reduce[d] the doctrinal points . . . into certain theses." When other ministers happened upon this manuscript (perhaps a copy made for the students), they asked for a longer version while also urging Shepard to "take off some obscurity arising from the brevity and littleness of them [the theses], by greater enlargements, and a few more explications." Once this was done, "all the elders in the country, then met together," urged him to publish the text in its expanded form. Off it went to England, there to be received as authentically his, a book (as an English minister declared in another book) "published by himself," an assertion not about publishing per se but about the provenance of the text. Yet as Shepard himself pointed out in telling the story of the text, the book emerged out of a collaboration with readers who recommended changes in the text—the Harvard College students who discussed the sermons after hearing them preached, and for whom he wrote the initial version in the form of theses, followed by the "elders" who encouraged him to enlarge the scope of the manuscript. Initially Shepard had assumed that he was preaching to (and writing for) "ordinary hearers among the people," but as the manuscript evolved into the published version, "many things [were] left out" that he had intended for "a plain people." Readers both learned and unlearned thus appear in the pages of the *Theses*, as do English writers whose views on the Sabbath he was challenging. But the "plain people" of Cambridge were more absent than present, excised, along with much of an earlier version of the text, in order for Shepard to satisfy other expectations. [41]

The history of *The Parable of the Ten Virgins* involved a manuscript that well-meaning friends worked on before it was ready for printing. The key intermediary in its making was Jonathan Mitchell. In his preface Mitchell was unusually explicit about when and how these sermons were preached: at "weekly lectures . . . begun in June, 1636 and ended in May, 1640," during the "time [when] there was a leaven of Antinomian and Familistical opinions stirring in the Country." As Mitchell and his unnamed co-editors read over the manuscript, they wondered whether the references to Antinomianism should be "expunged" given the passage of time and their own reluctance to expose, yet again, the sorry evidence of conflict among the colonists. They worried, too, that English readers would not be interested in "passages" that were "of special application to the Countrey, and to those first times of it." In the end, however, Mitchell and his partners left things as they were, reasoning that "the world has already in Print been informed" of the turmoil of the 1630s and that any local stories may still "be profitable to others in like cases elsewhere, and of special benefit to the New-English Reader." Textually, a complicating circumstance was that Shepard had never written out these sermons. Among his papers were simply "the Authors own Notes, which he prepared for preaching," with "only about a Sheet himself wrote out in his lifetime." Such a provenance meant that the sermons as published were missing "some lively passages that were uttered in preaching" and stylistically had a certain "Curtnesse of expression." These limitations (and probably others Mitchell did not specify) may have tempted him to improve the text, for he or someone else had "carefully reviewed and corrected it" before the manuscript went off to London. Though he complimented the "industrious and intelligent persons" (probably students at the College) whom he had engaged to transcribe Shepard's notes, he said nothing about the challenge of comparing their work as copyists with the original. At best, therefore, the printed version of the *Parable* embodies three stages of intervention: Mitchell's in reviewing and correcting the manuscript, the copyists', and the handiwork of the London printing shop.[42]

Subjection to Christ (1652) was also a posthumous text. Again the fashioning of copy text was undertaken in Cambridge, though we are not told the name of the "godly brother" who did the work. Whatever his name or capacities, he worked "partly from the Authors own notes, and partly from what he took from his mouth." Well aware that the copy text was a composite, whoever wrote the (second) preface, quite possibly Mitchell, acknowledged that "posthumous editions are farre short of what the Author was wont to do, and of what the Sermons were in preaching," adding too that "the sense be not every where so full, nor every thing so thorowly spoken to, nor the stile so good by far, (as the Authors manner was)." In a preface preceding this one, William Greenhill and Samuel Mather acknowledged that "These notes may well be thought to be lesse accurate, then if the Author himself had published them, and to Want some polishments and trimmings, which it were not fit for any other to adde."[43]

All this, and yet the archive was far from being exhausted. Shepard's son Thomas, by now the minister in Charlestown, retrieved a letter defending infant baptism Shepard had written an unnamed correspondent in 1648 or 1649 and published it to strengthen the party of ministers arguing in favor of the baptismal policy that, almost a century later, was nicknamed the "half-way covenant." To underscore its relevance in 1663, the year it was printed, Thomas II added a preface that equaled his father's letter in length. More than eighty years later, the archive was still being mined for books, the last of them his *Meditations and Spiritual Experiences* (Boston, 1747), "transcribed" (as the title page declared) "out of his own book, written with his own hand, and left by him to his son Thomas Shepard," with a preface by David Brainerd, who would die in the household of Jonathan Edwards a few months later.

One more story of text-making, this time told from the vantage of an author's instructions to his brother, expands on four features of collaboration: the importance of fair copy, the uncertainties of sermon notes, the free hand of intermediaries, and the uneasiness of an author who was commissioning someone else to prepare his sermons for publication. Increase Mather's brother Nathaniel went to England in 1647 and was a minister in Dublin for many years before moving in 1687 to London. When he approached Increase in the early 1680s about the possibility of a local printing of some of his sermons, he spoke frankly of the qualities of the manuscript he was forwarding from Dublin. These were sermons "as they were prepared for preaching, without the least thought of their ever beeing published . . . :P[ray do] you with them as you see good." The sermons were far from ideal in other respects: "one of them at least that is not yet perfected so as to bee legible," while others contained "some vacancyes, and lacunae, and also some curtness of expression, which should bee filled up." Perhaps because of these problems, Nathaniel authorized his brother in Boston "to detract or ad[d], or otherwise alter any thing as you think fit, so it bee not contrary to what I have written." Meanwhile, Nathaniel had taken on the task of preparing his late brother Samuel's manuscript on the "types" of Scripture for publication, a manuscript in "many places being [broken or gaping] in his notes, and many ill written, and many things left to [be] inserted from other and loose papers." Eventually he found himself dealing with a London bookseller who worked with painful slowness on a manuscript of near folio dimensions. As for the manuscript in Boston, Increase took the easy road, incorporating only a single sermon by his brother into a book of his own, *The Doctrine of Divine Providence* (Boston, 1684), remarking in a preface that "Twould have bin more Polite and perfect, had the Author himself emitted it" and offering the excuse that "what is here published is done from the Notes which himself wrote without having the least thought of its ever being Printed." True in one sense but distinctly false in another, the statement may have been Increase's way of masking how little he had done to improve the text for printing.[44]

These stories of provenance remind us of certain problematic aspects of text-making, like the practice of using sermon notes as copy text. Such stories of provenance (and those cited in earlier sections of this chapter) remind us as well of the importance of intermediaries—Joseph Sewall and Thomas Prince for Willard, Increase Mather for his brother, and Mitchell, Thomas II, and William Greenhill for Shepard. Anyone who wanted to publish through the London trade necessarily relied on someone to play this role unless it was possible to negotiate with printers and booksellers in person, as Increase Mather certainly did during the years (1687–1691) he lived in the city as agent, formal and informal, of the Massachusetts charter government. But the distance between writer and printer usually meant that these negotiations fell to others.

Who were these intermediaries, and how did they understand their role? Connections mattered in the book business and, in the decades when the Cambridge printers were unable or unwilling to undertake much more than almanacs, catechisms, and government printing, good connections with the English trade, or with English men and women of influence and means, were essential. Fortunately, the colonists could depend on the many alliances fashioned within the "spiritual brotherhood" of ministers in the Church of England who, in their preaching, emphasized the "new birth" and the righteousness that God expected of all Christians. The spiritual brotherhood was never a formal organization, but in the southeastern counties where gentry families and town corporations supported its program, the brotherhood relied on a network of connections to find posts for promising young ministers and (although this is less certain) to encourage the publishing of sermons in the vein of the practical divinity.[45] Some of these connections suffered from the divisive politics of the Civil War years, but others were strengthened, most importantly the affiliation between ministers who on both sides of the Atlantic identified themselves as Congregationalists or "Independents." Anyone writing from New England could depend on having friends within this group—and as the colonists learned in the 1640s, the hostility of Presbyterians and moderate Anglicans. By the early 1640s, colonial writers could also begin to rely on former colonists who returned to England, some to participate in the refashioning of the Church of England, others to serve as soldiers in the Parliamentary armies or represent the interests of the orthodox colonies.[46]

Before 1660, the person who may have been most involved in helping New England writers was William Greenhill, who shared with many of the colonists a Cambridge education and a sympathy for the "Congregational Way." He wrote the preface to Shepard's first published book, *The Sincere Convert*, saying nothing about provenance but praising Shepard as "able to enlighten the dark corners of the little world," reappeared as the person to whom Shepard dedicated *The Sound Beleever*, and was present a third time as one of five authors of the opening "To the Reader" in *The Parable of the Ten Virgins*; the other four included two well-known ministers of Congregational sympathies, Edmund Calamy and Simon Ash. Greenhill turned up again as co-author of the "To the Reader" in *Subjection to Christ*, where he told the story of Shepard's life in a way that suggests he had access to Shepard's spiritual autobiography. He added his name to two of the tracts reporting on John Eliot's missionary outreach to the Native Americans, and served as intermediary for a book by Thomas Allen.

Other significant collaborators emerged within the group of colonists who relocated to England in the 1640s and 1650s. Winslow played such a role with the Eliot tracts, and, early on, Hugh Peter became the midwife for the collection published in 1643 as *Church-Covenant and Church-Government Discussed*, while Thomas Weld's was the pen that transformed *Antinomians and Familists Condemned* into *A Short Story*. Though no orthodox writer may have wanted them to do so, dissidents turned up in London with texts the trade promptly published. Roger Williams, who arrived in London in 1643, incorporated the "Model of Church and Civil Power," written by a group of ministers, into *The Bloudy Tenent, of Persecution, for cause of Conscience, discussed* (1644), and arranged for the printing of a letter John Cotton had sent him.[47] Soon, too, Williams was passing on information to the Scotch Presbyterian Robert Baillie about events and people in New England that Baillie used in *A Dissuasive from the Errours of the Time* (1645).

By the close of the 1640s several of the earliest graduates of Harvard College had also found their way to England in search of employment as ministers, and others would follow for the same reason. Benjamin Woodbridge, a member of the first class to graduate from the college (1642), entrusted a bookseller with a short letter from his uncle Thomas Parker, the minister of Newbury, to his sister, an outspoken religious radical, published as *The Copy of a Letter* (London, 1649). He was also the intermediary for a manuscript written by another uncle in New England, James Noyes's *Moses and Aaron*. But it was Benjamin's brother John who brought the most significant *literary* manuscript with him to London in 1647, the collection of poems by his sister-in-law Anne Bradstreet that became *The Tenth Muse Lately sprung up in America* (1650). One of the Mather brothers, either Increase or, more likely, Nathaniel, slipped a copy of the deliberations of an assembly of ministers in 1657 to a bookseller, who issued it as *A Disputation concerning Church-Membership and their Children in Answer to XXI. Questions* (1659). Some of these men stayed on after the Restoration of Charles II; others, like Increase Mather, returned to Massachusetts.

Thereafter Increase maintained a wide-ranging correspondence with English Nonconformists. During his second trip abroad he became good friends with some of them, to the point of being honored by Richard Baxter in the dedication of his final book. Among the second-generation clergy, Mather was the first to secure prefaces from older, more distinguished ministers— John Davenport writing one for his first major publication, *The Mystery of Israels Salvation* (London, 1669), with other tributes from Greenhill and William Hooke, and the great English Nonconformist John Owen for *Some Important Truths about Conversion* (London, 1674). Meanwhile, a few of the immigrants exploited other kinds of connections. The title page of *New Englands Teares, for old Englands Feares* (London, 1641), a fast day sermon preached in 1640 by William Hooke, an Oxford graduate and gentleman's son who immigrated in the 1630s and became the first minister in Taunton, Massachusetts, reported that Hooke had "sent [the manuscript] over to a worthy Member of the honourable House of Commons, who desires it may be [printed] for publike good." Four years later, another of Hooke's sermons, *New-Englands Sence, of Old-England and Irelands Sorrowes*, was described on the title page as "Intrusted in the hands of a worthy Member of the Honourable House of Commons, who desired it might be Printed."

Connections were invaluable, but they did not always work and could have unexpected consequences. Everyone who served as a go-between had an agenda of his own that left its mark upon the text he was facilitating. The most benign of these agendas was the strong interest among many English Protestants in the project to bring Christianity to the New England tribes. The founding of the New England Company and its success in raising funds was an emphatic sign of this interest, but another was the willingness of so many prominent ministers to abet the Eliot tracts—the ten ministers, some

of them Presbyterians, others Congregationalists, who signed the preface to
The Clear Sun-Shine of the Gospel; John Drury, the great internationalist, who
added an appendix on the origins of the Native Americans to the third in the
series; and the important Congregationalist Joseph Caryl, who provided a
dedication for another. This enthusiasm extended past the Restoration, when
Robert Boyle and Richard Baxter, among others, lobbied to have Charles II
re-charter the company, which happened in 1662, with Boyle stepping in as
governor.

Others were less benign. Thomas Allen's churchmanship was tilted
toward the conservative end of the Congregationalist spectrum, which may
be why he was entrusted with a manuscript of John Cotton's that broached
the rapprochement of Independents and Presbyterians, a text to which Allen
added a section of his own composing.[48] The politics of Roger Williams and
Robert Baillie, though in most respects utterly at odds, were as one in exposing the colonists as something other than what they pretended to be. Thomas
Goodwin and Philip Nye distanced themselves from some of John Cotton's
ideas about the "Congregational Way." William Greenhill and Samuel
Mather spoke frankly of Shepard's reputation, reporting in their preface to
Subjection to Christ that "it is a wretched stumbling block to some, that his
[Shepard's] Sermons are somewhat strict, and (as they term it) legall."[49] Baxter was deeply involved in efforts to temper the strictness of high Calvinism
and the Congregational principle of a gathered church. He lent his name to
Cotton Mather's *Memorable Providences* (1689) at a moment in his own life
when he was searching for evidence to validate the existence of witchcraft.
Baxter did not fiddle with Mather's text, but the presence of his voice in the
printed book—and of voices that were not the author's in other books—
imposed on readers the challenge of making sense out of such differences.

Anyone who intervened in the making of a text wanted to affirm its
authenticity. Most of the time these intermediaries professed their respect for
the writer and extolled the person that readers would encounter in the
printed page. Often, though not always, they responded to anxieties about
authenticity by insisting that the writer had reviewed the copy text or entrusted an original manuscript to them. Some of these assertions were worth-
less, mere booksellers' bravado; others moved in the space of a page from
assurances of accuracy to evidence that contradicted those assurances. A col-
laborator who masked his own role by professing respect for an authentic
original, and who voiced his respect for the very privacy he was violating, as

Humfrey did—such hybridity was present in most descriptions that intermediaries or collaborators provided of their role.

This was a hybridity some writers intentionally licensed when they invited friends and other intermediaries to "improve" a text. This, too, could have unexpected consequences (as when, in our own times, a historian advised a colleague at his university not to publish a manuscript, advice that, had it been taken, would have thwarted the receipt of a major prize), for some writers abandoned a text in response to criticism, as Winthrop did for two of his in response to Shepard's urging him to "forbeare wrighting for a while" or, at the very least, "have a few second thoughts of some passages."[50] When Cotton Mather was preparing biographies of political leaders for Book II of the *Magnalia*, he shared a draft of his life of Thomas Dudley with members of the family, probably because of tensions that dated from the Dominion of New England, which Joseph Dudley had supported and the Mathers had opposed. The family's response persuaded Cotton to write a much briefer version. In the early eighteenth century, the Boston minister Benjamin Colman reviewed some of the manuscripts of his two literary daughters, Elizabeth and Abigail, and may have kept a few from publication.[51]

Another practice was to entrust a manuscript to someone else and empower that person to make changes in it, as Nathaniel Mather did when he dispatched manuscripts of his sermons to Increase. Shepard did this as well with *The Sound Beleever*, telling his "deare Friend, Mr. W[illiam] Greenhill" that he left it "wholly with your selfe [to] . . . adde or detract any thing you see meet, (so as it bee not crosse to what I have writ)." Davenport authorized John Cotton to review the scriptural citations in what was eventually printed as *The Knowledge of Christ Indispensably required of all Men that would be saved* (London, 1653): "I leave it wholly to your wisdom, to add, or alter, as you find expedient." When Daniel Maud of Dover, New Hampshire was writing his will in 1654, he asked someone to transmit a manuscript of his to John Davenport, "that he would peruse, and for putting it forth I would leave it to his wise and godly ordering," a step rendered necessary by the illness that ended with his death. At an extreme, a colonist could leave it up to someone else "with libertie to print, or suppresse it," as John Eliot did with a manuscript he sent Thomas Thorowgood, who decided to include it in *Jewes in America* (London, 1660). Though some of these gestures of delegation were prompted by having a manuscript published three thousand miles away, the practice had a broader significance, as Davenport indicated in asking Cotton's help.[52]

The final service that collaborators were called on to provide was proofreading, a task that, more often than not, New England writers left to someone else. No London printer expected a writer living three thousand miles away to do this work. Nor, for many books, did the printers in Boston and Cambridge even when a writer lived nearby. "Reader, The Authors distance from the Press, and difficulty of the Copy [the more likely reason], having occasioned the following Errata's," a statement inserted by Samuel Green in Samuel Whiting's *Abraham's Humble Intercession for Sodom* (Cambridge, 1666), was echoed by John Foster, the printer of the Dedham minister William Adams's fast-day sermon *The Necessity of The pouring out of the Spirit* (Boston, 1679): "Reader, The old Plea, The Authors absence from the Press, being stil in force, occasions the further desire of this, viz. that before thou readest thou wilt with thy pen mend these following faults." Foster was a good deal more plausible when he made the same excuse for William Hubbard's *A Narrative of the Troubles with the Indians in New-England* (Boston, 1678), for Hubbard had gone off to England. More than just geography was involved in decisions about who did proofreading, and how. Some seventeenth-century English writers received sheets and sent them back with corrections, as John Milton did with *Paradise Lost*, but it was also common practice to delegate this chore to a workman in a printing shop known either as "Reader" or "Corrector." Larger shops employed correctors who did little else but review printed sheets; in others, the task fell to anyone "well skill'd in true and quick Reading" or perhaps with a decent command of grammar, spelling, and punctuation.[53]

As practiced in these shops, the purpose of proofreading was never to standardize spelling and punctuation or to align them with fair copy. Compositors and proofreaders spelled and punctuated as best they knew how. So did authors, which meant that compositors were constantly working with manuscripts that varied widely in their accidentals. For printers, the key concern was to identify mistakes in the printing process—an inadvertent shift of type face or type that was accidentally disturbed, signatures numbered incorrectly, catch-words missing, running heads and pages out of order. Efforts to correct spellings, diction, and punctuation were commonly incomplete, carried out for some sheets but not for others, especially when the printing was being done on different presses or divided between shops. These circumstances lie behind the instructions to readers to proofread for themselves, as urged in a 1673 edition of Milton's *Poems:* "Some other Errors and mispoints the Readers judgement may correct."[54]

For the colonists, the possibilities of correcting London-printed sheets were nil, or nearly so. When Davenport's *The Knowledge of Christ* was printed in London in 1653, he warned readers that "My far distance from the Press" meant that any errors were not his own doing but "committed by the Printer." In what may be the sole example of its kind, Thomas Cobbet, the minister of Lynn, reviewed the sheets of *A Just Vindication of the Covenant and Covenant-Estate of Children* (London, 1648). So it was asserted in "To the Reader," followed by a "catalogue . . . collected by the Author himself nine months since," a claim made plausible by the extraordinary length of the catalogue, which nearly filled an entire page. But how or why, in this one instance, sheets traveled across the Atlantic and back again, cannot be determined.[55]

Proofreading brings us at long last to the booksellers and printers who made their presence felt in every printed book.[56] From a writer's point of view the most important decision these tradesmen made was whether to publish a manuscript or not. If the answer were yes, printers and booksellers had to decide what copy text to use, which in practice usually meant the version that came into their hands. Thereafter, decisions followed thick and fast about what a book should look like: typeface, printers' ornaments and illustrations, the layout of the title page and sometimes its wording, the size of the page, the spacing of lines, and the wording of the running heads. Printers and booksellers chose the quality of paper—the most expensive aspect of book-making—and kind of ink. They fixed the number of copies to be printed, decided what share of a print run should be bound up in advance, and set the sale price. As Nathaniel Mather learned from his efforts to get Samuel Mather's *Types* published, printers also dictated the pace at which a book would be produced—frustratingly slow for books as lengthy as the *Types,* but astonishingly prompt for newsworthy or time-bound items like execution sermons and almanacs.

Every bookseller knew that, year in and year out, some books were steady sellers, especially bibles, psalm books, and manuals of devotional practice. Within the London trade, the rights to steady sellers were sometimes sold or exchanged while the rights to others, like the Bible, were granted by the Crown to specific printers or, as time went on, claimed by a "conger" of tradesmen. Thomas Hooker's *The Poor Doubting Christian* was a steady seller throughout the century (at least fifteen editions by 1695), outsold in this respect only by Shepard's *Sincere Convert*. But the New England trade could not count on any local steady seller until the eighteenth century, making do instead with books of this kind imported from London, like the thirty-nine copies of three titles by the popular Nonconformist John Flavel that the Boston printer/bookseller Michael Perry had in stock in 1700. Closely spaced reprintings were rare in the Boston trade, which contented itself with small print runs, slow-selling imprints, government-related printing, and ephemera.[57]

At every stage of production, printers and booksellers were capable of deviating from the copy text. A tired or lazy compositor, or someone of dubious literacy, could stumble into mistakes in setting type, and the persons who arranged the type in the forms from which printing was done sometimes changed or misnumbered the order of the pages. Expediency competed with craftsmanship, with consequences for uniformity within copies of the same edition (issue). As sheets were passed through the press, anyone standing by could reach in to adjust or remove pieces of type that had become dislodged. Usually, someone was reading each sheet for errors that could be promptly corrected. But the pace of printing could easily yield some sheets with corrections and others not, with both kinds bound up in gatherings or signatures that, in the final stages of production, became the complete book. Or it might be that the printer waited until all the sheets had been printed before taking note of "errata" and listing these in a preliminary or concluding leaf.

Expediency was at odds not only with craftsmanship, but also with attribution and authority. Booksellers and printers wanted a reliable text and said as much whenever they added the notations "authentic" or "corrected by the author" to a title page. So did writers, and so of course did readers who had learned from sad experience that some versions of a text were superior to others and that writers were not above fabricating the truth of a story. Within the trade, however, the descriptive term "authentic" had no hard and fast meaning. For a Shakespeare play, it sometimes signified that the printed version coincided with the stage version—or one such version given the proliferation of quartos. "Corrected by the author" was no less imprecise, as seen from the re-issues of Shepard's *The Sincere Convert*. On occasion, printers and booksellers availed themselves of the expression "corrected by the author" merely to market a new printing.

These attitudes and practices (and an underlying culture of expediency) help to explain why John Allin's name was eliminated from the second printing of a book he co-wrote with Thomas Shepard, which also acquired a new title.[58] They explain, too, the variations in different copies of Hubbard's *A Narrative of the Troubles with the Indians*, which John Foster's Boston shop put on sale in March, 1677; a London printing, with an altered title, followed in midsummer. The local printer struggled with the copy text, but the compositor(s) in London who worked from the Boston imprint did so to an extraordinary degree, transposing "twenty-five . . . perfectly intelligible American place names . . . to almost ludicrous mis-spellings." Foster's printer misnumbered some of the pages, dropped important elements of punctuation, and omitted a line that was corrected on some of the sheets. When the bibliographer Randolph G. Adams compared a large quantity of extant copies, he learned that the Boston-printed copies were haphazardly assembled out of sheets of several kinds. Summarizing his discoveries, Adams imagined being in the presence of a "customer [who had] . . . gone into John Foster's bookstore in Boston in 1677, on the day upon which Hubbard's book appeared for sale." There "he might have picked up not two or four possibly variant printings, but any one of twenty five. In the fifty copies of the book which we have examined, we have counted at least nineteen textual and typographical differences and emendations, which seem capable of appearing in almost any possible combination." Adams concluded that the variations could not be plotted in terms of a sequence of printings; all emerged from a single moment of production.[59]

For two other New England printed texts that have been studied in a similar manner, the variations between sheets or putative editions are again abundant. During the printing of *A Whole Booke of Psalmes* in 1640, one of the ministers responsible for the translation intervened to alter the wording of Psalm 69; the two lines that in some sheets read, "their loynes also with trembleing / to shake continuallee" were revised to "with trembling also make their loynes / to shake continuallie." A more substantial change was the redrafting of two lines from Psalm 19, where "And from presumptuous-sins, let thou / kept back thy servant bee" was replaced by "And from presumptuous-sins, kept back / O let thy servant bee." Nineteen other changes of a very minor kind turn up in this printing, and more were introduced when a second Cambridge edition was published in 1651, for the translators had agreed that their initial efforts had not always served their readers well.[60] Mary Rowlandson's *The Sovereignty & Goodness of God* was printed four times in 1682, initially in Boston, twice in Cambridge, and once in London. The Boston printer was using Rowlandson's manuscript (or a fair copy); that she or the copyist reviewed the sheets or had anything to do with the local printing is quite unlikely since she was living in far-way Wethersfield. No copies survive of the first (Boston) edition, but four leaves do, surplus paper the printer reused as "lining papers" in Boston-printed books of the same year. When the pages used as liner are compared with the London and Cambridge printings, two facts emerge: the London printing was much closer to the Boston first, from which the Cambridge second varied at a rate of more than twenty differences a page (punctuation, spellings, words and phrases). Paradoxically, the Cambridge printing carried on its title page the phrase "The second Addition [sic] Corrected and amended," a statement that may only mean that the printer had taken account of the "Errata" specified in the Boston edition.[61] (For the second Cambridge printing, "Addition" has been corrected to "Edition.") As bibliographers demonstrated many years ago for settings of Shakespeare's plays, so for Rowlandson's *Sovereignty* the lesson learned is that compositors set the same text quite differently.

The trade had other practices that affected copy text and attribution. Edward Johnson, who immigrated to New England in the 1630s and became a prosperous layman and civic leader in the town of Woburn, Massachusetts, wrote a book-length history of Massachusetts that he or someone acting on his behalf sent to London at some point between mid-1651, when Johnson ceased working on the manuscript, and early 1653, the year that the London bookseller Nathaniel Brooke issued *A History of New-England. From the English planting in the Yeere 1628 untill the Yeere 1652*, without any mention of an author. Brooke had fiddled with the title, initially thinking he would call it *Historicall Relation of the First Planting of the English in New England*. When sales proved slow, he reissued the text five years later, using unsold sheets, as part of a larger four-part volume, *America Painted to the Life*. Three of the four sections carried the names of Sir Ferdinando Gorges and his grandson Ferdinando as their authors, and the casual reader might well have assumed that one of the Gorges had written the fourth part, though neither would have agreed with its enthusiastic description of the colonists. Not until the early eighteenth century did the antiquarian Thomas Prince learn from the aged magistrate Samuel Sewall that Johnson was the author and write a note to this effect in his copy of the book, and not until the mid-nineteenth century did the text regain the title Johnson seems to have intended, *The Wonder-Working Providence of Sions Saviour in New England*.[62]

Brooke was using well-rehearsed tactics for unloading unsold stocks of printed sheets and, less commonly, unsold stocks of bound books. One step was to reissue the sheets under a different title. *A Short Story of the Rise,*

Reigne, and Ruine of the late Antinomians and Familists had already been published by the bookseller in January under a different title; to this version Thomas Weld added an introduction and title, but the heart of the book was made up of left-over sheets from the January printing. The same practice was followed with *A Conference . . . Held at Boston* (London, 1646), reprinted the same year using the same sheets with one mis-numbering corrected.[63] Boston printers attempted the same alchemy with various of Cotton Mather's publications. *Small Offers*, a sermon series first issued in 1689, was re-issued eleven years later "with the dedication, the Errata, and the original title-page cancelled, and another title-page, this time anonymous with a changed title and title-page text," along with the new date and bookseller. Unsold sheets of Mather's *Batteries upon the Kingdom of the Devil*, first published in Boston in 1695, were repackaged *in Boston* for sale in London two years later with a new title page and an imprint advertising (falsely) that the book had been printed there; amusingly, the Boston printer forgot to change the date.[64]

Together with the ways of doing business within the book trades, these shop-floor practices affected every printed text. The stories of "broken notes" as copy text (and more such stories are to come), of uncorrected sheets and misattributions, of interventions to improve or criticize a text, all these cast in doubt the authority of almost every book by a colonist that was printed in London and of many that were printed in New England. Nonetheless, some of the time and for some imprints, provenance and accuracy mattered. They did for the compilers of the First Folio and for the London bookseller Richard Chiswell, who advertised Increase Mather's *Brief History* as "according to the Original Copy Printed in New-England" (though he soon realized that his copy text did not include the *Exhortation* mentioned in the title) and the printer in 1645 of John Davenport's confession of faith, done "as it was drawn from his own Copy." Similarly, the embarrassment of Shepard's *The Sincere Convert* "awaken[ed]" William Greenhill to the imperative of putting out an adequate version of *The Sound Believer*.

The force of these statements must always be balanced against the abundant evidence that printers were expedient and writers provided poor copy text. Authenticity did not immediately signify mean authorial control or the transmission of an uncontaminated original, especially since *no such original* existed for many of the sermons that were printed. But the expressions of anxiety about the provenance and condition of texts—voiced for certain kinds of handwritten texts as well as for those that were printed—were something more than rhetorical gestures. Author, intermediary, and printer all shared a horizon of expectations that encompassed the principle of authenticity. But just as in the "shadow of the law" much happens that is not perfectly congruent with the law as written, so for printed texts much happened in the shadow of the authentic and authoritative, as we learn in more detail from the case studies that follow in the next chapter.

CHAPTER FOUR

Textures of Social Authorship

Case Studies

THE COMPLEXITIES of book-making affected every writer in New England. To generalize about this process is to risk losing sight of specific circumstances—the motives of intermediaries, the lapses of compositors, the ambitions of booksellers, the writer's own role, the reliance on auditors' notes—that case histories can reveal. Thanks to the traditions of bibliographical scholarship, some of those circumstances are unusually visible in the literary careers of two first-generation ministers, John Cotton and Thomas Hooker, and the most prolific writer in New England at the beginning of the eighteenth century, Cotton Mather, co-minister with his father Increase of Second Church, Boston. Three poets figure in this chapter as well, each with a particular sense of audience: the ministers Michael Wigglesworth and John Danforth, and the housewife Anne Bradstreet. Wigglesworth's career as a published writer was brief (1662–70), Bradstreet and Danforth's lifelong. All five may be described as social authors, yet not in simple or uniform ways.

Scribal publication served versifiers well throughout the century. Anyone wanting to circulate poems of substantial length could finally have them printed once the local book trade, and John Foster in particular, began to publish poetry in book form and broadsides.[1] John Danforth (1660–1730), who served for nearly fifty years as minister of Dorchester after graduating from Harvard College in 1677, included some of his verse in the almanac he prepared for 1679. Thereafter, he published nearly two dozen elegies, some of them commemorating parishioners for whose gravestones he also composed verse tributes, some honoring members of his family, and some written for patrons with last names like Sewall, Eliot, Foxcroft, Hutchinson, Bromfield, and Mather. He distributed this verse either in handwritten copies or as single-sheet printed broadsides. No versifier made any money from these imprints; anyone wanting to own two elegies honoring Foster and printed in 1682 would have paid two pence apiece and three if bought together.[2] In keeping with a long-standing rule, Danforth signed some poems with his initials and allowed others to appear unsigned. He may have reached a wider audience once he began to incorporate verse into collections of his sermons (1697, 1702), and the longest of his poems, the 264-line "Love and Unity Encouraged, and Contention and Division Disswaded, in a Poem," appeared in another minister's book (1712).[3] Cotton Mather solicited his services in the mid-1690s to provide a brief commendatory poem, partly in Latin, for the *Magnalia*, and in similar exercises he honored the "Renowned" Samuel Willard and "two excellent Persons" who died within a month of each other in 1727, the ministers of Taunton and Milton, one of them his brother Samuel. Always writing within the framework of the vernacular tradition, he commemorated the dead as models for the living, declaring of the ministers who died in 1727, "Their Lives-Right-Steps shew'd Men the way to God: / They both were to their Flocks unblotted Paterns: / And of all Godliness and Virtue Patrons." Here too, he used their deaths as warning signs from heaven.[4] Thematically, sermons and verse were identical, each of them a means of arousing readers to renew their relationship with God.

Wigglesworth's *The Day of Doom*, printed in Cambridge in 1662, was the first of four book-length poems local printers issued in the seventeenth century. Of these four, *The Day of Doom* was the only one to be reprinted in England and New England. Constrained by illness from full-time preaching as minister of Malden, Massachusetts, where he went in the mid-1650s after serving as a tutor at Harvard College, Wigglesworth turned to poetry as his public voice. Though he wrote a few elegies that circulated in manuscript, Wigglesworth never relied on the sociability that animated Danforth. No patron came forward to introduce or finance "Gods Controversy with New England in the Time of a Great Drought" (1662), which remained in manuscript; and he may have paid the printer's bill for the first edition of *The Day of Doom*. A narrative poem that dramatized Christ's return to earth at the day of judgment, it was singular in reaching a large audience; by Wigglesworth's own reckoning, some 1800 copies were sold, a figure that may conflate two or more printings.[5] A more certain measure of its success in the marketplace is that printers on both sides of the Atlantic began to issue new editions on their own account. In 1666, if not earlier (the sequence of editions cannot be described with certainty),[6] the two Cambridge printers, Samuel Green and Marmaduke Johnson, published a version to which Wigglesworth added "Scriptural and marginal notes." The London printing of 1666 incorporated other new material: an introductory "To the Christian Reader," a tribute by the Cambridge minister Jonathan Mitchell, who had known Wigglesworth during his years as tutor at Harvard, "On the Following Work, and It's Author," and a poem by someone else, a bookseller's sleight of hand to increase the size of a book. Not until 1701, however, did any local printer undertake a third printing, which was also the first of the New England versions to have Wigglesworth's name on the title page. Meanwhile, the Cambridge printers had published in 1670 the last of his verse to be printed, the devotional *Meat out of the Eater*, which had four printings by 1701 in Massachusetts but none in London. Wigglesworth was emphatically a public poet who instructed the colonists on God's providence and warned of the perils of "declension"—public in relying on the book trades and in his message, but not associated with patrons as Danforth and Benjamin Tompson were, and not relying as Anne Bradstreet did on a coterie.

Bradstreet preceded Wigglesworth as a poet with a printed book of verse. Arriving in Massachusetts in 1630 as the young bride of Simon Bradstreet, she was the daughter of Thomas Dudley, an early investor in the Massachusetts Bay Company, who came the same year and, until he died in 1653, was a significant presence within the leadership of the new colony. Dudley had written poetry, none of it printed, during his years in England, and did so again in Massachusetts, dying (it was said) with a scrap of verse in his pocket. Of his work Anne was familiar with a description of the "Four Parts of the World,"[7] a poem mirrored arithmetically in four series of four poems, the longest of them "The Four Monarchies," she "humbly presented" to "her most honoured father" in homage to his verse. Though Thomas Dudley may have been her ideal reader, the poetry she was writing in these years was also known within her family circle, which included a sister who was also writing verse, now lost. By the mid-1640s she was being read outside this coterie. So we learn from her brother-in-law John Woodbridge's explanation for why he arranged to publish a collection of verse she herself had confined to manuscript copies: "I found that diverse had gotten some scattered Papers, affected them wel, [and] were likely to have sent forth broken [i.e., incomplete and inaccurate] pieces to the Authors prejudice." "Sent forth" may refer to the proliferation of handwritten copies or, less likely, to the possibility of her verse being printed without anyone close to Bradstreet having oversight or approving of the venture. The copy text Woodbridge carried with him to England and arranged to have printed as *The Tenth Muse Lately Sprung Up in America* (London, 1650) was partly of his making, for it omitted the domestic verse (most of which was yet to be written) and included poems that were incomplete, Bradstreet herself noting that the last of the "monarchies" was marked by a "confused brevity" the poet attributed to "shortness of time" and "inability" (lines 3427–28). She spoke more critically of her verse in a poem that appeared in the second edition, *Several Poems compiled with great variety of wit and learning* (Boston, 1678), "The Author to her Book," describing the printed version of 1650 as full of "blemishes" she could not eliminate despite her best efforts at rewriting and lamenting that a text she had "cast . . . by as one unfit for light" was now "exposed to public view . . . in print" (lines 13–14, 5, 9–10). These were sentiments she shared with male writers. Like so many other colonists, she had no direct control over a London-printed book, though whether she resented having the manuscript "snatched" from her "side . . . by friends" or was voicing a familiar trope is uncertain.[8]

Bradstreet was a social author because of how her books were fashioned. Initially she wrote for a coterie of kin, but as often happened with English writers in the same situation, her work was appropriated and reproduced by well-meaning admirers and the book trades. Without the intervention of Woodbridge, *The Tenth Muse* would not have been printed. The *Several Poems* was explicitly a collaborative project, for someone (possibly the minister in Ipswich, John Rogers) had selected and transcribed "other poems found amongst her Papers, after her Death." It is tempting to suppose that she worked over *The Tenth Muse* and that John Foster, who printed *Several Poems*, incorporated her corrections, for the title page represented the book as "Corrected by the Author, and Enlarged." But the bibliographical evidence is equivocal on the first of these assertions and, as her most recent editors point out, the book is best understood as a "collaborative production."[9]

Bradstreet's was a different voice from Wigglesworth's, for nowhere in her verse and prose did she fret about declension or evoke the colonists as a covenanted people. When she spoke of her verse as "private," she drew on three meanings of that multi-sided word: that her father and immediate family were her principal readers (no sermonizing stance for her, as though she were addressing a congregation!), that as a woman she should not appear in public, and that her verse would remain in manuscript. Yet much about her poetry moves beyond the merely private. The "formal poetry" implied a different audience than her family circle, for these were "poems that, logically, ought to have been produced in a European court, under patronage by the royalty, and by a male."[10] The commendatory poem that Jonathan Mitchell, the minister of Cambridge, provided for *The Day of Doom* celebrates Wigglesworth as a "Preacher" who has substituted "Verse" for a "Sermon" the better to teach the "Truth" about "our death and pain." Wigglesworth becomes another David who turns "affliction" into "poetry," as contrasted with "Poets" who write "Fables." The nine commendatory poems and two anagrams that, with Woodbridge's preface, constitute the paratext of *The Tenth Muse*—the most extensive apparatus of this kind in any book by a colonial writer printed in the seventeenth century—likened Bradstreet to the poet she herself took as a model, the sixteenth-century French Huguenot Guillaume Du Bartas, evoking as well Apollo, Homer, Chaucer, and the "graces." Here, too, she was celebrated for writing about the "noble acts / of Kings and Princes," though in much of the paratext the men who wrote these poems marveled that a woman could be so skillful a poet.[11]

The ambiguities of public and private reappeared in the domestic poems, which exploited the maternal voice in a manner already familiar to English readers of Elizabeth Joscelin's *The Mother's Legacy to Her Unborn Children* (1624) and similar books of advice. To speak as a mother to children, counseling them on how to be (or become) good Christians, was in keeping with the assumption, widely articulated in seventeenth-century England and New England, that mothers were distinctively responsible for the spiritual welfare of their children and, by implication, the spiritual welfare of the household.[12] Sarah Whipple Goodhue drew on the same assumption in "A Valedictory and Monitory Writing" (c. 1681), which ended with Goodhue charging her husband to ensure that their children fulfill the obligations of the baptismal covenant.[13] Thus construed, a woman's voice was legitimately public, for another core assumption within Bradstreet's culture was that a godly commonwealth depended on the moral health of the well-regulated household. Speaking as a wife, mother, and grandmother, therefore, she situated herself in the space between the familial (or the private) and the public these roles opened up for her. She did so as well in a series of prose meditations meant only for her children, dedicating the manuscript to her "dear son Simon Bradstreet," affirming in the opening sentence that "parents perpetuate their lives in their posterity," and signing it "your affectionate mother." The two manuscript copies that survive have a family provenance, one in the hand-writing of her son Simon and another in that of a daughter.[14]

With Thomas Hooker and John Cotton we return to the complexities of auditors' notes as copy text for printed sermons and to questions, never easy to answer, about which of their texts, and in what versions, each of them sought to have printed. Already "in print" before they left for New England, the two depended entirely on the London trade for the rest of their lifetimes. Cotton Mather's is a story marked by new opportunities but also fresh problems. By the time he came of age as a writer, the local trade was able to undertake most of he wrote. Yet his ambitions were larger, ambitions that in the years after 1700 were never fully realized. He remains unique in how he rehearsed his self-understanding as a writer in a diary that preserves his negotiations with the many people—printers and booksellers, friends and enemies, intermediaries in England and New England—who became his collaborators.

Thomas Hooker came to New England in 1633 on the same ship as Cotton. Forced out of his English lectureship in 1629 because he refused to conform to the rules of the Church, Hooker went in 1631 to the Netherlands, where he quickly became controversial within the English community in Amsterdam for his Congregationalist perspective on church government and church membership. He spelled out his thinking in a manuscript that circulated in the early 1630s[15] and contributed an unsigned preface to *A Fresh Suit against Human Ceremonies* (1633), William Ames's strenuous critique of church liturgy. Hooker had already made his mark as a preacher in East Anglia, and a collection of his sermons, *The Poor Doubting Christian Drawn to Christ* (1629) was on its way to becoming a steady seller. By the beginning of the 1640s his texts were a favorite of the London trade, with booksellers trading rights to copy for certain sermon series. Like early Shakespeare, early Hooker imprints never bore his full name, though by 1637 he was being identified as "T. H."

Auditor's notes were the source of copy text for all but one of the printed sermons published in the 1630s.[16] Generalizing about those sermons, two of Hooker's English editors remarked that the notes had been "taken by an unskillful hand." Prompted by their warning, Cotton Mather alerted readers of the biography he wrote of Hooker (printed separately in 1695, it reappeared in the *Magnalia*) to the same circumstances, noting of the English-printed sermons on Hooker's favorite theme, the "application of redemption," that "many wrote after him in short-hand; and some were so bold as to publish many of them without his consent or knowledge." From Mather's perspective, the troubling aspect of these early printed sermons was that "his notions came to be deformedly misrepresented in multitudes of passages; among which I will suppose that crude passage which Mr. Giles Firmin, in his 'Real Christian,' so well confutes, 'That if the soul be rightly humbled, it is content to bear the state of damnation.' " [17] Thanks to modern bibliographical scholarship, the limitations of auditors' notes have been specified for a particular sermon, *The Danger of Desertion*, which Hooker preached on the eve of his departure for the Netherlands. When it was printed ten years later, with his full name appearing for the first time on a title page, the copy text lacked much of the phrasing and scriptural citations that appear in a second set of notes that survive. More by chance than by design, the bookseller George Edwards had followed the practice of the trade and accepted the copy text that came to hand. In a piece of book-making that again was customary practice, Edwards paired this sermon with a sermon written by an unidentified writer. Half a century later, Mather knew what modern scholars have confirmed, that the second sermon was not Hooker's but someone else.[18]

The most circulated of his sermon series owed more to a bookseller than to Hooker's own initiative. The first edition of *The Poor Doubting Christian*, based almost certainly on an auditor's notes and printed anonymously as part of a multi-author collection, *The Saints Cordiall* (London, 1629) was a fragment of a longer sermon. When the first independent printing occurred in 1635, the text acquired five major additions, possibly but not certainly his doing. Not until 1646, however, did his name appear on the title page, and this for an edition that Sargent Bush characterized as "bastard" after demonstrating that it consisted of the original *Poor Doubting Christian*, the additions made in 1635, and "major portions" from another sermon series, *The Soules Effectuall Calling*, all done to "justify raising the price on a book which had by now proven perennially popular." The changes also encompassed the recasting of sentences and longer passages that, as the literary historian Winfried Herget has remarked, pass beyond redaction to "tampering." In the course of the century, the least authentic edition of *The Poor Doubting Christian* became the version most frequently reprinted, a circumstance that, as Bush rightly notes, reveals "the uncritical tendency of printers and editors . . . to use recent rather than early editions as printer's copy."[19]

In his Hartford years, Hooker responded to the flood of unauthorized and imperfect publications by preaching anew on "the application of redemption," hoping, as Cotton Mather astutely realized, "to perfect with his own hand his composures for the press, and thereby vindicate both writer and matter from the wrongs done to both, by surreptitious editions heretofore." Presumably he wrote out full versions of some of these sermons, manuscripts that almost certainly were included in the archive he mentioned in his will of 1647, the year he died. In that document he entrusted "such manuscripts as shall bee judged fitt to bee printed" to his wife and secondarily to Edward Hopkins and William Goodwin, two wealthy laymen of his congregation, ceding them also the "[financial] advantage that may come thereby."[20] That his congregation already knew of Hooker's intentions is clear from the will of another Hartford layman, William Whyting, who left him twenty pounds in 1643 "towards the furtherance of setting forth for the benefit of the church his worke upon the 17th of John, with any thing else hee doth intend."[21] When Hopkins and Goodwin looked into the archive, they realized that none of the manuscripts were "fair copy." Fortunately a freelance copyist was available, the same man who in 1637 had served as clerk during the Antino-mian controversy. Within a year or two, John Higginson had transcribed "near two hundred" of the sermons. His version may have served as copy text for the 1656 London printing of *The Application of Redemption . . . The first eight Books*, with a title page boasting, in bookseller's inflated language, that it was "Printed from the Authors Papers, Written with his own Hand," with an attestation to the same effect from two well-known English Congre-gationalists that the bookseller had probably solicited.

The attestation is interesting in its own right, for Thomas Goodwin and Philip Nye (who would also introduce John Cotton's *Keyes of the Kingdome*) knew of the uncertain provenance of other Hooker texts, including some on the same themes. They spoke frankly of how his sermons had been corrupted and, in contrast, how this new text had come into being:

And whereas there hath been published long since, many Parts and Pieces of this Author, upon this Argument, Sermon-wise preach'd by him here in England. . . . Yet having been taken by an unskilful hand, which upon his recess into those remoter parts of the World, was bold without his privity or consent to print and publish them (one of the greatest injuries which can be done to any man) it came to pass his genuine meaning, and this in points of so high a Nature, and in some things differing from the Common Opinion, was di-verted in those printed Sermons from the fair and cleer draught of his own Notions and Intentions, because so utterly deformed and

mis-represented in multitudes of passages; And in the rest but imperfectly and crudely set forth.

Then came the reassurance—never fully to be trusted—that "Here, in these
Treatises, thou hast his Heart from his own Hand, his own Thoughts drawn
by his own Pensil. This is all truly and purely his own, not as preached only,
but as written by himself in order to the Press." The two Englishmen knew
enough of how the manuscript had come into being to report that, "provoked" by the publishing of illicit or inadequate editions, Hooker had resolved "to go over again the same Materials . . . in order to the perfecting of
it by his own hand for publick Light, thereby to vindicate both himself and it
from that wrong which otherwise had remained for ever irrecompensible."[22]
Goodwin and Nye said nothing of Higginson's role in creating the copy
text, though his was probably the "hand" that "perfected" the *Application of
Redemption*.

Meanwhile, friends continued to rummage in the Hartford archive.
Thomas Shepard, Hooker's son-in-law, may be the "T.S." who retrieved the
sermons that became *The Saints Dignitie, And Dutie* (London, 1651), and
another New England minister, Zachariah Symmes of Charlestown, may be
the "Z. S." who cleaned up the manuscript that became *The Christians Two
Chiefe Lessons* (London, 1640). Symmes (or quite possibly someone else) defended his "meddling in another mans labours" on the grounds that, had he
"not taken some paines in the perusal and transcribing thereof, after it came
into the Printers hands," the work "would have passed the Presse more imperfectly then now it doth." He insisted as well that he and others he did not
name had added nothing "of our owne; onely we amended such errours as
would have beene imputed to the Authour through the oversight of the
Scribe."[23] The Hartford archive also contained the manuscript that became
The Survey of the Summe of Church-Discipline, Hooker's defense of the Congregational Way against its English critics. After sharing a draft version of the
text with some of his colleagues in 1643, Hooker had sent a complete manuscript to England on a ship that disappeared at sea. Edward Hopkins and
William Goodwin took on the task of preparing a fresh copy, only to realize
that Hooker had never completed the text. In their "To the Reader" they
acknowledged that the printed text could not be considered entirely authentic: "The Reader may well conceive, had the judicious Author lived to peruse
the Copy now sent, the work would have been more compleat, and perhaps
some additions made in some parts thereof. But we have not yet had the

happinesse to finde among his papers what was intended in that kinde." Reassurances about their own role followed: "let the Reader know, that nothing is added to, or taken from, the Authors primitive Copy for the substance of it."[24] "Primitive copy" was surely their choice of words to connote the unfinished qualities of the manuscript. As printed in London the printed book was curiously unfinished, for the pagination in some copies skips from page 139 to page 185, possibly because the bookseller was expecting to pair it with something by John Cotton.[25]

Shipwrecks, the expediencies of booksellers, the labors of a copyist, the well-meaning interventions of lay men and ministers on both sides of the Atlantic, the merits and demerits of auditors' notes, the indifference of the London trade to much of the manuscript that Higginson or others assembled, for "some half" of the sermons Higginson had transcribed never made their way into print—none of these circumstances prevented Hooker from thinking of himself as an important writer who, some day, would be able to provide authoritative texts to the London trade. The instructions in his will imposed this same ambition on Hopkins, Goodwin, and Higginson. Yet posthumously as well as during his lifetime, unreliable printings of his sermons went through edition after edition. Perhaps because "T. H." had become a vendible mark, the London trade also credited him with books he never wrote.[26]

After John Cotton's death in 1652, he was remembered as a "man more moderate, and patient," and as "a most skilfull compounder of all differences."[27] He was also the most controversial of all the ministers who participated in the founding of New England—challenged about his orthodoxy in the 1620s,[28] accused of complicity in the "Antinomian" uprising of 1636–37, taunted by Roger Williams for his views on liberty of conscience, and denounced by Presbyterians in the 1640s for being so fervent and early on, so radical, in promoting the "Congregational Way." As Cotton Mather would remark at the end of the century, the "bitter spirit" of adversaries would "expose the name of the incomparable Cotton unto irreparable injuries."[29]

When he was called upon to help the Massachusetts Bay Company fend off rumors that the company was a vehicle for Separatism, he used to advantage the different technologies of publication, entrusting a printer with *Gods Promise to His Plantations* (London, 1630) and relying on manuscript circulation for his letter to Samuel Skelton, a minister employed by the Company who organized the first gathered church in Massachusetts in 1629. Eighteen years later Cotton referred to the letter he sent Skelton as "private," but it was private only in the sense of not being printed, for as pointed out in Chapter 2, he licensed the making of copies. The middle-of-the-road Puritanism he voiced in this letter disappeared once he reached New England. Soon, a new-found partisanship for the very practices he criticized in 1630 was being voiced in letters to England reporting the colonists' experiments with church government; none of these were printed until 1641, but handwritten copies were circulating on both sides of the Atlantic well before this.[30] Soon, too, he was articulating the principles of the "Congregational Way" and its corollary, a "Christian common-wealthe." Less predictably, he was questioning the spiritual well-being of the colonists in his weekly sermons. So he insisted in a sermon he gave in Salem in 1636 and in his weekly preaching, implying as he did so that mistakes were being made by his fellow ministers.[31] On three fronts, then, Cotton ventured onto daring ground: articulating a form of church government that assigned lay men a great deal of authority and restricted church membership to "visible saints," laying out the principles of "godly rule," and pressing on everyone a model of the spiritual life that disparaged "works," "duties," and "sanctification" as sources of assurance and extolled the "witnesse of the Spirit."

To run with the radicals was to draw attention to every word he said or wrote and to increase the risk that others would want to publish his manuscripts. Already in his English ministry a manuscript set of "answers" to theological problems had, to his discomfort, circulated in handwritten copies. "Little did I think," he complained some twenty years after the fact, "that a private letter of mine written to a very friend, should ever have been divulged abroad. But it seemeth some got copies of it; and in process of time, one copy multiplied another."[32] Early on, therefore, he experienced both sides of scribal publication—its utility when he wanted to publicize his letter to Skelton and its powers of exposure when others circulated a document he himself regarded as "private." The same possibilities recurred with text after text, some distributed with his permission but others not, or else in versions that varied from what he had actually written.

For "a model of Moses his judicialls," a program for godly rule he entrusted to the Massachusetts General Court in October 1636, the several states of the text point to another possibility, that no clearly identified original existed, though its history also suggests some of the complexities of scribal reproduction and social authorship. One copy traveled with a group of colonists who moved from Lynn, Massachusetts in 1640 to Long Island; there, a clerk entered it into the new town's book of records, without attribution.

Another copy came into the hands of a London bookseller who printed it, unattributed, in 1641 with a misleading title, for the provisions Cotton sketched in *An Abstract or [sic] the Lawes of New England, As they are now established* had never been approved by the Massachusetts government. Fourteen years later a New-Englander-turned-Fifth Monarchist, William Aspinwall, now in England, published an edition that he or the bookseller entitled *An Abstract of Laws and Government. Wherein as in a Mirrour may be seen the wisdome & perfection of the Government of Christs Kingdome.* Cotton was identified as the author in Aspinwall's preface, but whether the Scriptural citations and other material not in the 1641 printing were his or Aspinwall's additions cannot be determined. The two printed versions may have stemmed from imperfect scribal copies, a possibility suggested by Thomas Hutchinson's version of the text. He had seen what he regarded as "the first draught of the laws of Mr. Cotton . . . corrected with Mr. Winthrop's hand," a manuscript that cannot presently be identified. Comparing this manuscript with the 1655 version, Hutchinson made a number of changes based on Winthrop's emendations of the "first draught."[33]

That manuscripts of varying quality were reaching England and that printers accepted whatever came their way is suggested by the curious history of another text that originated in the 1630s, *The True Constitution Of A particular visible Church, proved by Scripture*, printed in London in 1642 from a manuscript that seems to date from early 1635. Using a question-and-answer format, Cotton emphasized the equality of church members in a congregational system and the "spirituall" nature of the church itself. Reprinted in 1642 as *The Doctrine of the Church*, the bookseller announced in 1643 that he was bringing out a "second edition" "Printed according to a more exact copy; the Marginall proofes in the former Edition misplaced, being herein placed more directly." A "more exact copy" seems a plausible source of the many changes in the text, especially words and phrases that filled out or modified some of the questions and answers. Nothing was revealed, however, of the authority or provenance of that copy. When the text was reprinted a third time in 1644 by another bookseller, again with a title page declaring that the text was "more exactly corrected," the changes seem much more erratic—for example, entries reappear from the edition of 1642—possibly because the bookseller was working not from a third manuscript but creating a composite of the two previous versions.[34]

The year 1642 saw the publication of *The Powring out of the Seven Vials* thanks to John Humfrey, a text based on notes "taken from his owne mouth," or so Humfrey alleged in the preface. That the sermons Cotton was preaching on the Apocalypse in 1639 were attractive to radicals and, conversely, making moderates in the colony uneasy explains the provenance of a manuscript in Thomas Shepard's handwriting, a summary of a sermon on Revelation 4:2 he copied from another source into his notebook of Cambridge church relations. Perhaps in response to the "hidden Antinomianism" of this sermon, Shepard remarked in a note appended in 1639 to his spiritual autobiography, "Mr. Cotton repents not, but is hid only."[35] Earlier, in 1636 and 1637, Shepard was among the ministers who were paying close attention to Cotton's preaching; and as he himself would recall some years later, part of the run up to the synod of September 1637 had been the efforts of his colleagues to "gather out of my Sermons to the people, and my conferences (in word and writing) with the Elders, all such opinions of mine as were conceived by some, to bee erroneous."[36] Text-making in these years was thus a process that involved others, some of whom, such as Shepard, were intensely suspicious of Cotton. Did he accede to the pressures on him and conceal the drafts of the sermons he had been preaching in the mid-1630s? That the Salem sermon was not printed until 1713 and that other sermons or sermon notes of the 1630s appeared after his death implies something akin to self-censorship.

The public voice these texts of the 1630s ascribed to Cotton was not the same voice his readers would encounter in the books he began to write in the early 1640s. As the tone and substance of his statements began to change, so did his attitude toward unauthorized publication. Using intermediaries in London, he intervened to explain which of his statements on church government were authoritative and which were not, a process also akin to self-censorship. This phase of publication involved three books printed out of sequence. The earliest to leave Cotton's desk was a manuscript that circulated in handwritten copies for a year or two before being printed in London in 1645 as *The Way of the Churches of Christ in New-England*. Already, however, a bookseller had brought out *The Keyes Of the Kingdom of Heaven* (1644). Four years later the same agent published *The Way of the Churches Cleared* (London, 1648), with a preface by two English Congregationalists that explained how this sequence came to be, and why it was necessary for Cotton to write *The Way . . . Cleared*.

Why *The Way* of 1645 was belatedly printed, and why the printer's copy text fell short of the fair copy standard was narrated in a preface by two people who identified themselves only by their initials, though one was almost certainly Nathaniel Holmes, a minister who signed his full name in the final treatise of this series:

> If all things in this Treatise, as now printed, doe not answer punctually word for word, to the first written Copie, let the reverend Authour, and the candid Reader pardon us, because wee had not the fairest Copie, nor knew wee, till the Book was neer done, that there was a better to be had, nor to this day yet ever saw it. Therefore wee were forced to shift with this, so as to keep the mind of the Authour, make it *constare sibi*, and by an interpretive leave in his absence, not onely to doe as wee would be done by, but also as he himselfe would have done (wee are confident) if he had been in our case, or present here.

In an offhand way, the two editors acknowledged what any reader who compared this text closely with the *Keyes* of 1644—and some were doing so—would realize. Cotton was moderating a few of the arguments he had been making in the 1630s, especially his enthusiasm for lay rule of local congregations. To indicate their own position, the two editors inserted asterisks next to passages (as on page 81) they did "not yet fully close with." Holmes and his co-editor also had to explain why, in light of the *Keyes* and without being asked to do so by Cotton, they had arranged for publication despite "Diverse Objections . . . laid against the Printing of this Book (to the saddening of the Authour)." The best they could say in their own defense was that the manuscript had already come into the hands of Presbyterian critics and that "others" were "conscientiously and candidly cry[ing] out for information" on New England practices.[37]

Nothing was reported of the provenance of *The Keyes*, but the editors of *The Way . . . Cleared* said a great deal about its history. Thomas Goodwin and Philip Nye, who wrote the opening "To the Reader," had known many of the colonists, and probably Cotton, in the years before the great migration. By 1644 the two were also leading figures in the "Congregational" party, Goodwin as a member of the Westminster Assembly. Though they described themselves as agreeing with Cotton that the "Congregational Way" was God's plan, Goodwin and Nye spoke frankly of differing with him on a series of topics. The censoring voice was theirs, not Cotton's, though implicitly the book was his rewriting of *The Way*. *The Way . . . Cleared* began with a "To the Reader" that spoke directly to questions of provenance and authority:

"Here (Reverend Brethren) is presented unto you in Print, that very Copie, which the worthy Author . . . sent together with his letter under his own hand unto me." Nathaniel Holmes, who wrote this preface, followed these assurances with advice and a cautionary word about provenance: "let us be warned (by that good account this Book renders unto us) of facile credulity, either to reports, or letters, or Books, unlesse they be handed to us from the Authors themselves." Holmes let readers discover for themselves that much of the book was Cotton's response to the humiliation of having his friendship with Anne Hutchinson splashed across the pages of Robert Baillie's *A Dissuasive from the Errours of the Time* (1645).[38]

Questions of provenance and authority multiplied with Cotton's printed sermons. As so commonly happened in the early seventeenth century, people in his English parish had taken notes that, ten or twenty years after the fact, London booksellers accepted as copy text without asking Cotton's opinion of them or questioning their provenance. The Englishmen who wrote prefaces to these books may have wanted to reassure potential readers about provenance, but the more they said about copy text, the more they unsettled the authority of the sermons that followed. *The way of Life. Or, Gods Way and Course, In Bringing The Soul Into keeping it in, and carrying it on, in the wayes of life and peace*, published in London in 1641, was introduced by a William Morton who spoke candidly about provenance and the quality of the text: "I could have wished (if it might have been) that it had passed under his own censure, and then it needed not feare the censure of any other; but seeing it was designed for the Presse, that desire I had of the publike good, and that respect I have ever owed the Author, inclined me to lend it the best furtherance I could, that others might receive as much benefit." Commending the text as "full of precious, sweet, experimentall truths," Morton acknowledged being unsure whether Cotton would be "gratefull . . . that this work of his should come abroad into the publike view and censure."[39]

This same year, another London bookseller issued *Gods Mercie Mixed With His Iustice, Or, His Peoples Deliverance in times of danger. Laid open in severall Sermons*. Whoever wrote the prefatory "To the Christian Reader" acknowledged that the sermon series was based on "broken Notes of his powerfull soule-searching Sermons taken from his mouth by the diligent hand of some well disposed hearers and followers" in England.[40] The peculiarities of *Some Treasure Fetched out of Rubbish* (London, 1660) began with what the unnamed bookseller said about provenance: "These ensuing Treatises were found laid by the Walls, and covered with dust, in the study of an old Non-Conformist (there being diverse Copies of each, under several unknown hands.)" The same person insisted that Cotton was the "known Author of the first Discourse" and, less insistently, "(as it is verily believed) of the second also," and that "Mr. Robert Nichols studiously composed the third." Thomas Shepard II, whose copy of the book survives, was uncertain whether to accept this story: "sd to be Mr J. Cotton's B.D.," he wrote on the flyleaf. What seems certain is that Cotton's name was not written on the manuscript of the second sermon and possibly not on that of the first.[41]

The uncertain authority of "broken notes" and half-hearted attributions extended to other sermons, sermon-series, and treatises. Other than a reference to "comfortable Notes . . . in the hands of a friend to the Authour," nothing at all was said of provenance in *The Covenant of Gods free Grace* (1645), almost certainly a bookseller's composite, for it contained three unrelated texts. The initial text was a sermon preached in England, for it refers to everyday social practices (e.g., apprenticeship) of a kind that would not yet be significant among the colonists; the third was John Davenport's confession of faith before an unnamed congregation in New England. In *A Practical Commentary . . . upon The First Epistle Generall of John,* published in 1656 by the London bookseller Thomas Parkhurst, Charles Scott's comments on provenance in his "To the Reader" were remarkably unspecific, reporting only that "these following Notes" had fallen "by providence" into his hands. Scott or Parkhurst (or possibly neither; we may be in the presence of an invented episode) had taken the unusual step of asking the advice of "Reverend Divines"—"such men whom the whole Nation may justly honor for piety"—whether the book "might be found usefull for the Publick," and therefore published. Scott himself was virtually unknown, and the tactic of asking others who were unnamed to authorize the book has the ring of a bookseller's cover-up. Was it brick or straw (or more dust in the reader's eye) that, on the page following Scott's "To the Reader," Edmund Calamy, a leading minister, testified that "It is sufficiently evident by the preceding Epistle, and by many other arguments, that the ensuing Sermons were preached by Mr. John Cotton"? Cotton Mather was doubtful; though he described the sermon series as having been "preached in his youth, and not published by himself, there are some things therein, which he would not have inserted."[42] The intermediaries responsible for publishing Cotton's commentaries on Ecclesiastes and Canticles (the Psalms) were no more forthcoming, though the staccato nature of *A Brief Exposition . . . of Canticles* (London, 1655) points toward an auditor's notes as copy text.

Too many manuscripts, too many intermediaries (few of whom professed to have known John Cotton), and accumulating signs of booksellers' expediency—this was the situation of books that emerged from manuscripts of the 1620s, like the sermons on John, published some thirty years later. Well before the 1650s, though especially in that decade, booksellers were attempting to reassure the reading public about the state of his printed texts. That this anxiety was widely felt is suggested by Nathaniel Holmes's insistence in *The Way . . . Cleared* that the manuscript had reached him directly from Cotton. Booksellers were offering similar assurances, as when the bookseller inserted on the title page of *The Churches Resurrection* the statement that the copy text was "there [in New England] corrected by his own hand." Similar language—never to be trusted—turned the title page of *An Exposition upon the Thirteenth Chapter of the Revelation* (London, 1655) into another site of reassurance: "Taken from his mouth in Short-writing, and some part of it Corrected by himself soon after the Preaching thereof, and all of it since Viewed over by a friend to Him, and to the Truth: wherein some Mistakes were amended, but nothing of the Sense altered."

Were we to put ourselves in Cotton's place as book after book arrived from London, we would be discriminating among them as he surely was inclined to do himself, differentiating five manuscripts he sent to England to be printed from all the others that bore his name or were associated with him. These five were two discussions of the Congregational Way, the *Keyes* and the *Way . . . Cleared*, his two responses to Roger Williams, *A Letter of Mr. John Cotton's . . . [to] Mr. Williams* (1643) and *The Bloudy Tenent, Washed, And made white* (1647), and *Singing of Psalmes A Gospel-Ordinance* (London, 1647).[43] We know he was unhappy with Humfrey's theft of *The Powring out of the Seven Vials* and embarrassed both by the printing of *The Way* and a text that Roger Williams handed over to the London trade, *The Controversie Concerning Liberty of Conscience* (1646), the letter Cotton had angrily insisted was "private." Nor would he have appreciated the publishing of his answers to the sixteen questions of 1636–37 in 1644 and again in 1646, the year his answers to other questions were printed as *Gospel Conversion*. It was hurtful to have William Twisse publish a critique of his analysis of the doctrine of justification twenty years after the fact, in 1646, and he regretted that Thomas Shepard's name was left off *Singing of Psalmes A Gospel-Ordinance*, for he was recorded some years later as saying, "I am troubled that my bro. Shepard's name is not prefixed to it," the reason being that Shepard "had the chief hand in the composing of it."[44]

The weight of all these disappointments can be felt in a step he took in 1651. As Thomas Allen, who ministered in Charlestown, Massachusetts, was leaving for England in 1651, Cotton handed him several manuscripts intended for the book trade. In all, Allen would play a central role in the making of five texts (two of them incorporated in the same book) printed after Cotton's death in 1652. Which of these Allen received from Cotton and which have a more complicated provenance can only be decided by listening carefully to Allen's accounts of provenance and by taking with a grain of salt his assertions of friendship, for he insisted that he was close to Cotton, testifying, for example, that he knew Cotton's preaching extremely well, having lived "in the Towne next adjoining to Boston, and so had thereby the happy priviledg of enjoying the benefit of the precious labours of Mr. Cottons, in his Lecture upon every fifth day of the week."[45]

The one text Cotton may have placed directly in Allen's hands was *Certain Queries Tending to Accommodation Between The Presbyterian & Congregationall Churches* (1654). The title page represented the book as "Published by a Friend, to whom the Author himselfe sent them over not long before his Death." When it was reprinted in 1655, Allen was more emphatic, declaring in his "To the Reader" that he "had" it "from the Reverend Author himself" (accompanied by a letter giving permission to print), adding, "at my coming over from that Country (which was about a year before his death) he delivered unto me the same for substance." Yet the printed book was based on another manuscript, for Cotton had subsequently recast the twelve "Propositions" of the initial version into "eleven queries." In a near-perfect expression of social authorship, Allen had decided to "add one more to make up the number even and round."[46]

For each of three other books, Allen told stories of provenance that never eliminated uncertainties of provenance and authority. In the "To the Reader" for *An Exposition upon The Thirteenth Chapter of the Revelation* (1655), Allen reiterated the anxieties that booksellers so commonly were voicing about their Cottoniana: "being earnestly desired by the Christian brother, the publisher of this Exposition, who having the pen of a ready Writer, did take those Notes from the mouth of the Preacher, to give my testimony to the world that these were indeed the very Sermons of that holy Servant." To the ambiguous conflating of "publisher" and note-taker Allen added other unsettling language. These, he declared, were "for the substance of them (giving allowance for such defects of the Amanuensis, which cannot but be expected ordinarily, (and yet I confess are but very few in this Treatise)."[47] For another text he midwifed, *The Covenant of Grace: Discovering The Great Work of a Sinners Reconciliation with God* (1655), Allen offered would-be purchasers "a brief account of the publishing of them to the world, that the Reader may undoubtedly assure himself that these are neither spurious Copies, nor surreptitiously put forth." Here he specified that the manuscript, an auditor's notes, was "afterwards presented unto him [Cotton] with desire of his perusal and emendation of it; which being done (and indeed the interlinings of his owne hand doe plainly testifie his correcting of it) he delivered back, not long before his death, into the hands of a Gentleman, (one of the Church in Boston there)." Subsequently, this unnamed person had delivered the manuscript to Allen, now in London, "to take order for the Printing of it."[48]

It was not Thomas Allen but the London bookseller John Allen who spelled out the complex making of *A Treatise of the Covenant of Grace* (1659), an expanded version of the 1655 *Covenant of Grace*, both of them probably containing sermons from the 1630s. Yet again a title page became a site for insisting on textual authority: "Corrected also by the Authors own hand," with Thomas cited as the person who "fitted" the copy text for the press. In "The Stationer to the Reader," the other Allen was quite specific about provenance and copy text:

> I have of late received (from a neer Friend and Relation, one of the reverend Elders of that Church) another copy of the said Treatise, far larger then the former (above a third part) corrected also in some places by the Authours own hand before his death: the reason of which enlargement, is not from any addition by any other hand, but (as may easily be conceived) from the diversity of the *Amanuenses*, who did take the Notes of his Sermons, some writing the same more largely and exactly than others, and several Copies so taken, being presented to the reverend Author to correct, He, as he had leasure (willing and ready to gratifie the desire of his Friends) did peruse and rectifie the sense with his pen, as he went cursorily over the same.

The truest of these statements may be the comment that some auditors' notes were better than others, for it seems unlikely that Cotton edited the "several Copies" and created a composite out of them, a feat Allen himself seemed to doubt by suggesting that Cotton had "cursorily [gone] over the same." In their fuller as in their earlier, more constrained condition, these sermons seem closely connected to the turmoil of the mid-1630s. Their appearance after Cotton's death again suggests an intentional delay in bringing them into print —probably Cotton's, possibly his auditors', and certainly Thomas Allen's.[49]

As these stories of provenance so clearly reveal, Cotton was a social author par excellence. Allen, Humfrey, Aspinwall, Williams, Holmes, Goodwin and Nye, Greenhill, John Owen (who assisted with a posthumous text), Anthony Tuckney, William Twisse, Robert Baillie, note takers in old Boston and new, booksellers and printers known and unknown, though especially Matthew Simmons in the 1640s—all of these men intervened in one way or another in the process of bringing Cotton's texts into print. Almost to a person, his collaborators praised him for his qualities as a spiritual teacher even as they were treating his texts with a mixture of expediency and respect, with expediency often winning out. For Cotton, the lesson he learned again and again was that he could not control how or when his manuscripts were published. He tried self-censorship, but the possibilities for doing so were undercut by the quantity of manuscripts that circulated in Puritan circles and the London book trades. In a sentence that captures some of the ironies of Cotton's situation, Charles Scott speculated in his preface to *The way of Life* that Cotton might be "gratefull . . . that this work of his should come abroad into the publike view and censure," though adding immediately thereafter, "I know not." The hesitation implied by these three words was surely a hesitation Cotton shared as, year after year, he experienced the advantages and disadvantages of having his work made "publike." Others, too, were uneasy—the men who introduced his books, the booksellers and printers who manufactured them, and, at the end of the century, the ever alert Cotton Mather, who realized that "few of them [Cotton's books] were Printed with his own Knowledge or Consent," specifying, in particular, the imperfections of the "Sermons on the First Epistle of John, in Folio . . . being Preached in his Youth, and not Published by himself, there are some things therein, which he would not have Inserted."[50]

At the turn of the century, the conditions of text-making were beginning to change. Nowhere are these changes more visible than in the publishing career of Cotton Mather (1665–1728), who in 1685 was ordained and officially joined his father Increase in the ministry of Second Church, Boston. Not the astonishing abundance of his publications but the contingencies of his life as a writer make him interesting to us. In that role he was constantly deciding whether to identify himself on the title page or remain anonymous. In that role, too, he tinkered with his own texts, altering some as they passed through a printing shop and re-arranging others to fit into a different imprint. For some of his books he drew on manuscripts that came his way; in doing so, Mather the author became redactor and compiler. More than any other writer in New England, he relied on patrons to finance his publications and represent him with the London book trade. He was singular, too, in self-publishing much of what he wrote. His successes were many, but they were overshadowed by one great failure, an immense manuscript (eventually filling six folio volumes) no one in the London trade would undertake to publish. For twenty years or more he repeatedly pressed the importance of the "Biblia Americana," as he named this compilation of commentaries on Scripture, upon his English friends and the London trade, to no avail.[51]

Mather's life as a writer was marked by multiple contradictions. Inheriting those that were intrinsic to the Protestant vernacular tradition, he encountered or created others that were particular to his times. Though he declared that his purpose in writing was to sustain "evangelical Religion," early on making it his goal to "promote the Publication of a good Book, whereby the Soules of many in the Countrey may bee edified" and hesitating to advertise his presence as author, he also craved recognition abroad as well as in New England, feeling, as his son Samuel remarked after his death, that it was not "sufficient to be useful and active at home: he was for appearing publickly, and to the European World."[52] The search for patrons and intermediaries who would vouch for him in England thus acquired a significance it did not have for Cotton or Hooker. At once cosmopolitan and provincial, he never crossed the Atlantic. His cosmopolitanism was constrained, moreover, by his commitment to an idealized New England and the "Congregational Way," even though he also complained incessantly of "declension" and approved of measures like the "half-way covenant." He endorsed the charter of 1691 that incorporated Massachusetts into the English empire, yet detested the Anglicans who, by the 1680s, were becoming a presence in New England. Ever a partisan figure in local politics, he tried to implement themes and practices that would overcome factionalism among the colonists. Never able to do so, he experienced again and again the "bitter spirit" of adversaries that, as he remarked of his grandfather John Cotton, "expose[d]" him to "irreparable injuries."

Title pages and other formal features of his books bespeak the contradictions of his life as writer. Should he practice the anonymity that betokened self-effacement or foreground the rewards of celebrity that came his way, like the honorary doctorate he received from the University of Glasgow in 1710 and his election to the Royal Society of London? Should he incorporate an author's portrait into his books, as some of his father's booksellers were doing,[53] or would this demonstrate an ungracious vanity? Should he self-publish the short, inexpensive texts he wrote in great abundance, or should he trust the book trade despite the comment (of English provenance) he quoted in his diary, that "Booksellers are generally such, that a celebrated Author, thinks the most opprobrious Term he can give unto them, is to say, in one word, they are Booksellers"?[54] Printed or unprinted, the physical books and manuscripts—some languishing unpublished, others choked with errata or abridged by someone else—testify to the double-sided nature of this relationship. And on whom could he depend in England and New England to treat him fairly? The Nonconformist community was the obvious answer, but would that relationship survive the differences, at once theological and political, that began to emerge within English Dissent by the 1690s? Compounding all of these anxieties was the contradiction between the spiritual exercises that accompanied his forays into writing and publishing, exercises predicated on the hope that God would respond and resolve any problems, and his attempts to manipulate printers and patrons.[55]

These contradictions were not unique to Mather, but the times in which he lived gave them fresh importance. Unlike his great predecessors, Mather could rely on the local book trade to print the vast majority of his sermons and incidental writings. The Cambridge printing office closed down in 1692, but Boston became home to several printers and booksellers, some of whom moved there from London. The Nonconformist Benjamin Harris, who got into trouble by criticizing James II, arrived in 1685 and remained until 1694, when he returned to London carrying with him some of Mather's manuscripts. In 1686 another Nonconformist bookseller, John Dunton, turned up for six months, bringing with him a stock of books to sell and, during his time in Boston, undertaking others. Early on, Mather depended on Bartholomew Green to print much of what he wrote, and in England Dunton, Harris, and Thomas Parkhurst, the most substantial Nonconformist bookseller, were usually available. For the most part the local sermons he or his patrons paid for were never bound, had print runs of as little as 200 copies and were distributed free of charge or sold cheaply to notables or congregations like his own. For a funeral sermon commemorating one of the Connecticut Winthrops, Mather envisioned distributing some of the 200 copies, which another Winthrop had financed, to "Every Magistrate, and Minister, and Deputy in Connecticut colony," with others being sent to "particular

Friends, both here and in England."[56] Manuscripts of the size of the *Magnalia* and the "Biblia Americana" could only have been printed in London, at a cost that Mather himself could not afford.[57]

In his early twenties Mather was already practicing the textual strategies he would use the rest of his life. As was customary, the poem that marks the beginning of his literary career (1682) identified the writer by initials, in this instance "N. R.," the final letters of his name; another poem of 1685 used his proper initials, but the Cambridge-printed almanac he prepared for 1683 had no identification. Then came an unexpected opportunity, the public execution in 1686 of a convicted murderer, James Morgan, that drew thousands of people to Second Church, Boston, to hear Cotton preach a "suitable sermon" in Morgan's presence. The event was a bookseller's dream, for the "people, throughout the Countrey, very greedily desired the Publication of my poor Sermon." John Dunton obliged them by partnering with a local bookseller, Joseph Brunning, to issue *The Call of the Gospel*, a package of sermons, two by senior ministers and a third by Cotton with a separate title page under his name. A second edition followed, a rarity in the Boston trade, but a risk Brunning took because of the "speedy sale of the lst Impression" and because he was excited by new material in Mather's hands, a "Discourse of the Minister [Cotton] with James Morgan on the Way to his Execution" that, in Mather's words, was "procured (utterly against his knowledge)" by a "harmless Strategem." Yet Mather exaggerated his resistance, for the manuscript had been carefully prepared and he reprinted it in two subsequent publications, hoping, as he noted in his diary in 1686, that the book would do "a World of Good."[58]

Meanwhile he was beginning to acquire patrons and sponsors. The first book Mather wrote solely on his own, and also the first to have his name on the title page, *Memorable Providences, Relating to Witchcrafts and Possessions* (Boston, 1689) was also the first of his publications for which he sought the sanction of intermediaries. Its descriptions of diabolical possession in a Boston family, together with two "Discourse[s] and a father's testimony," were "Recommended by the Ministers of Boston & Charlestown," four of whom signed a "To the Reader" that implicitly confirmed the truthfulness of Mather's narrative. For the first time, too, he singled out a local notable, dedicating the book to "the Honourable Wait Winthrop, Esq.," the chief justice of Massachusetts's highest court. Surely as satisfying as the textual presence of these guardians was the willingness of Thomas Parkhurst to reprint it two years later, though for the London printing he omitted one of Mather's "examples" and made other changes. Another novelty of the London version was an attestation by Richard Baxter, a Nonconformist minister of great renown who agreed with Cotton on the validity of possession stories. Baxter was already a client of Parkhurst's, but it may have been his friendship with Increase Mather, then in London as an agent of the Massachusetts Bay government, that explained his presence in the book. Cotton also turned to John Dunton, who sponsored the first printing anywhere of Cotton's spiritual biography of his younger brother, *Early Piety, exemplified in the Life and Death of Mr. Nathaniel Mather* (London, 1689), a text to which Cotton added three sermons on the lessons to be learned from the "Pattern" of his brother's brief life. Again with Increase on hand to help out, the Nonconformist community intervened to signal its support. The distinguished minister Matthew Mead wrote a "Prefatory Epistle" for the second London edition praising Cotton's "Modesty" in allowing his brother to speak for himself, and Cotton's London-based uncle Samuel compared Nathaniel to "famous young Janeway" for his spiritual capacities.[59]

By 1691, therefore, Cotton had set in motion a literary career on both sides of the Atlantic, a career situated in the context of a literary tradition that had been reenergized within English Nonconformity by writers, some of them best-selling celebrities, such as Joseph Alleine, John and James Janeway, John Flavel, and Richard Baxter. That Mead, Baxter, Parkhurst, and Dunton were willing to help him had much to do with the politics of religion in the aftermath of the Glorious Revolution, which promised greater toleration of Dissent and, for a moment, the possibility of reshaping the Church of England to include Dissenters. 1691 marked as well the drafting of an agreement between Congregational (Independent) and Presbyterian clergy to end the conflict between them and, implicitly, to temper their criticism of the Church of England. Increase had participated in the discussions that led to the "Heads of Agreement," and Cotton publicized them in New England as a basis for unity among the colonists. The two Mathers could count on other friends and patrons, especially William Phips, a parishioner of theirs who had been knighted in 1690 and returned from England in 1691 to begin a term of service as the first royal governor of the province.

Some of these contours of Mather's career would persist for the rest of his life, but others vanished or were weakened by events like the witch-hunt of 1692 and the fracturing of English dissent along theological lines. *Wonders of the Invisible World* sits aside the fault line of Mather's career, a work that "exposed" its author to an extraordinary degree, as the history of its making and reception demonstrates. According to Mather, he wrote it at the behest of William Phips, who responded to accusations of witchcraft in and around Salem by appointing a special court to decide who was innocent and who guilty, with William Stoughton, an ally of the Mathers, as its chief justice. Toward the end of the summer, at a moment when Phips realized that the decisions of the court were being widely questioned, he asked Mather to write an account of the trials. So did several of the judges on the court.[60] Thus came into being a book printed in Boston in late 1692, though dated 1693 to avoid the appearance of violating Phips's order of October 14 that nothing be published about the trials. Mather and his publisher, Benjamin Harris, did everything they could to surround the book with emblems of official sponsorship. On the reverse side of the title page appeared the words, "Published by the Special Command of His EXCELLENCY, the Governour of the Province of the Massachusetts-Bay in New-England." A commendation by William Stoughton, not only chief justice but also lieutenant governor, followed, and Stoughton reappeared, along with Samuel Sewall, a fellow judge, near the end to endorse Mather's account of the court's proceedings. (Mather had shown Stoughton parts of the manuscript.)

As he was working on the book, Mather assured Stoughton that the court was God's "instrument for the extinguishing of as wonderful a piece of devilism as has been seen in the world" and that he wrote to allay the "fury which we now so much turn upon one another." The summaries of the trials had come to Mather from Stephen Sewall, clerk of the special court. Soliciting these from Sewall in a letter of September 20, Mather had suggested that Sewall write a "narrative by way of letter to me," a text, had Sewall written it, that Mather would probably have incorporated as such into *Wonders*. By this time he knew that whatever he said would be controversial. Seeking reassurance, he asked Sewall to "intimate over again, what you have sometimes told me, of the awe which is upon the hearts of your juries" and how this, in turn, bore out the "validity" and "credibility" of evidence that others were doubting.[61] As printed, however, the summaries seem to be Mather's redactions of whatever Sewall sent him, recast to emphasize the guilt of the executed. As he waited for Sewall to respond, with the printer impatient to set type, Mather cast around for other material—sermons he had preached, a digest of some English trials, an account of a Danish witch hunt, and the like, all assembled in great haste to keep up with the printer. Together, writer and printer may have taken no longer than three or four weeks to assemble and manufacture *Wonders*.[62]

Wonders was a modest success in the London market, noticed in a periodical, reprinted with astonishing rapidity by John Dunton in London in December 1692 (dated 1693), with an altered title page, and reprinted twice more in a version Dunton abridged by excising one of the sermons and several of the extracts from other writers. Dunton cared little for authorial control, but by the time copies reached him Mather was not of a mind to make strong claims for the book. From the start, he hesitated to acknowledge it: "I Live by Neighbors, that force me to produce these Undeserved Lines," he wrote in a singular "Authors Defence" that appeared at the beginning of the book (pp. iv–v). Here and elsewhere he repeatedly cast himself as an instrument of others, the men in high places whose approval and authority he inserted at every possible point into the text. That the book was doing him no good may account for his decision about the same time to circulate in manuscript two descriptions of local cases of what he took to be witchcraft, the "Brand Pluck't Out of the Burning," which detailed the struggles of the teenage Mercy Short, and "Another Brand pluck't out of the Burning," about Margaret Rule. He wrote on the cover of "Brand" the words "to be returned to the authour," but any hopes of keeping these stories private was thwarted by the animus of the Boston merchant Robert Calef, who incorporated the story of Mercy Short into his viciously anti-Mather *More Wonders of the Invisible World* (London, 1700). [63]

Accepting or denying responsibility for a text was linked with Mather's practice of anonymity, which he used in several different ways. He and his father colluded to hide their presence in *A Brief Discourse Concerning the Unlawfulness of the Comon Prayer Worship*, printed probably in Cambridge in 1686 shortly after Anglican church services began to be held in the town; it was written by Increase, who left his name off the title page and charged Cotton with the task of seeing the pamphlet through the press. To remain concealed but to attack was a style that reappeared in 1690 with the newssheet *Publick Occurences*, which the government immediately suppressed because it contained an unfavorable story on military operations against the Indians. Mather painted his own involvement as minimally accidental: "the publisher had not one line of it from me, only as accidentally meeting him in the high way; on his request, I showed him how to contract and express the report of the expedition." Two years later, as discontent was mounting with the new charter of 1691, he wrote and circulated in manuscript a collection of anonymous fables defending the charter and his father's role in securing it from William III. [64] Within his family and circle of friends there could have been little doubt as to what he was publishing, so little, indeed, that after he died his son Samuel was able to publish a bibliography of what he had written. In some situations Cotton concealed his presence in keeping with the ideal of self-effacement he inherited from the vernacular tradition. But when anonymity turned political, his enemies were quick to expose Mather's presence. Calef did so gleefully when he named Cotton as author of *Pietas in Patriam: The Life of Sir William Phips* (London, 1697), a defense of Increase's presidency of Harvard and his efforts to gain a new charter for Massachusetts as well as a vindication of a member of their congregation whose term as governor had gone badly: "Which book," Calef wrote, "tho it bears not the Authors name, yet the Stile, manner and matter is such, that were there no other demonstration or token to know him by, it were no Witchcraft to determine that the said Mr. C. is the Author of it."[65]

By the mid-1690s Mather's identity as a writer was being tested by other circumstances he could not control. His hopes for "unity" within English Nonconformity began to founder as fresh outbursts of theological controversy began to signal the divisions that, by the early eighteenth century, were carrying some English Dissenters out of the "evangelical orthodoxy" he himself favored. For the moment, his connections with English Nonconformity continued to serve him well. *Pietas in Patriam*, which Phips's widow may have helped subsidize, came with an attestation signed by three English ministers who evoked Mather's "well known Integrity, Prudence, and Veracity" as reasons for expressing their "Confidence" in "the truth of what he here Relates," a confidence qualified, however, by their adding, "there is not any cause to Question" that truth—the "truth" thus put in doubt being Mather's account of the Salem witch-hunt. A defense of his father's agency in England and of Phips's mishandled governorship, *Pietas in Patriam* contained a dedication to "To his Excellency the Earl of Bellomont . . . General Governour of the Providence of Massachusetts," composed by Cotton's London-based uncle Nathaniel but certainly in keeping with Cotton's wish to insinuate himself with an outsider who as yet had no local base of support.

Having good connections at home and abroad was critical for Mather's life as a writer as well as for his sense of himself as a significant figure in international evangelicalism and in mediating the colonists' relationship with the English empire. At home, his literary career was benefiting from new patrons like John Winthrop of New London, of "a family in the world which I have endeavored always to treat with all possible service and honor," as he informed this Winthrop in a letter of 1707 soliciting funds to publish a fu-

neral sermon on another member of the family.[66] By the early eighteenth
century Mather could count not only on Winthrop but also on Boston-based
merchants and young peoples' societies to pay the printers' bill for certain
kinds of sermons. Overseas, he found allies both literary and political in two
influential men with a background in Dissent, Henry and Sir William Ashurst, both of them active in the New England Company. Using the instrument of a dedication (though compromising its significance by remarking on
the practice as over-used), Cotton honored William in *Bonifacius* (Boston,
1710), to which he added an appendix on Native American affairs and the
earliest advertisement for the commentaries on the Bible he was preparing,
the "Biblia Americana."[67]

Again, however, particular books reveal the complications of relying on
intermediaries. Those complications played a large role in the making of the
Magnalia Christi Americana, printed in London in 1702 seven or so years
after Mather began to prepare the manuscript, which he sent off to London
in 1700. (In all, the *Magnalia* as finally printed contained seventeen previously published texts; though the opening sentence of the General Introduction evoked a high understanding of authorship, the actual making of the
book was more in keeping with Mather's casual approach to the authority
both of his own publications and of texts he collected from others.) By mid-
1700 he had learned from a London bookseller that printing it would "cost
about 600 lb." When word reached him in 1702 that, at long last, Thomas
Parkhurst had undertaken the project, he also learned that none of the conditions he had specified were being met. The man on whom he was counting,
the English Nonconformist John Quick, who was personally known to Increase Mather, had done his best (or so he claimed) to meet those conditions:
that Mather would receive one hundred guineas "or so many Books well-
bound," that six would be printed on "larger paper richly bound" for Mather
to give his favorite patrons, that Quick himself would have access to "every
sheet . . . hot from the Presse to be revised and corrected," that the quality of
the presswork and paper be of the standard Mather had specified in "printed
Proposalls," and that the book as printed be illustrated with, among other
images, "the best Topographicall Dellineation of Boston and your effigies in
mezzotint." But as Quick reported in a letter, he had been entirely excluded
from the process of production. The consequences were so dismaying that
when copies of the printed book (not in the quantity Mather had hoped for)
reached him that fall, he hastily arranged for a Boston printer to issue a two-
page folio errata (Fig. 6) correcting some of the many compositors' mistakes.

THE *Holy Bible* it self, in some of its Editions hath been affronted, with Scandalous *Errors* of the *Press-work* ; and in one of them, they so Printed those Words, Psal. 119. 161. *Printers have persecuted me.* The Author of this *Church-History* ha's all the Reason in the World then to be Patient, tho' his work, be depraved with many *Errors* of the *Press-work.* The common Excuse in such cases is, The Distance of the *Author* from the Press ; Here there was the Distance of a thousand Leagues. Tho' the *Errata* are mostly, but *Literals* ; and there are few, but what an Intelligent, and Charitable Reader, would correct without any Direction from the Author ; yet it was thought fit here, to offer a collection of them ; (omitting the *False-Pointings*, which are more Numerous, and less Important.)

p. stands for *Page. c.* for *Column. l.* for *Line.* (*f. b.*) is as much as to say, count the Lines *from* the *bottom.*

IN Poems *p* 5 l. penult f. *Seems*, r. joins. *p.* 6 l. 1 r. *Literarum p* 7 l. 18 r. *Dumque.*

In General Introduction, *p.* 1 *c.* 2 l. 2 r. Fare. *Ibid* l. last f *decreed* r. decried. *p.* 2 *c.* 2 l 62 blot out, NOT. *p.* 3 *c.* 1 l. 43 f. implies, r. employes. *p.* 4 *c.* 1 l. 41 r Lyncei, *p.* 5 *c.* 1 l. 32 r *Jurieu, p.* 6 *c.* 2 l 54 f Christ r. Assist. *p.* 7 *c.* 2 l. 41 f *tu* r. in.

BOOK I.

PAge 1 *c.* 1 l 1 r. It was *as* long ago, *Ibid c.* 2 l 2 r. compilasse, l 27 r. ill-boding. *p.* 3 *c.* 1 l 4 r terrarum. *Ibid c.* 2 l 21 f Served, r Scrued. l 42 r One Captain. *p* 5 *c.* 1 l 5 (*f. b.*) The Sentence is to End at, Impugned. *p* 6 l 12 r Adventurers. *p* 12 *c* 1 l 12 f. and r. in. *c* 2 l 17 r Showes. *p* 14 *c* 1 l 40 f Ther, Though, *p* 15 *c* 1 l 2 (*f.b.*) r Horror. *p* 17 *c* 1 l 29 f Peace r Face, *p* 20 *c.* 1 l 8 (*f.b*) r Infantiæ. *c* 2 l 3 (*f. b.*) r *Nov-Angles. p* 21 *c.* 2 l. 14 r Zone for the poor- *p* 22 *c* 2 l 33 place the (;) at, *Alive*; *p* 27 *c.* 2 l 23 r *Willard p* 28 *c.* 2 l 28 r *Lyme. p* 36 *c* l 39 r. their.

BOOK II.

TItle-page l 13 r *Secli.* l 14 r *damus.* l 16 r *Dignitate- panormitan.* *p* 1 *c* 2 l 28 r. works, *p* 7 *c* 1 l 21 r. *Fortis,* *c* 2 l 13 r *Magno, p* 9 *c* 2 l 39 f. imitate, r. intimate *p* 10 *c.* 1 l 51 r make. *p* 11 *c* 1 l 38 r. if it be, *p* 13 *c* 1 l 8 r *Humility. p* 17 *c* 1 l 19 (*f.b.*) r *Eudoxia.* 14 r *Schurman p* 21 *c* 2 l 23 r *Successively.* And again at l 32. *p* 27 *c* 1 l 46 r Loving. *p* 32 *c* 1 l 9 r *Adeptist c* 2 l 2 r Loving. *p* 41 *c* 2 l 4 (*f. b.*) r 1687. *p* 61 *c* 1 l 4 r Invisible. *p* 64 *c* 2 l 3 r Invisible. l 9 (*f. b.*) f. under, r. unto, *p* 69 *c* 1 l 38 r *Agellius, p* 70 *c* 1 l 3 (*f. b.*) f. few *but* would— *c* 2 l 45 f. of r. or *p* 72 *c* 1 l 44 f. him r. them.

BOOK III.

PAge 1 *c* 1 l 14 r *Calvinianus.* l 34 f. *ac* r *ab.* l 35 f *meus,* r *mens c* 2 l 1 f. our r one. *p* 3 *c* 1 l 27 r *Maverick. c* 2 l 8 (*f. b.*) r *Hanford p* 4 *c* 1 l 6 r. Signalize. *p* 5 *c* 1 l 31 r *Mapalia,* l 3 (*f.b.*) f. Patrons r Nations. *p* 13 *c* 1 l 11 r. It is better. l 47 f Faith r. Truth. *p* 15 *c* 2 l 32 r no less than— *p* 18 *c* 1 l 23 r *Temporibus p* 22 *c* 1 l 2 r Sincere, l 3 (*f.b.*) r the Name. *c* 2 l 20 r *Varia. p* 23 *c* 1 l 7 r *Presbyteros.* l 28 r a *Synodo. p* 25 *c* 1 l 20 r. was by the, l 16 (*f.b.*) r. Expound. *p* 28 *c* 1 l 41 f. of r off. *p* 30 *c* 2 l 25 r. more instructed and.— *p* 33 *c* 1 l 42 f. two r. a— l 44 r. unexceptionable. *p* 43 *c* 2 l 4 r Bishops. *p* 45 *c* 1 l 14 Blot out, *Me. p* 46 *c* 2 l. last r. *wish no one Ill. p* 49 *c* 2 l. 7 r *Antiquitati. p* 55 *c* 2 l 49 f. will r

might. *p* 57 *c* 1 l 2 (*f. b.*) r. pleasantly said. *p* 58 *c* 1 l 2 r. it is in one. *c* 2 l 43 f. for r. from the Spirit. *p* 59 *c* 2 l 38 f. one r. our. *p* 63 *c* 1 l 16 Blot out, *And his own.* l 18 f. her r. his. *p* 64 *c* 2 l 10 (*f. b.*) r, it was NOT long. *p* 66 *c* 2 l 24 f. yet r. not. *p* 67 *c* 2 l 12 (*f. b.*) r. Souls. *p* 68 *c* 1 l 10 r. that's. *p* 71 *c* 2 l 3 (*f.b.*) f also r. tho' *p* 74 *c* 1 l 37 make a Comma (,) at, *New-England, p* 76 *c* 1 l 14 r. for as the. *c.* 2 l 13 r. *Paleas. p* 77 *c* 2 l. 5 r. *Enatare. p* 80 *c* 2 l 5 Blot out, *Not. p* 84 *c* 1 l. 9 Blot out, *Not. p* 85 *c* 2 l 38 make a *Comma* (,) at, *Conversion, p* 90 *c* 2 l 6 Blot out, *Mis.* l 43 r *Exeundum. p* 91 *c* 1 l 38 f. me, r. Him. *p* 93 *c* 2 l 7 (*f.b.*) r. Circumstance. *p* 94 *c* 1 l 3 r Transaction. l 4 f. her r. His *p* 95 *c* 1 l 3 r. *rogitas. c* 2 l 21 r. *Abraha. p* 96 *c* 2 l 36 r Vicar-General *p* 98 *c* 2 l 6 r *Nominis.* l 33 r *Tellus.* l 36 r *Irati p* 100 *c* 1 l 29 r. Mistakes. l last, Blot out, *as p* 104 *c* 2 l 5 (*f b*) r. depulerant. *p* 105 *c* 1 l 14 (*fb*) r *Cupsit. p* 106 *c* 2 l 9 r. of his. l 41 f. mentioned, r maintained. *p* 108 *c* 2 l 20 r *Periclitati.* l 23 r *fidis* l 48 r *desideratissimos. p* 109 *c* 2 l 2 r *Excitarem.* l 14 r *Regum. p* 113 *c* 1 l 17 (*f.b.*) f. and r. in. *c* 2 l 6 (*f. b*) r. make. *p* 114 *c* 1 l 23 r. weariness. *p* 116 *c* 1 l 34 r *Irrefragabilis c* 2 l 17 r. *esset. p* 119 *c* 2 l 18 r. many an. l 20 f. we r. He. l 3 ⊙ t. Twice r. Thrice *p* 120 *c* 1 l 14 r. move. *p* 121 *c* 2 l 28 f. Souls r Seals. *p* 122 *c* 1 l 18 r Likeness. *p* 123 *c* 1 l 15 (*fb*) r. Orbilian. l 17 (*f. b.*) r *multa. p* 126 *c* 1 l 21 r. by the. *c* 2 l 19 (*f. b.*) f if. r. of. *p* 127 *c* 1 l 29 r. find him. *p* 133 *c* 1 l 30 r. *navarunt* l 36 r. *delibuti* l 38 r. *arripiane. c* 2 l 10 r. did. l 21 r. tearful. *p* 134 *c* 2 l 1 r. *Paula.* l 9 (*f. b.*) blot out, *So.* l 3 (*f. b.*) r *Hebraicas. p* 138 *c* 2 l 8 r. ὀρθοποιεῖν — ὀρθοποιεῖν. l 10 r. make the. *p* 141 *c* 2 l 18 (*f. b.*) r. calling. *p* 143 *c* 1 l 20 (*f.b.*) r. Foster,— *Descensu. p* 144 *c* 1 l 34 r. *Sinceriotis. p* 145 *c* 1 l 2 blot out, *Luthi. p* 151 *c* 1 l 27 r. *Abase, p* 152 *c* 2 l 23 f. her r. their. *p* 153 *c* 2 l 28 r. *Cælos.* l 32 r ×ωσι· l 36 r. *Indus. p* 155 *c* 2 l 25 r. grew. *p* 157 *c* 2 l 40 f. of r. and *p* 158 *c* 1 l 19 (*f.b.*) r. that which. *p* 159 *c* 1 l 17 (*f. b.*) r. Solam *c* 2 l 9 (*f.b.*) r. *Nuge. p* 160 *c* 1 l 14 (*f. b.*) r. Transaction. *p* 161 *c* 1 l 11 (*f.b.*) r *homely, p* 162

c 2

Figure 6. A Boston author corrects the errors in a London-printed book: the broadside errata Cotton Mather prepared after receiving the *Magnalia Christi Americana* (London, 1702). Courtesy of the Massachusetts Historical Society.

The sales in England were so disappointing that someone (Mather? Park-hurst) floated the idea of an abridgment. Cotton's brother Samuel, who lived in England, set to work on the project and slashed his way through the folio pages. Nothing came of this effort, though Samuel did succeed in publishing two abridgments of other books by Cotton.[68]

To be sure, a few of Mather's books were achieving a certain success in the marketplace, as judged by the willingness of booksellers on both sides of the Atlantic to issue second or third printings. One such success was *Family Religion Urged* (Boston, 1705). In the course of the eighteenth century, book-sellers in New England also reprinted *A Token for the Children of New England* (Boston, 1700), an imprint that demonstrates in a special way how the presence of a putative author (or compiler) could be erased as printers and booksellers rearranged and rewrote what Mather had prepared. The book contained tales of pious children's deathbed experiences Mather had gathered from various sources, a collection he and his bookseller paired with a much-reprinted Nonconformist text, James Janeway's *A Token for Children*. Mather's name was on the title page of his portion. Thereafter, it vanished from the five re-printings in the eighteenth century, with the package of stories also changing—more of them added from uncertain sources or, by the end of the century, substantially shortened. *A Token* thus became a book without an author in two respects, formally in being "anon" and practically in being a collection anyone in the book trades felt entitled to refashion. Together, trade practices and the contents of the book—deathbed stories were a much relished genre within the vernacular tradition—rendered Mather virtually invisible.[69]

Elsewhere he was quite visible or determined to make himself so. By the second decade of the eighteenth century he was announcing himself on title pages as "D.D." to signify his Glasgow honorary doctorate of 1710, some-times adding "F.R.S." to commemorate his election to the Royal Society. He continued to correspond with Nonconformists in England and figures in the Church of Scotland, often enclosing copies of locally published books and extolling, directly or indirectly, his accomplishments as a writer. In many of these same letters he pleaded, never successfully, for assistance with the "Biblia Americana," which he also publicized in a printed prospectus directed at the practice of subscription publishing that had become an important means of financing larger books within the English trade. When he wrote in 1714 to an English minister with whom he had no previous connections asking that he "accept the t[rou]ble of advising, directing, ordering [what] shall be done about" the "Biblia Americana," he laid out a series of tasks: to find a bookseller, agree on terms "as if it were your own," and "give effectual injunctions for the press work, to be done fairly, neatly correctly, and according to the directions I may in time give concerning it." The anxiety about press work sprang from the many disappointments he had experienced, first and foremost with the *Magnalia*. The anxiety about "terms" arose from his awareness that no one had stepped forward to pay the printer's bill and that books of great length could not be sold in any quantity in New England, a fact he tried to conceal by mentioning the possibility of "subscriptions for many more than one hundred sets of the work" among the colonists.[70] Time passed, the manuscript languished, and although he "bombarded a host of correspondents," among them Ashurst and Jeremiah Dummer, he experienced a growing sense of betrayal from those who had helped him at the beginning of his career: "From the Dissenters I must expect nothing, for such reasons as I am not fond of mentioning," a complaint to which he added a note of unease that marked the provincial writer: "our correspondents on your island seem very much to cast us off, and count us what we really are, of too little use or worth for them to converse withal."[71]

The contradictions Cotton Mather experienced were distinctive to his times, but to see him as different is to ignore the continuities that linked his experiences in book-making with those of Thomas Hooker and John Cotton. All three worked within the Protestant vernacular tradition. In Mather's case as in theirs, this tradition informed how he approached anonymity, genre, audience, and originality. As it did for them, his commitment to the Puritan/Nonconformist tradition gained him the support of intermediaries at home and in England. Yet he had no great cause of the kind that animated Cotton and Hooker as founders of the "Congregational Way" and framers of the practical divinity. In some ways his world was much smaller than theirs, and it was certainly a world far more defined by a deference to the English empire; as Kenneth Silverman has astutely pointed out, the *Magnalia* is as much an act of courtship of the Church of England as it is a hymn to Protestant primitivism.[72] Mather's was the more entrepreneurial career—his suggestion to John Quick that a bookseller pay him a hundred guineas for the *Magnalia* has no parallel in their literary careers—a difference in keeping with the enlarging scope of the book market and the success of bookseller-publishers such as Dunton and Parkhurst. Mather was also more intentional in directing books at particular audiences; in the parlance of our own times, he exploited every possible niche in the market. Unlike theirs, however, his voice as author was persistently unsettled, mediated as it was by the practices of compilation, self-censoring, re-writing, and self-advertising, the differing materialities of brief, unbound sermons and substantial books with good bindings, and the contradictions of domestic and international politics he was constantly having to negotiate.

Mather's hopes for the *Magnalia* remind us again of the complexities of the middle ground between the authoritative and the unstable. At one end that middle ground was bounded by *A Token for the Children of New England* and, at the other, the gesture of authorial control evident in the errata he inserted in some copies of the *Magnalia*. For his father Increase, it was bounded by his insistence on the accuracy of the letters printed in *The First Principles of New-England* and the merits of the woman who took good notes in shorthand on his sermons and, at the other extreme, by variations in texts of his that passed through a printing office or were reprinted in London and his own refashioning of manuscripts such as John Mason's narrative of the Pequot War. The same complexities are revealed in the practices of the book trade: on the one hand the many title-page assertions about accuracy and authority, the preference for fair copy, and the correcting of errata, all of them signaling that the trade wanted to produce texts that were sound; and, on the other, the many signs of expediency. It is tempting to give greater emphasis to the "broken notes" that served so often as copy text for books of the first-generation ministers and to printing-shop practices of the kind Randolph Adams described for William Hubbard's *Narrative*. But it is just as important to emphasize the frustration of a John Cotton and Thomas Hooker when they saw what happened to their texts, a frustration that prompted each of them to find better ways of transmitting their books. To acknowledge that frustration is to acknowledge that certain rules about authority and authenticity existed in the seventeenth century, rules not always followed, but present nonetheless. Change over time figures in this argument, for the second- and third-generation writers and their intermediaries were notably less anxious about the state of their texts than Cotton and Hooker were, probably because the great majority of their texts were printed locally. But for any sermon, the text as spoken or performed was never identical with the text as transmitted in handwritten or printed form.

To recognize the ever-present framework of the Protestant vernacular tradition is also to realize that the promise and practice of authenticity was always conjoined with the criterion of usefulness. We misread writers and the book trade in the seventeenth century if we ignore the point made again and again in prefaces, that the uncertainties of a text did not stand in the way of its doing the cultural or religious work the writer had intended. Introducing a printed book of Thomas Shepard's to the English reading public, the minister William Greenhill fashioned a hybrid of these two perspectives, the useful and the dubiously authoritative: "These notes may well be thought to be less accurate than if the author himself had published them, and to want some polishments and trimmings, which it were not fit for any other to add; however, thou wilt find them full of useful truths."[73] The many problematic copy texts and the expediencies of the book trade so apparent in the publishing histories of books by Hooker and Cotton must be understood in the context of a culture that assigned originality and authority other meanings than they have for us today.

CHAPTER FIVE

Between Unity and Sedition

The Practice of Dissent

IN THE MIDST OF THE Antinomian controversy, a group of men handed the Massachusetts General Court a "petition and remonstrance" complaining of the censure of John Wheelwright. Petitioning was a well-rehearsed practice in England, resorted to by people high and low who sought redress of a grievance or solicited a favor, a practice customarily verbalized as a "humble" expression of loyalty and good will toward the government. In form and substance, petitions were ostensibly apolitical.[1] Each aspect of petitioning, the practice and the formulary, reappeared among the immigrants as soon as civil government was established and, within a decade, responding to petitions had become a principal activity of each of the colonial governments. Something was unsettling about the petition of 1637 even though it opened with the formulaic expression of deference, its signers representing themselves as "humbly beseech[ing]" a certain action of the government, to which they pledged their "due submission." Yet what followed was contentious. Insisting that Wheelwright had said nothing that warranted the verdict of sedition, the petitioners associated the decision of the Court with the presence of the Evil One: was it not "the old method of Satan" to have "raised up such calumnies against the faithfull Prophets of God"? To this strong language they added the warning that acts of injustice would provoke a righteous God to punish the colony.[2] Nothing they said changed the thinking of the Court, which responded in November by characterizing the petition as a "seditious libel" and punishing everyone whose name was on it.[3]

Too often the story of the "petition and remonstrance" of 1637 ends at this point and, as the dissenters made their way to Rhode Island, returned to England, or abjectly apologized, modern historians assume that all roads to dissent in Massachusetts had been closed off in favor of a newly consolidated "orthodoxy" quick to accuse any dissident of fomenting "sedition."[4] The full record of the Court's deliberations that November is at odds with this interpretation. Near the close of the session the magistrates and deputies agreed to a carefully worded legitimizing of petitions and complaints: "It is not therefore the intent of this Court to restraine the free use of any way of God, by petition, or other private advertizement, nor the free use of any lawfull publike meanes, where private shall not prevaile, for the reformation of any . . . failing in any Court, or member of the same."[5] Four years later, the Court would renew its commitment to the "free use" of petitions, embedding the right to do so in a code of laws, the "Body of Liberties." Liberty twelve offered resolute support for the broad interpretation of the practice: "Every man whether Inhabitant or Foreigner, free or not free[6] shall have liberty to come to any publique Court, Council, or Town meeting, and either by speech or writing to move any lawfull, seasonable, and materiall question, or to present any necessary motion, complaint, petition, Bill or information, whereof that meeting hath proper cognizance, so it be done in convenient time, due order, and respective manner." Other provisions broadened the possibilities for dissent or criticism. According to the seventieth Liberty, "All Freemen called to give any advise, vote, verdict, or sentence in any Court, Counsell, or Civil Assembly, shall have full freedome to doe it according to their true Judgements and Consciences, So it be done orderly and inofensively for the manner." Number seventy-five guaranteed the liberty of participants in the Court itself to "make their contra Remonstrance or protestation in speech or writeing, and upon request to have their dissent recorded in the Rolles of that Court" if they disagreed with the vote of the majority.[7]

Thus in a single session of the Court and within a few years' time the leadership of Massachusetts juxtaposed two modes of understanding dissent. The response to Wheelwright and his supporters was predicated on the assumption that dissent could undermine the authority of government. Protecting the right to petition was predicated on the assumption that, unless people were allowed the right to speak freely (and therefore to dissent), government would become "arbitrary." The tensions arising from this juxtaposition were not new to the colonists. Nor were they short-lived, for both assumptions would persist until the end of the century, neither of them easily dispelled or triumphing over the other. To take them seriously is to broach the possibility that the political culture of the colonists encompassed a space for debate that cannot be termed a "public sphere" in the usual meaning of that phrase,[8] but that nonetheless allowed ordinary people and dissidents among the leadership to disagree in public with policies they disliked. The workings of such a space—tenuous or denied at some moments, insisted upon and actively exploited at others—is what this chapter is about.

For reasons that go beyond the petition and remonstrance of 1637 and the labeling of John Wheelwright's sermon as a seditious libel, the Antinomian controversy is a useful point of entry into the making of this space. During 1636 and 1637, the many debates among the clergy were mostly held in private settings, as were some sessions of the General Court. Any public protests got people into trouble. As John Winthrop remarked of Wheelwright, his sermon had offended the magistrates because he had no "care of the publick peace" as shown by his "publishing" (making public in his fast-day sermon, and probably by other means) his opinions on the covenant of works. The determination to quell the Antinomians was visible anew in May 1637, when another group of people sympathetic to Wheelwright and Henry Vane carried a petition to the General Court asking that it vote on (probably to receive) a "grievance" before elections of a new governor and other officers took place. The Court refused to do so.[9] In September, the ministers who convened the synod that met for three weeks proceeded in a different manner. Aware of the anti-clericalism fanned by Anne Hutchinson and manifested in accusations that some of them were acting "grossly Popish," the men in charge opened its sessions to anyone who wanted to attend, doing so "for the satisfaction of the people" and granting "liberty of speech (onely due order observed) as much as any of our selves [the ministers] had, and as freely." Remarkably, the synod gave this privilege to "all the Opinionists." If Thomas Weld's judgment can be trusted, these steps did much to bring the controversy to an end: "the worke of the Assembly . . . gained much on the hearers, that were indifferent . . . and on many wavering, to settle them." As would happen in November when the General Court affirmed the privilege of petitioning, so at the synod the clerical leaders of the colony sanctioned the practices of debate and criticism.[10]

Though always under pressure, a space for doing so reappeared during the disputes about civil government that divided Massachusetts in the 1630s and 1640s, in disputes elsewhere in the 1640s and 1650s, and in all of the orthodox colonies after 1660. John Winthrop was a central figure in several of these disputes, central not only because of the offices he held but also because of how he exploited the possibilities of handwritten texts to defend his understanding of "authority." The magistrates and deputies in the General Court who disagreed with him exploited the same possibilities and, on one occasion, called something of *his* a "seditious libel" as a way of indicating their displeasure. Within Massachusetts, four major episodes of tension or conflict happened during this sweep of time: the resistance to Winthrop's understanding of the magistrates' authority that divided the General Court in the early 1640s; the "petition and remonstrance" of Robert Child and a handful of others, brought to the General Court in 1646; the angry response to the decision of a synod of ministers in 1662 to make baptism the key to church membership; and the uprising against the Dominion of New England in April 1689. Scribal publication figured significantly in each of these episodes, as did communication in the less tangible form of."ill report" and "rumour."[11] Printed books were also involved, for in 1662 and again in 1689 both sides turned to printers in Cambridge and London. Indeed the publication of John Davenport's *Another Essay For Investigation of the Truth* (Cambridge, 1663) marked the first time that any colonist on the losing side of a major debate was able to do so locally rather than in London.

The two modes of politics that became visible in 1637 were each a legacy from English political culture. The circumstances of political life in the colonies, together with the circumstances of political life under Charles I and Charles II, would ensure that each persisted, one or the other sometimes weakened or reenergized by local and international events, like the civil war that broke out in England in 1642, a frightening example of factionalism transmuted into something much worse. Always, the boundaries of the space for debate were made uncertain by the struggle to reconcile two quite different social rules: the rule that "publick peace" of the kind that Wheelwright had disrupted must be maintained, with its corollary that peace entailed submission (deference) to authority; and, in contrast, the rule that "liberty" to "consent" (and to dissent) was the crucial safeguard against power turned tyrannical or, as people were saying in 1630s Massachusetts, authority deemed "arbitrary."

Deeply invested in an ethic of social peace and consensus, the colonists shared with their peers in Stuart England an appreciation of hierarchy and order. Social peace depended on deference to those in authority lest "disorder follow," as Shakespeare observed in *Troilus and Cressida*. Speech and writing were potentially subversive, each easily transformed into a contagion or disease that could ruin a Christian commonwealth. Hence the long-standing insistence of the English Crown and Parliament on licensing what printers could publish and curtailing what could be reported as news. No one could legally report the debates in Parliament to others, no one could publish a book without having it licensed, and although members of Parliament were allowed free speech during its sessions, this privilege irritated the Stuart kings, who sometimes violated it.[12] English law defined false news as defamation or libels. Because all such libels called into question a ruler's authority, they were also "seditious libels." When the government was really angered by unauthorized news or publications, it could accuse people of treason, for which the punishment was execution.[13] Another framework of assumptions, as meaningful to the colonists as to the Stuart kings, affirmed the responsibility of the Christian magistrate to uphold the truth of religion and to employ coercion to this end if necessary. Truth brought happiness and health, whereas error was a disease akin to gangrene, as so often was said. From the king's point of view, the animus against episcopacy was such an error. Worse, it was equivalent to sedition. Though it was his father who reportedly said, "no bishop, no king," Charles I was of the same mind.[14] In general, the English government aspired to sustain what the sociologist David Zaret has characterized as a "culture of secrecy," secrecy in the broad sense of wanting to control the flow of information and limit the possibilities for dissent, but secrecy too in the sense of keeping much state business "private."[15]

Because none of these practices and attitudes accomplished what the Stuart kings expected of them, a history of the suppression of dissent in the seventeenth century is also a history of the many exceptions and failures in doing so. Social peace, though deeply valued, was a visionary abstraction, the reality an ever-shifting factionalism as different groups contended for the rewards that went with power. Hence the constant stream of oral rumor and texts, both printed and handwritten, that rang endless changes on themes such as anti-Catholicism. Together, unceasing factionalism and the laxness of local administration made for inconsistency in how a government behaved.[16] Within the book trades, the system of licensing had many loopholes that printers and booksellers exploited to the point of issuing a third of all printed books without entering them in the register of the Stationers Company. Nor could the government count on judges and juries to approve the verdict of treason; Elizabeth I wanted John Stubbs brought up on this charge, but a court rejected her request. News of Parliamentary debates continued to circulate in the form of handwritten "separates" that gave the gentry this information.[17] By the late 1620s, news had taken on a fresh significance in light of the policies Charles I was pursuing with Parliament and the Church of England. Angered by those policies, in the late 1630s the dissident Puritan lawyer William Prynne was "secretly scatter[ing]" pamphlets—one of Winthrop's correspondents referred to them as "libels"—in which he denounced "awdacious usurpers . . . upon" the king's "loyall subjects lawfull liberties." A fierce critic of episcopacy in general and of certain bishops in the Church of England in particular, Prynne had already published *Histrio-Mastix* (1633), which somehow gained a license despite its implied criticism of Court culture under Charles I and his queen. Four years later, Prynne was punished by the Star Chamber for publishing unlicensed attacks on the Church and its leadership. From an English friend Winthrop learned of the consequences, the heavy fine imposed on Prynne, the loss of both his ears, "his boockes to be there burned before hym, and to suffer Imprisonmente during his life besides," Prynne's own behavior as he was being punished ("the gentleman lyke a harmeles lambe, takes all with suche patience"), and the retribution rendered from heaven on someone who had participated in "sheddinge Mr. Prinnnes bloodde."[18] Even though imprisoned, Prynne and other radicals who suffered with him resumed their protests, circulating some in manuscript and others in surreptitiously printed versions.

Every aspect of this politics reappeared in New England, the possibilities for criticism enhanced in the 1630s by the colonists' hostility to Charles I but the possibilities for suppressing criticism enlarged by the precarious situation of the settlements. No Puritan, and especially not the aristocrats and gentry who supported the movement in regions like East Anglia, wanted to overthrow the monarchy; no one proclaimed the sovereignty of the people. Yet the movement had become accustomed to ferment from beneath, some of which its leaders encouraged, and to exploiting local possibilities for bypassing the policies of Crown and Church. Moreover, the congregational versions of the movement relied on lay "consent" in church governance. For many of this persuasion, episcopacy was a "human invention," a structure imposed without regard to Scripture. Well aware of Charles I's ideology of divine right, the colonists brought with them to New England a heightened fear of the authoritarianism they associated with the king and Catholicism. The constitution-making that unfolded in New England, together with the provisions of the "Body of Liberties" and the insistence on keeping church and state apart, bespoke their concern that no version of "tyranny" reappear in their new home. If not republicans *à la lettre*, something of the republican spirit was at work among them.

Yet as Winthrop and other leaders recognized, it was also crucial that the colonists act as one and not allow their differences to paralyze the government. Those differences were many, far more than anyone knew would be the case as the migration was unfolding. The quest for purity led some into deep waters—Roger Williams for one, the magistrate John Endicott for another when he began to insist that the colonists eliminate the cross of St. George in their flags.[19] Reconciling the ministers to the scheme that became known as the "Congregational Way" was no easy matter, and reconciling lay leaders to the constraints on their power alienated men like Roger Ludlow and Sir George Downing, who complained in 1645 to John Winthrop, Jr., that the form of government in Massachusetts "remaines so popular" that "authority is debased." The many young people who came as hired servants proved unruly, and as the colonists dispersed across the landscape in search of more or better land, some leaders fretted that the ethic of "mutuality" and self-sacrifice had given way to greed. For sure, the towns began to chafe against the regulating powers of the central state. These forces, but especially the challenge of organizing coherent systems of church and civil government, worried the ministers and magistrates, all of whom wanted to sustain the strength, at once ideological and practical, of their offices.[20]

One clear sign of this goal was the determination of the leadership to defend the close connections between church and state. For Winthrop and John Cotton alike, it remained a foundational assumption that the civil magistrate should preserve the "truth" and use coercion in doing so, a truth made all the more precious by the disarray that arose in England during the 1640s. The Cambridge Platform of 1648 minced no words, asserting in chapter XVII that magistrates were obligated to suppress "Idolatry, Blasphemy, Heresy, venting corrupt and pernicious opinions, that destroy the foundation."[21] At about the same time, the magistrate William Pynchon and the minister Thomas Shepard were adamant that the orthodox colonies not take the path of toleration some in 1640s England were beginning to prefer. Writing Winthrop in mid-1646, Pynchon described the religious situation in England as one of "lawlessenesse" and predicted that those in favor of liberty of conscience "will change their iudg[men]ts and say that liberty of conscience will give liberty to Sathan to broch such horrid blasphemose opinions as never were the like in any age." "There is but one truth," Thomas Shepard insisted in a letter to a former colonist now in England, where he had become sympathetic to a policy of toleration, "and is it not your daily prayer to God to blot out all errors . . . from off his earth?"[22] Pynchon would become a dissident himself, but the great majority of the colonists continued to accept Shepard's version of the truth and the imperative to protect it.

That imperative was acted upon by the Massachusetts General Court in 1644 when news reached New England that the license of civil war was enabling Baptists (or "Anabaptists," as the colonists preferred to say) to become a public presence. Forecasting the arrival of Baptist publications and fearing their consequences, the Court ordered in November that anyone who expressed a range of views (some Baptist, some not) would be banished. Another law of 1646 proscribed heresy. The Court had already put in place other means of ensuring obedience and uniformity, like the oaths that adult men swore never to conspire against the government.[23] Behind such actions lay an understanding of "sedition" that Winthrop articulated in defending the censure of Wheelwright. As he (and his colleagues) put it in the "briefe Apologie," sedition had two elements: "going aside to make a party" (i.e., rejecting the authority of the center), and attempting to alarm the "minds of the people" so that they become "kindled" and "fierce" against any who oppose them. This rhetoric of "heat" that made minds "inflamed" flowed from a distrust of the people that many others shared. Those who thought this way were certain that if the people were allowed to rule or factionalism to prevail, the holy commonwealth would collapse from within.[24] Hence the anxieties among the colonists about dissent in general and especially about dissent that was published or publicized. Allowing this to happen within New England could provoke the people to throw off authority.

Allowing dissent to be publicized *outside* the colonies could also be destructive. As everyone on both sides of the Atlantic knew, the well-being of the orthodox colonies, and especially their well-being as near independent jurisdictions, depended on how they were regarded by their friends and enemies in England. As Puritan-affiliated letter writers from England remarked again and again, the reports of the colonists' radicalism that were reaching England threatened their relationship with the moderate Puritans who by 1643 were in charge of Parliament and most of the mechanisms of governance.[25] To agree that publicity was against the best interests of the colonies was not the same, however, as agreeing to silence all dissent. Indeed, the provisions of the "Body of Liberties" made this impossible. Thus it happened that a fundamental contradiction arose between publicity and silence, the liberty to speak and the power to suppress, a contradiction that impinged directly on the making of texts.

* * *

John Winthrop arrived in Massachusetts determined to avoid the near anarchy that had brought the Virginia Company's settlement in Jamestown to the verge of collapse. Although he wanted church and commonwealth to conform to the standards set by Scripture, he had reason to worry that the reforming energies of the Puritan movement would divide the colonists into factions. Reason to worry, because this had nearly happened at Salem in 1629 when the first "gathered" church in New England was organized, and nearly happened again in the person of Roger Williams, who by 1633 was publicly associating Charles I with passages in the Book of Revelation that represented kings as fornicating with whores and as agents of the Antichrist. Some months later, Williams was voicing more "dangerous opinions" that led to his being banished from the colony.[26] Yet Winthrop did not foresee that the small group of men who held office as magistrates would fall out among themselves. Nor did he anticipate the acts of defiance that arose from local communities wanting a voice in who held office and how taxes were levied. Meanwhile, everything depended on preserving the good will of merchants and other creditors in England on whom the colonists were relying for supplies, and preserving, too, the flow of immigrants in the face of reports sent back from the colony (or carried by people who returned) that New England offered little by way of economic opportunity. These circumstances put extraordinary pressure on communication both within the colony and with supporters in England, pressure that helps account for the reluctance of the magistrates and ministers to publicize the Antinomian controversy and the recurrent censoring of people who relayed complaints about policies and situations to people in England.[27]

These pressures are registered as well in how Winthrop chose to communicate with the people he was governing. He did not intend to show the freemen the charter of the Massachusetts Bay Company, though popular agitation forced him to do so in 1634. At Thomas Shepard's suggestion, he suppressed two texts he wrote in response to the Antinomian controversy lest they make things worse. Angered by the petition and remonstrance of 1637, he told three of its instigators that they were wrong to "invite the bodye of the people, to joyn with you in your seditious attempt against the Court, and

the Aut[horit]y here estab[lished] against the rule of the Ap[ost]le, who re-
quires every soule to be subject to the higher powers and every Ch[ristia]n
man, to studye to be quiet." Here in essence, Winthrop summed up the
principles that would guide his text-making as governor and magistrate: remain as quiet as possible, try never to mobilize the common people, deploy
speech and writing to "quench [any] . . . sparks of contention," and use his
pen to enhance the "Authority" that was singularly his as magistrate and
sometime governor.[28]

Authority was the crux of the matter, in part because many of the colonists disagreed with his policies and practices. Could it be sustained against
the centrifugal tendencies that were animating political and religious life in
the new colony? As means to this end, he wanted the magistrates to have a
"negative voice" or veto over decisions by the General Court, where they
were soon outnumbered by the deputies. As another means, he helped constitute a "standing council" of magistrates empowered to make decisions between sessions of the Court and did his best to thwart the demand for a
written (i.e., published) code of laws. In doing so he fell out of step with the
mood of colonists who had learned from the personal rule of Charles I that
legitimate authority all too quickly became "arbitrary." For them, the key
goal was to guard against this possibility and, specifically, to protect a different form of authority, the consent of the people. When the founders of
Connecticut were creating their form of government in 1638, they deprived
the governor of the power of veto, made him merely a presiding officer, and
limited him to a single year's term, though allowing re-election after a year
out of office. Thomas Hooker, who removed to Connecticut in 1636, declared in a sermon of 1638 that "the foundation of authority is laid . . . in the
free consent of the people." More pointedly, he told Winthrop that his stance
was "a way which leads directly to tyranny." Acknowledging that the people
"should referr matter of counsell to their counsellours," Hooker insisted that
"in matters of greater consequence" not the "few" but the "multitude"
should decide.[29] The same fear of arbitrary rule, and the same preference for
resting authority on something like the will of the people, would influence
the colonists in Plymouth and Rhode Island as they organized (or in the case
of Plymouth, re-organized) their governments by 1640. Its consequences for
the political development of Massachusetts included, in particular, the drafting of the "Body of Liberties," a process under way by 1639. In response to
local pressures, the General Court agreed to solicit comments on a preliminary version of the text from each town. No evidence remains of how the

towns responded, but as enacted by the Court in 1641, the "Liberties" conceded significant privileges to local communities and, as already noted, guaranteed a version of free speech to every adult male, freeman or not. After a synod of ministers finished drafting the Cambridge Platform in 1648, the General Court followed the same practice, approving it in principle but arranging for copies to be sent to each congregation for comments.[30]

The "Body of Liberties" emerged out of a collaborative process of text-making that involved (as Hooker would have said) a "multitude of counsellours." But the possibilities for consultation and debate remained uncertain. In the early 1640s some petitions were accepted and others rejected, just as some writings were condemned as seditious and others not. The manifestoes of the radicals who became known as Gortonists were easily rejected, for almost everyone agreed that "their blasphemous and reviling writings, etc., were not matters fit to be compounded by arbitrament, but to be purged away only by repentance, and public satisfaction, or else by public punishment." Here, the line between authority and criticism could be firmly drawn. On other occasions that line was ambiguous or provisional, made so by the persisting uneasiness about "arbitrary" rule and the near impossibility of suppressing rumor, speech, and writing as means of contesting the politics of the Massachusetts magistrates. Writings flowed thick and fast in the late 1630s and into the mid-1640s as the Court debated the scope of the magistrates' authority, a dispute about the ownership of a stray sow, the government's alliance with a French adventurer, Charles La Tour, and the choice of officers for the militia company in Hingham. For the first time Winthrop's decision-making was challenged by a significant number of deputies and magistrates who knew they had widespread support among the colonists.

One year after the General Court ratified the "Body of Liberties," it debated whether to classify a handwritten "book" as a seditious libel. The grounds for doing so were substantial: the book was anonymous and it criticized the recently instituted "Standing Council" as a "sinful innovation." Both aspects irritated John Winthrop, who proposed that the Court determine who had written it and censure him. But in a step that broke with the usual rules for dealing with such texts, the deputies refused to go along, proposing instead that the writer "were first acquit from any censure concerning the said book.." Everyone participating in this dispute already knew that one of the magistrates, Richard Saltonstall of Ipswich, had written the offending book. For the deputies, the compromise was to validate the standing council "from all dishonor and reproach cast upon it or them in Mr. Saltonstall's book," but simultaneously to invoke a key principle of the "Body of Liberties." Winthrop recorded the nuances of their thinking and the quotation of a Liberty in his journal entry narrating the debate:

> When he [Saltonstall] did write and deliver it, (as was supposed,) there was an order in force, which gave liberty to every freeman to consider and deliver their judgments to the next court about such fundamental laws as were then to be established, (wherein one did concern the institution and power of the council,) therefore he should be discharged from any censure or further inquiry about the same, which was voted accordingly, although there were some expressions in the book which would not be warranted by that order, as that the council was instituted unwarily to satisfy Mr. Vane's desire.

To be "discharged from any censure or further inquiry" for publishing an unsigned critique of the magistrates was a step wholly at odds with the culture of secrecy and suppression. The deputies were aware of what they were doing, for they ignored the "answer" that the magistrate Thomas Dudley wrote and only "with some difficulty" agreed to let the minister Edward Norris of Salem read his response in court.[31]

Meanwhile, tensions were emerging this same year (1642) around the case of a stray sow claimed by two different people. After the Court awarded the pig to the wealthy merchant Robert Keayne and a jury granted him damages for having been accused of theft, a fresh petition revived the basic issue, that the government was mistreating a "poor woman" who continued to insist that the long-dead pig had been hers. The "clamours" reaching Boston favored Mrs. Sherman and her husband Richard, a noise Winthrop associated with a "great expectation in the country" that the decision would be overturned. Repeating what he had done during the Antinomian controversy, Winthrop and "others of the magistrates . . . publish[ed] a declaration of the true state of the cause, that truth might not be condemned unknown"—published in this context meaning, sharing copies of a handwritten text. Separately, Winthrop drew up a "breviate" supporting Keayne that also circulated in handwritten copies.[32]

But the case refused to die. A man acting on Mrs. Sherman's behalf petitioned the Court in May 1643 that it rehear the case, a petition the deputies but not the magistrates accepted. Insignificant in itself, the dispute had by this time become entangled with the deputies' protest against the magistrates' "negative voice" or veto, a means of thwarting majority rule in the General Court. Winthrop spoke out on this issue, too, writing "A small treatise, wherein he laid down the original of it from the Patent, and the establishing of it by order of the General Court in 1634, showing thereby how it was fundamental to our government, which, if it were taken away, would be a mere democracy." As he noted in the journal, "this would not satisfy, but the deputies and common people would have it taken away." Another magistrate—in all likelihood Richard Bellingham—wrote "an answer" from the deputies' point of view "that [they] made great use of." This chain of text-making concluded with a long "Replye" that Winthrop wrote, though the more significant step may have occurred in the fall of 1643 when the Court ordered (in the context of tensions over the negative voice) that "it shalbee no offence for any, who shall, either privately or in any lawfull assembly, deliver their minds soberly and peaceably therein, or to deliver the same in writing . . . so it bee under their hand" (no more unsigned texts!). Yet again, the Court was affirming the possibilities of a space where criticism could unfold in public.[33]

Peace-keeping of a more customary kind had already been attempted in October 1642 when the ministers had intervened to "take a view of all the evidence" in the sow case and to dissuade Saltonstall from agitating against the standing council.[34] From Winthrop's vantage their intervention was welcome, for too much "open" criticism was arousing "the country." Saltonstall agreed to acknowledge the "failings" in his book, and "so . . . was reconciled with the rest of the magistrates." Then in May 1643 it was Winthrop's turn to apologize for what he had written about "the case of the sow . . . wherein some passages gave offence." The speech he gave was so important to him that he "set [it] down verbatim" in the journal to prevent misrepresenting. Admitting to excessive "pride" and to acting out of "distemper" in how he complained of others' judgments, he told the deputies and other magistrates that he "desire[d] to remove" whatever was offensive about the breviate, though he added that he found "no ground to retract" any of its specifics. Wanting to sustain the process of reconciliation, he was realistic about having to participate in the new politics of criticism and publicity: "therefore I desire I may enjoy my liberty herein, as every of yourselves do, and justly may." In the event, the question of the negative voice was resolved by a compromise: the magistrates retained their veto, the deputies gained the same privilege, and the two groups began to meet apart.[35]

All this occurred while other issues were emerging to test the ethics of peace and deference. Faced with two rival claims for authority over French-held Acadia and Nova Scotia, Winthrop and a handful of magistrates decided to favor Charles de La Tour. To others, and especially the people in Essex County to the north of Boston, doing so rendered them vulnerable to attacks from La Tour's rival, Charles d'Aulnay, with whom La Tour was skirmishing. Many others were irritated by the welcome shown La Tour, a Catholic, when he visited Boston in 1643, John Endecott reporting from Ipswich that "The Countrie hereabouts is much troubled that [the French] are so intertained," and Winthrop himself took note of "rumor" about the honors shown La Tour. Popular unrest was accompanied by high-level protest, for a coalition of Essex County ministers and magistrates insisted that the colonists should not take sides in a conflict that was "unjust." The rebuke drew from Winthrop a letter that began with gestures of peace-making. He had not meant "to contend," Winthrop told his critics, and was always open to "submit[ing] unto the wise and loving advise and admonitions of any of my brethren." Thereafter he reaffirmed the tactic of privacy he himself preferred. Was it not wrong, he asked, for a small group of magistrates to "contradict" the majority in a "publick Instrument"? Did not doing so blow "a trumpet to division and dissention amongst ourselves, magistrates protesting against magistrats, Elders against Elders, blameing, condemning, exposeing brethren to the peoples curses, and casting them downe to hell it selfe"? The magistrates and ministers who publicly dissented about La Tour had staged an "unwarranted Protestation" instead of observing "the way of God and of order, and of peace," unwarrantable because they had appealed to the public instead of arguing their point of view within the confines of the General Court.[36]

This rhetoric failed to quell the new-found politics of publicity that Winthrop was having to practice himself. As happened also with the English and French monarchies in the course of the seventeenth century, he was realizing that those in power needed to manufacture publicity of their own. The next wave of controversies also taught the lesson that, depending on the situation, each side could play the part of the conservative by evoking the ethos of privacy or, alternatively, the part of the radical by summoning up the dangers of "arbitrary" rule. In June 1644, Winthrop and most of his fellow magistrates were defending themselves anew against "the aspersions cast upon them, as if they intended to bring in an arbitrary government, etc." Though his preference was otherwise, Winthrop had learned that the best response to hostile text-making was to respond in kind. When he and most of the magistrates signed a "declaration" and threatened to "publish" it, the deputies demurred. Compromise ensued, with publication at its center, the two groups agreeing that "the declaration should remain with the secretary [of the Court], and not be published . . . except [the magistrates] were necessitated thereto by the deputies' misreport of our proceedings."[37]

The tensions between local versions of governance and Winthrop's became sharply evident during the controversy which broke out in 1644 over who would name the captain of the Hingham militia. Winthrop had done so against the wishes of a great majority of the men in the town, who sent a "humble" petition to the Court asking it to restore the captain of their choice and accusing Winthrop of overstepping his authority. After the Court decided against the town and in his favor, he made his "little speech on liberty." Speech making before the "great Assembly of people" who crowded into Boston meeting house was possibly without precedent.[38] Before the Court decided what to do, the crowd listened to arguments about the proper scope of magisterial authority. After Winthrop was "publicly" cleared, he spoke his mind about the relationship between liberty and authority. He did so even though it troubled him to violate the line between the public and the private; the affair "should have been reserved to a more private debate" and not allowed to become a matter of "public agitation."[39]

Looking back on these years of controversy and text-making, Winthrop felt he could observe "the workings of Sathan, to ruine the Colonies and Churches of Christ in New England," his presence evident in the "unreasonable obstinacy" of the "people." Winthrop's choice of words suggested how far he was from acknowledging the legitimacy of opposition. Within a few days he was hard at work writing yet another statement of his views, a "treatise about Arbitrary Gouvernment" to add to the series of handwritten texts he had composed in the hope of shoring up authority and deterring his critics. Yet again, however, an act of text-making had the opposite effect. Perhaps because he sensed its power to provoke, he shared the "treatise" cautiously at first, asking for advice from some deputies and "most of the magistrates and Elders," and revising it in response to their readings. When the moment came for "present[ing]" it to the General Court, he discovered that "the Deputyes had gotten a Coppye, which was presently read amongst them, as a dangerous Libell of some unknowne Author." Suddenly the tables were turned: he, not Saltonstall or Wheelwright or Samuel Gorton, was being accused of sedition![40]

The deputies were not seriously interested in pressing such a charge, but the tactic was a perfect demonstration—as Saltonstall's book of 1642 had been as well—of the two-sided politics Winthrop found so troubling. It was deeply bothersome that he and his allies among the magistrates were constantly being opposed by other magistrates and many of the deputies, and disturbing that he had to accept a politics of publicity at odds with the modes of communication he preferred. Together, his uneasiness and the deputies' indifference to "seditious libel" signified that a space for criticism and debate had come into being in Massachusetts politics. As the deputies indicated when they quoted the "Body of Liberties" in defending Saltonstall, this space presumed the assurance that the people could petition the government and otherwise speak out.

Yet this space remained provisional, ever dependent on the willingness of the General Court to receive a petition or acknowledge dissent. Any petition that called into question the fundamental policies of the colonists or that insulted someone in authority trumped that willingness. The leaders of the Hingham petitioners found themselves accused of submitting a "false and Scandalous" petition, and Winthrop complained that the practices associated with the protest, especially the willingness of the deputies to "receive" the petition, were "mutinous and seditious." He would have preferred that a "Booke . . . about Arbitrarye Gouvernment" written by Bozon Allen, a deputy to the Court from Hingham, be "burne under the Gallhouse" and, in the privacy of the journal, remarked—shades of William Prynne!—that "it would have cost Allen his eares, if not his head" had one of the magistrates written such a statement.[41] The minister in Hingham, Peter Hobart, who himself had been fined, continued to complain that the General Court had violated his rights, including the right to petition; "he could never knowe wherefore he was fined, except it were for Petitioning: and if they [the Court] were so waspishe that they might not be Petitioned, he knew not what to saye to it." All that he gained in return was another fine for "speeches" that "tended to sedition and contempt of Authoritye."[42]

Other disaffected groups were also employing the instrument of petitioning, with uncertain success. To the October 1645 session of the Court, "diverse merchants and others" presented a petition complaining of the bad effects on English opinion of the 1644 law proscribing Baptists and asking that it be "suspended." When the ministers arrived en masse to insist that "the Lawe might continue still in force," the Court decided not to act on the petition, though nothing was done to punish the men who signed it. Seven months later, in May 1645, a counter petition asking for "dew strengthening" of the 1644 law arrived signed by seventy-eight lay men from several towns, a sure sign, among others, that the politics of debate and dissent was teaching the ministers how to mobilize lay support. In response, the Court voted to persist in enforcing the law.[43]

The "Robert Child affair" of 1646 and early 1647 tested anew the possibilities for petitioning. Robert Child, a friend of John Winthrop, Jr., and someone of broad learning who came to Massachusetts as a visitor in the 1630s and returned in late 1645, did not like the system of Congregational church membership the colonists had established or the rule that restricted the privileges of freemanship to church members. Both disrupted the Presbyterian mode of church governance he seems to have favored, and for which he hoped to find support among the "non-members" who, by his reckoning, outnumbered those within the churches. The same year Child returned to New England, a colonist sympathetic to Presbyterianism, William Vassall, had initiated a "written proposition" (probably in the form of a petition) to the Plymouth Colony government asking for "full and free tollerance of religion to all men that would preserve the Civill peace, and submit unto government," a measure Edward Winslow, an officer in the colony, "utterly abhorred" as making "us odious to all Christian commonweales."[44] Gathering around him Vassall and half a dozen other disaffected colonists, Child organized a "Remonstrance and humble Petition" to the General Court in May 1646. Rhetorically the document employed the trope of humility, but the substance was confrontational, for the group asked that the government allow anyone who had belonged to the Church of England the privilege of having his children baptized. The broader complaint was inflammatory, that the majority of the colonists were deprived of their "due and naturall rights" as Englishmen. Then or soon thereafter, the group made it clear that, if their petition were refused, they would inform Parliament that the colonists were flouting its authority. The petitioners filled the document with reports of adverse portents—ships lost at sea, and the like—and of severe conflicts among the colonists, all designed to cast doubt on their godliness and capacity to preserve social order.

At once a new war of words broke out, Child and his associates seeking to arouse the non-church members, the majority in the General Court, and, almost to a person, the ministers, mobilizing against the petitioners. Each side argued its case in texts distributed only in handwritten copies and almost certainly distributed widely, for Edward Winslow reported to Winthrop that "copies [of the Child petition] were dispersed into the hands of some knowne ill affected people in the severall governments adjoining; as Plymoth, Conectacut, New Haven, &c.," and Samuel Symonds wrote from Ipswich in January 1647 to tell Winthrop that "coppies of the petition [possibly a new version asking for toleration] are spreading here, and divers (specially young men and women) are taken with it." More to the point, Symonds recognized the importance of distributing documents that defended the Court and its policies: "I do desire you would be pleased to hasten the send of a Coppy of the Courts answere to the petition and remonstrance, alsoe of the Charge: of their answere thereunto: and also of a reply (if any be made unto it) if none be made, then a coppy of the reply to the answer to the first particular." As the references in this letter suggest, the ministers and the Court had been responding in kind, the former securing local "answers" to the petition and the Court producing by late fall a "Declaration" indicating in detail the agreement between Massachusetts laws and English common law. As part of this campaign, Winthrop busied himself (or more likely, had a clerk do so) distributing "extracts" to important leaders elsewhere in New England. In the Declaration the General Court insisted that the petition had been "received with all gentleness," but by early 1647, after intercepting letters and other documents the petitioners intended to send to England, the government fined Child and several others, and briefly imprisoned a few of them.[45]

Locally, the Child affair dramatized anew the tensions that accompanied gestures of protest: did the colonists enjoy a general liberty of petitioning, as Child had insisted they did when he was brought before the General Court in November, or was this liberty contingent on how the contents of any petition were evaluated by those in positions of authority, which is what the Court said in its defense in responding to his plea?[46] Winthrop would have maintained the second of these possibilities, Child the first. But the real significance of the Child affair is what it tells us about the imperatives of text-making in situations of controversy. Events in the 1640s had already compromised the culture of secrecy. Situations of protest now seemed to oblige civic and religious leaders to practice a culture of publicity, though in doing so they continued to insist on social peace and consensus.[47]

The tenuous space for public debate that was visible in Massachusetts by the mid-1640s was emerging elsewhere in New England in these years, though with similar difficulties. The records of colonial governments in Connecticut and New Haven note the arrival of petition after petition, most of them seeking personal benefits but some arising out of local and colony-wide disputes. In neither colony did the government agree to receive every petition, and in neither was protest routinely acknowledged as legitimate. Any act of speech or writing that "defamed" someone of high rank was suspect, as shown in disputes in two towns over the policies of a local minister. When a group of men in Wethersfield petitioned the General Assembly in 1643 about their minister Henry Smith, the Court responded by affirming the possibility for discussion and debate, giving "liberty to all who had any just greivences in ether kind against him to produce them in public." After holding this "full hearing," the Court decided that the complaints were "false" and acted to prevent their "further spreading" by requiring the leaders of the protest (who were fined) to circulate a handwritten statement to every town clearing Smith of their accusations. A decade later, with the Hartford church divided between friends and foes of its minister Samuel Stone, his critics took the unusual step of carrying copies of their complaints from town to town. Stone's response was to declare that "the withdrawers transgressed in publishing their papers."[48] In the short run, the outcome of the Hartford dispute was schism, with some people in the town leaving to found Hadley, Massachusetts. As conflict over baptism and church membership spread to other churches in the colony, the General Assembly embraced a limited version of the culture of publicity, calling in 1657 for a council of ministers to debate twenty-one questions and circulating its answers in handwritten copies to every church in the colony in the hope that this strategy would restore social peace.[49]

The politics of dissent in New Haven and Plymouth colonies followed a different path, mainly because neither colony had a charter from the Crown or Parliament and the people who settled in each did not agree on certain fundamental policies. In New Haven, a policy that some colonists disliked was a rule that limited the franchise to church members. For towns close to the Dutch in nearby New Netherlands, foreign policy was another irritant. In 1653 discontent reached the point in Stamford and Fairfield of a public protest against the taxes levied by the colony "because nothing is done against the Duch, and some saying they have bine in bondage a greate while." When one of the leaders of the protest, Robert Bassett, was summoned before the General Court, he found himself accused of "drawing company together against the commonwealth where he lives, and that he will be a reformer, not onely of commonwealthes, but of the churches also." Bassett admitted that he and others resented not having "our vote in our jurisdiction as others have," and the Court heard testimony that he had sought "to raise volunteeres to goe against the Duch . . . without any approbation from authority here." Bassett blamed an unsigned letter he had received for spreading such reports, a letter he refused to produce but described by the Court as "a seditious letter to disturbe the peace [and] . . . to turne things upsi[de] downe in church and commonwealth." Faced with the weight of the evidence against him, Bassett confessed that he had been "sinfull" and named others who had been "cheife actors in the buisnes." These gestures allowed him to escape being convicted for sedition, but the failure of the government to pursue a verdict of this kind also suggests it knew its weakness. As would happen elsewhere after 1660, dissent became more feasible in the context of structural difficulties.[50]

Dissent in Plymouth Colony entered a new phase in 1658 when the government enacted rules to suppress Quaker itinerants from proselytizing. The Commissioners of the United Colonies had recommended measures of this kind to the government, a message one of the Commissioners from Plymouth, James Cudworth, refused to sign. Cudworth was dismissed from this office, but in his home town of Scituate a magistrate also opposed the enacting of legislation to suppress the Quakers. The division of opinion on how to treat the Quakers quickly became a local issue when some of the townspeople in Scituate (perhaps at the prompting of the colony government) sent the Plymouth General Court a petition "expressing sundry greivances relating to" Cudworth's "entertaining of such persons as are commonly called Quakers," and a larger number counter-petitioned in his favor. As described by Cudworth, the struggle within Scituate and the Plymouth government was at root a struggle about how to deal with religious dissent. His own position was that fines and whippings were "carnal and anti-christian" measures that would never "convince gainsayers," though he was also careful to note that his own "dissent in sundry actings" of the government was "done with all moderation of expression, together with due respect unto the rest." The letter (1658) to an Englishman in which he voiced his dislike of the government's "persecuting spirit" circulated in handwritten copies, one of which, possibly unsigned, came into the hands of the government. Another letter drew the response that he was a "manifest opposer of the government." Dismissal from office as a colony magistrate and disfranchisement followed; in quieter times (1672) he came back into office. That Cudworth was intentionally exploiting the space between the private and the public is suggested by the history of the letter to his English friend, which reached the Quaker martyrologist George Bishop, who incorporated it into *New England Judged* (London, 1661).[51]

As with these acts of protest, so with many others the question before the government was where to draw the line: which petitions should be accepted, which protests termed "seditious," which (unsigned) texts a "libel"? From the point of view of those who protested, the question was how to press their case without endangering the peace they also valued. Apart from rumor, the means they had of publicizing their point of view were petitions, letters, and other handwritten statements, preferably signed, as petitions invariably were. In this material form, gestures of protest and criticism fell within the rules—or did so some of the time. But what if the local book trade began to publish texts that criticized a state-endorsed policy? And how would the growing presence of the English empire after 1660 affect the processes of communication and dissent?

* * *

The long-awaited translation of the Bible into Algonquian became reality in 1661, when Samuel Green and Marmaduke Johnson, the Cambridge printers, finished printing the New Testament. Two years later Green and Johnson completed the Old Testament, whereupon the two parts were bound together. An impressive book, the thousand or so copies of *Mamusse Wunneetupanatamwe Up-Biblum God* would mainly find their way into the hands of the Christian Indians. Eliot used others as gifts to reward the agencies and individuals in England who had financed the project and were paying the costs of the missions. His instructions in hand, together with a shipment of two dozen or so Bibles, the New England Company (or as it was officially named, The Corporation for Propagation of the Gospel) voted in March 1664 that "5 of the Bibles sent from N. England . . . bee Disposed according to Mr. Eliotes request," he having specified "Sion College, Jesus College Cambridge, one each to the universities of Oxford and Cambridge, and a fifth Lady Armin." Separately, the corporation authorized the head of the Corporation to present other copies to "such persons" as he "shall think fitt." Robert Boyle had just the person in mind, the king. He personally handed Charles II a copy, reporting in a letter to Eliot and the Commissioners that the king had "very gratiously" accepted the book.[52]

Three years earlier, in September 1661, the question before the Commissioners of the United Colonies, the group that oversaw the dispersing of funds sent by the New England Company, was to whom should the New Testament be dedicated? It did so having learned that all corporations had been dissolved by Charles II. The bad news came with a dose of good, for the company officer who wrote to tell them of the dissolution intimated that the king might allow the company to be re-chartered. Finger to the wind, the commissioners voted to "present his Majesty with the New Testament" and to include in the two presentation copies (of twenty printed in a larger format and "very well bound") a dedication to him, worded after some debate as an address to their "Dread Sovereign" and, in carefully chosen language, acknowledging "the Favour and Grant of Your Royal Father and Grandfather of Famous Memory," an allusion to the charter of 1629. The irony of doing so was compounded by the final sentence of the dedication: "Sir, The shines of Your Royal Favour upon these Undertakings, will make these tender Plants to flourish, notwithstanding any malevolent Agent from those that bear evil will to this Sion, and render your Majesty more Illustrious and glorious to after Generations." (Another irony is that other copies destined for England were dedicated to Robert Boyle.) Here, the unspecified "malevolent Agent" encompassed the many in Charles II's entourage who had good reason to be hostile to Puritan-style Nonconformity.[53] In all, the commissioners and the corporation distributed forty copies to notables in England, one of them the king's High Chancellor, Edward Hyde. Copies destined for the Indians themselves had neither the English title nor the dedication of those sent to England.[54]

As the wording of the dedication suggested, these gestures of gift-giving transformed the 1661 New Testament into an imperial book, revealing in its materiality the pressures and expectations placed upon the colonists in the aftermath of the Restoration of Charles II. The most important of these pressures was to acknowledge the king as sovereign, a step the Massachusetts government had been slow to take. To acknowledge the king was de facto to accept the supremacy of the English government over the chartered colonies. The possibility of doing so immediately divided the colonists, generating counter petitions by the mid-1660s and in other ways testing the space for dissent. Longer term, the return of Charles II to power would gradually force the New England colonies to make fundamental changes in their political culture, changes that encompassed the decision of the Crown to grant Connecticut a charter in 1664 that gave it authority over New Haven, the imposing of royal government (the Dominion of New England) on all of the colonies in the mid-1680s, and, in the aftermath of the Glorious Revolution, a process of negotiation that produced the Massachusetts charter of 1691. Culturally, too, the colonists were having to rethink much about themselves, beginning with the reasons why the founders of Massachusetts had left their native land. In the 1640s the answer was simple, that the Church of England had betrayed true Christianity. By the 1690s, this answer had become impolitic, so much so that Cotton Mather pleaded in the *Magnalia* that the immigrants of 1630 had not really wanted to leave a church they revered. Briefly, at least, change also swept over the tried-and-true genre of the almanac, which in the version printed in Boston in 1688 included for the first time a list of Anglican saints days and referred to "Oliver [Cromwell] the tyrant."[55]

Of the tension-making circumstances that aroused the English government to intervene and the colonists to quarrel among themselves, two were of particular importance, Indian affairs and the colonists' preference for local self-governance. Both of these circumstances came into being with the founding of the colonies. As early as 1638 the second had prompted the government of Charles I to consider revoking the Massachusetts charter, and as early as 1643, when a London printer issued *New Englands First Fruits*, the leaders of Massachusetts were defending themselves against the rumor that they were abusing the Native Americans and neglecting the goal—embodied in the seal of the Massachusetts Bay Company—of converting the Indians to Christianity. Seemingly distinct, Indian affairs and the preference for self-government were linked in the court of public opinion. Hence the political importance of the "Eliot tracts," printed in England at the moment that important figures in English public life like Lord Say and Sele were dismayed by the colonists' treatment of Baptists and other dissidents and when the colonists were contending against rival claims to parts of New England.[56]

In the aftermath of the Restoration of Charles II, the stakes were suddenly much higher. Dedicating the New Testament to Charles represented another attempt at using Indian affairs to mask the colonists' preference for self-government. Nor was the leadership of Massachusetts averse to soliciting Robert Boyle to do their business, as in asking him in 1664 to lobby for changes in the instructions to commissioners the Crown was sending to inquire into the loyalty of the several governments.[57] The English government undertook such a step again in 1676 in the person of Edward Randolph, who immediately informed the English bureaucracy overseeing the empire that the colonists were flagrantly disobedient. Not all of them, to be sure; in 1676 and again after he returned in the early 1680s, Randolph was assuring the English government that the majority of the colonists would welcome royal government and the Church of England. In the aftermath of an uprising against the Dominion of New England in April 1689, warfare on the New

England frontier once again connected Indian affairs and local politics: would the colonists act as allies of the empire and vigorously combat the French and Indians, or was a structure akin to the Dominion the only means of overcoming local laxness, as Edmund Andros would insist in justifying the policies he pursued as head of the Dominion?

Telling the story of this politics and the text-making that flowed from it takes us from the dedication of 1661 to the notebook of documents connected with the commissioners of 1665–66 assembled by Thomas Danforth and, a decade later, to the publications in London and Boston that narrated King Philip's War and the broadsides and tracts spawned by the overthrow of the Dominion of New England. More agitation followed once the government of William III granted Massachusetts a new charter in 1691, and the process of text-making experienced another spasm around the witch-hunt of 1692. Always, the practice and politics of writing drew on the same two technologies of publication that the colonists had been using since the 1630s, with London printers and, after 1689, the printing office of William Bradford in Philadelphia and New York serving as alternatives to the book trade in Boston. Always, too, text-making was situated in close proximity to the strongly felt categories of private and public and the uses of anonymity, with "sedition" and "libel" ever on hand as means of proscribing dissent or undermining someone's version of the "truth." The documentary record Danforth created of documents and debates within the Massachusetts General Court is emblematic of the pressures being brought to bear on these categories; for only the second time in the political history of Massachusetts (the first being 1637), a magistrate crossed a line by creating a written record of debate within the General Court, with each speaker identified by his initials.[58]

Well before the crises of 1689–92, however, dissent was being voiced in manuscript and printed book by high-ranking clergy. Agitation about baptism and church membership prompted a colloquy of ministers in 1657 to work out answers to a list of twenty-one questions, a text intended only for scribal publication but put into print in London by a young colonist.[59] Five years later, a synod revisited these issues. The provocation for debate was both practical and theological, practical because church membership was beginning to decline as children of first-generation church members delayed or never experienced the "work of grace" that in most congregations was a requirement for becoming a member, and theological because the churches were entangled in a contradiction: people had initially became members only after making a "relation" of the work of grace, but their children entered on the basis of their parents' covenant—for these children, an "external" covenant warranted by Genesis 17. For many of the ministers and some of the laity, these problems could only be resolved if the churches relaxed the rules for church membership laid out in the Cambridge Platform of 1648. Extolling the "external covenant," the majority at the synod of 1662 agreed that the children of any adult who had been baptized were entitled to baptism and church membership. Theirs would not be "full" membership, for the sacrament of the Lord's Supper would still be reserved for persons who testified about the work of grace. A compromise that broke with the past in one major respect, the synod's decision angered a few of the clergy who participated in the synod. Of more far consequence, the new ruling on baptism disturbed a great many lay people, who condemned it as distorting the purity of the "Congregational Way."

Once the synod finished voting, each side had to decide how to publicize its arguments. Almost certainly, the majority and the minority would have preferred to respect the usual restrictions on publicity, the majority because it was anxious about the effects of ministerial dissent on the "meaner" people. The Massachusetts government was just as anxious about publicity, for the General Court initiated a version of licensing in October 1662, ordering that any book the Cambridge printers wanted to publish had to be approved by the minister in Cambridge, Jonathan Mitchell, and a magistrate in the same town, to the end of preventing "irregularities and abuse to the authority of this country."[60] Yet for the first time in the history of the local trade, the Cambridge printers published each side's arguments. How something this unexpected happened is revealed in a letter Increase Mather, a dissident, sent to John Davenport in New Haven. As the synod was concluding its work, he reported to Davenport, its most significant critic, that "All dissenting is esteemed intolerable, and dissenters are accompted and charged to be the Breakers of the peace of the churches." Consistent with this stance, the majority was refusing to let the dissenters distribute copies—at this point, these were handwritten—of their criticism of the synod. Remarkably, the dissenters pressed on, turning to the General Court where they knew of allies among the deputies and magistrates. Increase and a few others gave the Court a critique of the new policy that Davenport and Nicholas Street, another New Haven Colony minister, had written, a document Davenport wanted to become "public," together with another manuscript statement of reasons for opposing the "innovation" signed by two Mathers and other colleagues. "I have given in yours and Mr. Streetes Testimony unto our General Court,"

Mather wrote in his letter, "with a preface subscribed by Mr. Chauncy, Mr. Mayo, my Brother and myselfe, in the name of others of the Dissenting Brethren in the Synod, wherein we declare that wee fully concurr with what is asserted by your selves in these papers."

Thereupon (in Mather's words), a divided General Court had backed off from any strong response:

> Some of the Court would very faigne have had them [the dissenters' arguments] throwne out againe, without soe much as reading them, but the major parte were not soe violent, they have voted that what the Sinod have done shall be printed: it was moved allsoe that what yourselves and wee have done might be printed allsoe, but all the answer that could be obtained was that wee might doe as we would, but they would not vote for such a thing, and wee must count it a favour that wee were not Commanded to be silent.

Mather was delighted. "It is our purpose therefore," he told Davenport, "to print what wee have given into the Court, of yours and ours. . . . As yet our wrightings have not beene publickly read in the Court."[61]

Thus it happened that in 1662 the Cambridge printers issued a document that materially was validated as official, the *Propositions concerning the Subject of Baptism* (Cambridge, 1662), but at almost at the same moment printing Davenport's *Another Essay For Investigation of the Truth* (Cambridge, 1663), with an unsigned preface by Increase. The material and verbal form of these texts embodied an uneasiness about their very existence. In keeping with the ethics of peace, each was anonymous, though it must have been no secret that Davenport and Increase Mather were responsible for *Another Essay* and Jonathan Mitchell and Richard Mather for the *Propositions*. As though to signify that Mather and Mitchell had acted reluctantly in publishing the *Propositions*, its title page incorporated the order of the General Court to have the manuscript printed. Moreover, the two men explicitly evoked "the peace and welfare of Religion" as reason for avoiding further controversy. Davenport and Increase Mather evoked the same ethics of peace in denying that they were "disturbers of the peace," though coupling their expressions of humility with stronger words: they would "say no more to Apologize for our Publishing of this Reply," a step they validated by associating themselves with the proto-Protestant martyr Jan Hus and the five Independents (Congregationalists) who had opposed the much larger Presbyterian majority in the Westminster Assembly.[62]

Once the private-public line had been crossed and once, as the majority complained, the case of the minority had been taken to the people, more texts turned up in Samuel Green's printing shop. Over the next two years he and Marmaduke Johnson would print two more books defending the synod. The printers could do so without looking over their shoulder, for in 1663 the General Court repealed its order of 1662 about licensing. Meanwhile, the multi-authored critique, *Anti-Synodalia Scripta Americana*, with an unsigned preface by Charles Chauncy, the President of Harvard, was printed in 1662 in London combined with the *Propositions*. Much remained in manuscript, most notably Davenport's initial response. It may be that Green and Johnson were reluctant to invest in more books of this kind, but they may have yielded to pleas they pull back from the conflict.[63]

The final word on the novelty of dissenters appealing in print to "the common sort of Readers" was John Allin's *Animadversions upon the Antisynodalia Americana*, which Green and Johnson jointly issued in 1664. The minister in Dedham since 1638, Allin scoffed at Chauncy's insistence that he and his fellow dissenters "had much rather this Treatise [the *Anti-Synodalia*] were suppressed." pointing out that "they declare a Resolution to have it Published, whatever should follow, concluding in the words of Esther, *If I perish, I perish*." Allin insisted that the synod had fully entertained the dissenters' "Writings." For him, the General Court's inaction was a sensible response to a conflict it did not wish "to countenance and encourage" lest it create "Division and Disturbances amongst us." But his real worry was that all the agitation about the synod's decisions—agitation rippling through congregation after congregation in the 1660s—was doing "much to weaken the Authority of" the clergy: "These Treatises, coming into the Peoples hands, if no Answer should be returned, will much strengthen the hands of such as are Dissenters, and discourage the hearts of others from the Practice of the Doctrine of the Synod." In a turn of phrase that underscored the dangers of publishing in print, Allin appealed directly to "the Reader [to] judge who are more like the Pharisees." And, although he painted the dissenters as proto-Baptists, he asked them to recognize that, compared to the "many discontented persons, and corrupt Opinionists, Familists, Anabaptists, Quakers, and the like" who delighted in spreading "evil Reports" about New England, both sides in the controversy had a stake in preserving a public stance of "Brotherly Love."[64]

For the Cambridge printers to publish an oppositional text was unnerving, so much so that nothing like it would happen again until near the end of the century. Indeed, no one in 1662 celebrated this step. On the contrary, the minority endorsed the ethics of peace and, in keeping with that ethics, tried to preserve their anonymity. Tempting though it was to appeal to the people, Allin's rhetoric, with its specter *à la* Winthrop of divisions extending outward among the people and undoing the authority of ministers and magistrates, had more weight especially once disputes and schisms began to roil local congregations in Connecticut and Massachusetts.

With the outbreak in June 1675 of the Indian uprising that became known as King Philip's War, Indian affairs returned to center stage. Once underway, the war radically disrupted the missionary project embodied in the fourteen "praying towns" Eliot and his Native allies had established by 1674—and disrupted in unexpected ways, for many of the colonists accused the praying Indians of being "preying Indians," as much involved in the attacks as groups that had never accepted Christianity. The violence this attitude licensed against *all* Indians became one aspect of a much broader debate about whether the colonists were engaged in a "just" war. Like the agitation about baptism and church membership, this debate was carried on in publications, some anonymous and others by persons who identified themselves, a few in manuscripts but most in pamphlets or books printed in Boston and London. It resembled that agitation in drawing on a factionalism among the colonists that no government could hope to control—differences among military and civil leaders on how to conduct the war, differences among the ministers about the reasons for such a divine judgment, and more frighteningly, differences about the Christian Indians that threatened to break out in mob violence against Daniel Gookin, the one Massachusetts magistrate who emphatically took their side. At best, the authorities could hope that those who spoke out would respect some of the customary restraints on speech and writing. At worse, the war and its politics threatened to undo all the political benefits of the missions and to persuade the English government that its intervention was called for.[65]

The first report to reach an English audience was an anonymous pamphlet printed in London in December 1675 and described on its title page as "Faithfully Composed by a Merchant of Boston and Communicated to his Friend in London." The doing of Nathaniel Saltonstall, *The Present State of New-England With Respect to the Indian War* was immediately defensive in how it represented (as announced on the title page) "the true Reason thereof, (as far as can be judged by Men.)." Opening with the death of a Christian

Indian Saltonstall blamed on King Philip, *The Present State* represented the colonists as victims and the Indians as aggressors. Christian or not, the Indians were the cruelest of killers and rapists. As though he were a latter day martyrologist recording the sufferings of the godly, Saltonstall evoked the spectacle of Native Americans "killing many People after a most Barbarous Manner; as skinning them all over alive, some only their Heads, cutting off their Hands and Feet; but any Woman they take alive, they Defile." He was certain, too, that the Indians who assaulted a particular town had committed an act of treachery by passing themselves off as Christians. Though a careful reader would have realized that the colonists were performing cruelties of their own, Saltonstall had words of praise for James Mosely, a militia captain whose name was becoming synonymous with extraordinary aggression: "This Captain Mosely had been an old Privateer at Jamaica, an excellent Souldier, and an undaunted Spirit, one whose Memory will be Honourable in New-England, for his many eminent Services he hath done the Publick." One token of this service was Mosely's summary execution of two Indians, a father and son who described themselves as Christians but who Mosely accused of fighting against the colonists. As for why the war had broken out, Saltonstall returned to a question Roger Williams had raised (and answered) in the early 1630s: had the colonists acted unjustly in seizing the land of the Indians? Williams had said they did, but Saltonstall disagreed: "The English took not a Foot of Land from the Indians, but Bought all, and although they bought for an inconsiderable Value; yet they did Buy it," adding as further justification that "the English" had turned the "Wilderness" into a garden "through their Labour, and the Blessing of God thereon." Yet the voice in which Saltonstall made these claims was curiously fragile, acknowledging the opposite (as in the "not" in "not a foot of land") in the very course of defending the colonists. Elsewhere this fragility reappeared in his remark that the colonial soldiers were having difficulty differentiating Christian Indians from those who were not.[66]

The counterpoint to Saltonstall's *Present State* was a text that circulated in late 1675 only in manuscript and possibly only in New England, John Easton's "A Relacion of the Indian Warre." A long-serving attorney-general of the colony of Rhode Island and a Quaker, Easton retraced the background of the war in order to dispute why it had broken out. Promising a "true relation of what I kno and of reports, and my understanding Conserning the beginning and progres" of the war, Easton suggested that Sassamon had not been murdered, as Saltonstall alleged. Insisting that the war was unnecessary and unjust and that the Indians had "grave Complaints" against the orthodox colonists, Easton pointed out that expeditions mounted by Massachusetts and Plymouth against Philip's warriors had disrupted a process of arbitration begun by the leaders of Rhode Island to redress land deals the Indians resented: "if the English be not carefull to manefest the Indians mai expect equity from them, they mai have more enemies then thay wold." Easton reversed the language of savagery that Saltonstall employed, terming the behavior of the colonial army "brutish" and deceitful. For him the rage of the English against the Indians exemplified the violence of a Puritan culture accustomed to "persecution." Remembering, no doubt, the role of Charles II in ending the worst of the colonists' treatment of his own religious community and certainly remembering that Rhode Island owed its political existence to the English government, he pointed out that the Indians had "submitted to our king to protect them," protection he called upon the king and on royal governors such as Edmund Andros in New York to provide against the colonists' aggression.[67]

Meanwhile, the London trade was continuing to publish the letters Saltonstall was sending, *A Continuation of the State of New-England; Being a Farther Account of the Indian Warr,* issued in London in early 1676, and *A New and Further Narrative of the State of New-England; Being A Continued Account of the Bloudy Indian War,* a text dated July 22, 1676 and printed in London near the end of that year and both, like the first, anonymous. In contrast to the initial report, in these he equivocated about the agency and situation of the Christian Indians, perhaps because he realized that tales of the Christian Indians as warriors and of colonists killing or torturing them at will were undoing decades of propaganda on behalf of the missions. Whatever his reasons, Saltonstall began the second letter by describing the "great Care our Authority hath, as well to make a Distinction visible, betwixt our Friends the Christian Indians, and our Enemies the Heathens, as also, to secure the one from Injuries." For him, however, the war owed its origins to a "Conspiracy" hatched by the Indians, who murdered Sassamon when it seemed he was about to reveal the plot. Turning to the colonists themselves, he called attention for the first time to the ritual of fasting they had been using as the war proceeded, assuring his English readers that the practice showed "what Fear of the immediate Hand of God upon us our Majistrates have; and truly Sir, we have great Cause to bless the Lord for that we have such Magistrates and Councellores that we are so well assured do aime at the Glory of God." This language and the reference to fast days suggests he was

aware of Increase Mather's vehement criticism of the Massachusetts government for ignoring the providential dimensions of the war. Yet he also reiterated the theme of Indian savagery, citing in the third letter the example of
two Native women who, after killing two colonists, cut off "their privy Members." "So vain it is," he added, "to expect any Thing but the most barbarous
Usage from such a People amongst whom the most milde and gentle Sex
delight in Cruelties." In the same vein were the rumors he reported that
Mary Rowlandson had been molested (raped) by her captors and forced to
marry one of them.[68]

Saltonstall was in good company. Benjamin Tompson's poetic rendering
of the war hinted at the Indians' "lust" for colonial women and, although he
may not have been responsible for the title page of the version printed in
London in 1676, its language of "unheard-of Cruelties by the barbarous heathens" was in keeping with his verse.[69] The popular animosity against the
Christian Indians re-emerged in Mary Rowlandson's captivity narrative. Recalling the scene of "black creatures" singing and dancing the night after
their successful assault on Lancaster, she described it as "a lively resemblance
of hell." For her, there was little point in differentiating the "barbarous"
Indians from those who were Christian; all were barbarous, "even those that
seem to profess more then others among them, when the English have fallen
into their hands." She pointedly agreed with those who blamed a local Christian group for a raid on Lancaster the previous summer and implicitly sanctioned the cruelties inflicted on that group by "Capt. Mosely." Among her
captors was a "rude fellow" she had "seen afterwards walking up and down
in Boston, under the appearance of a friend-Indian," and she described a
"Praying" Indian "so wicked and cruel, as to wear a string about his neck,
strung with Christian fingers." (Hers was also a voice that equivocated, for
she recorded numerous acts of kindness that culminated in her being ran-
somed.)[70]

Well before Rowlandson had completed her narrative, Increase Mather
and William Hubbard had published histories of the war that treated it in a
different light. Mather wanted to indict the political leadership, Hubbard to
defend it. Both agreed, however, that the war was just; Mather filled a "Post-
script" with documents testifying to this description, and Hubbard cited
similar texts to prove that land belonging to King Philip's tribe had been
acquired by "honest purchase." Both ministers were also dismayed by the
outbursts of popular violence and racism. Hubbard pointed out that the
Indians seized by Mosely in response to the 1675 raid on Lancaster had been

"quitted from the Fact," and he insisted that the women taken captive in the attack of February 1676 "found so much favour in the sight of their Enemies, that they offered no wrong to any of their persons." Nor had the Indians "attempted the chastity of any of them." Knowing already of Mather's diatribes against the government, Hubbard dedicated his book to the governors of Massachusetts, Plymouth, and Connecticut.[71]

Mather's motives for writing were several. He wanted to take issue with Easton, whose accusations he knew of and perhaps had read; he wanted to reassert a politics of "declension" that had already put him at odds with the government; and he wanted to challenge Hubbard's restrained evocation of divine providence and judgment. In a sermon printed with *A Brief History of the War with the Indians in New England* (Boston, 1676), *An Earnest Exhortation*, Mather used the privileges of the pulpit to criticize everyone he regarded as responsible for the waning of religious zeal, from parents who were neglecting to have their children baptized to people whose madness for land was greater than their respect for education or churches, much less Indian rights. But he aimed his anger especially at two groups: the colonists who, by abusing the Christian Indians, had undermined the missionary project (a point emphasized in the materiality of the text, which included a reproduction of the original seal of the Massachusetts Bay Company with its image of an Indian voicing the Macedonian cry), and the General Court for refusing to heed the lesson that the war signified God's anger at the colonists for their failure to reform. Toward his fellow colonists he was scathing: "what madness and rage hath there been against all Indians whatsoever . . . yea if in their [the colonists'] skirts be not found the bloud of the souls of poor innocents." He was just as critical of the Court.[72]

These publications embodied a clash of opinion played out in the culture as a whole rather than in sessions of a colony government or synod. None of them came close to being designated as libels, perhaps because the issues they touched on were more elusive than the challenges Winthrop had faced to his authority. But to ignore them as expressions of dissent is to ignore the place of contestation within local politics and, in the case of Mather, to ignore the possibility that ministers fully orthodox and complicit in most respects could also turn critic. Other ministers before Mather had used sermons to criticize public policy—John Cotton had done so successfully in 1639 when he objected to a law imposing civil penalties on persons excommunicated from the churches that, shortly thereafter, the General Court repealed—and, like some of his predecessors, Mather could fall back on the stance of prophet. But he knew he was alienating the political leadership, and he must have realized that his support for the Christian Indians put him at odds with many of the colonists.

Like John Easton before him, Edward Randolph wanted to connect the war and how it was conducted with the business of empire. He began to do so in the earliest of his reports, informing the Board of Trade in September 1676 that, had the leadership of the orthodox colonists heeded the advice of Andros in New York, the war would have "proved lesse destructive." Randolph had little sympathy for the Indians and the Christian Indians in particular, repeating the canard that the Natick community had turned against the colonists. But he also sensed that the colonists had dealt with King Philip unjustly in how they encroached on his lands. In this and every subsequent report, his larger points were always that the colonists were flagrantly ignoring the authority of the Crown, that the Congregational system was much resented, and that many people of wealth and status were "well affected" to the Crown.[73] He complained as well of how he was treated by the political leadership in Massachusetts. As happened with the commissioners of 1665–66, so with Randolph the governor and magistrates tried to frustrate any communication with the colonists. In "An answer to severall heads of enquiry concerning the present state of New-England" he sent that fall to his superiors in London, he reported that, "Being ready to return for England," he "went to the governor . . . for my dispatches, and was entertained by him with a sharp reproof for publishing [i.e., reading aloud] the substance of my errand into those parts, contained in your Majesties letters, as also in Mr. Masons petition . . . unto the inhabitants of Boston, New-Hampshire and Main, telling me that I designed to make a mutiny and disturbance in the country and to withdraw the people from their obedience to the magistracy of that colony and the authority thereof."[74] Via such reports, Randolph translated the obstinacy of the Massachusetts government into a rejection of what he and his superiors in London regarded as legitimate communication or publicity. In effect, Randolph was depicting the orthodox colonists as seditious for refusing to acknowledge his authority.

The connections among publicity, revolt, and authority, with Indian affairs a thread that wound its way into every aspect of imperial and local politics, would enter an acute phase of strain in the late 1680s, as evident in printed books that, for political reasons, had none of the customary information of author, printer, place, and date on their title pages. This phase of text-making was marked by the recurrence of anonymity in politically contentious printed books, the first appearance in New England of newssheets, and the production of handwritten texts as a means of giving voice to political opinion. Indeed, the politics of dissent accelerated—and became more difficult—once the government of Charles II revoked the Massachusetts charter in 1684. To replace it and to implement a grander understanding of empire, the Crown created the Dominion of New England headed by a royal governor.

Like the Stuarts whom they served, the men who ran the Dominion during its short life were reluctant to authorize dissent of any kind. Once up and running, the Dominion, with Joseph Dudley temporarily in office as governor, assigned Randolph the responsibility of licensing every printed book. An order of November 1686, the month when almanacs usually went to press, commanded Samuel Green, Jr. "not [to] proceed to print any Almanack whatever without having" Randolph's permission. A month after Edmund Andros arrived in December 1686 to take Dudley's place as royal governor, he and the Council declared that "no Papers, Bookes Pamphlets &c. should be printed in New England until Licensed according to Law." The Dominion government took strong action against expressions of dissent. For the first time since Wheelwright's fast-day sermon of 1637, a minister, Charles Morton of Charlestown, was indicted for "seditious expressions" he uttered from the pulpit (the jury failed to convict), and Cotton Mather was pursued on charges of libel for being the anonymous author of a diatribe against the Church of England. When local dissent to the levying of taxes that were not voted by a town or colony government broke out, Andros responded harshly. The most publicized of these events happened in Ipswich when the town meeting voted in June 1687 not to appoint someone to collect a tax, a step agreed upon beforehand by the minister of the town, John Wise, and several other town notables. Wise may have provided the reason for doing so, that "the said Act doth infringe their Liberty, as free born English Subjects." The leaders of the protest set out to distribute copies of the town vote to other towns, but got only as far as nearby Topsfield before a sheriff arrested Wise, the town clerk, and several others for having "put into writing and published" the vote. Convicted by a jury, the six were heavily fined and suspended from their various offices. A rumor that Andros was secretly allied with the Indians harassing settlements along the Maine frontier brought fines upon several men of Watertown who were inadvertently involved in spreading the story. When the first copy of the "Declarations" of William III reached Boston in early 1689, the passenger on a ship who shared it was arrested for "bringing Traitorous and Treasonable Libels and Papers of News" into the colony. Meanwhile the Dominion government was taking other steps to counteract the flow of rumor. Realizing that "many false Representations and reflections" were circulating of what Joseph Dudley had said in May 1686 to the final, despairing session of the General Court under the old charter, the government "thought it expedient that the Presidents speech taken verbatim by credible persons be forthwith printed and published."[75]

On April 18, 1689, the tables were suddenly turned. By mid-day most of the officers of Andros's government were under arrest and the magistrates of the old charter government re-installed at the Town House. Within a day or two, Andros had surrendered and the revolutionaries had gained control of the fort in Boston harbor. New England, too, had known its Glorious Revolution. Or had it? This was a question not finally answered until 1776, but in the weeks and months that followed the overthrow of the Dominion the colonists were confronted with a crisis of publicity more severe than any in their past. Whose version of the revolt would win out, the rebels' or the version Andros and his allies were quick to provide? On that question hung the legitimacy of the revolt and what favors the colonists could expect of William III. Would he reinstall Andros or someone like him and disregard the colonists' preference for representative government? On it hung too the possibilities for unity among the colonists themselves, for the revolutionary fervor of April subsided as moderate and radical factions emerged to contest in writing the nature of good government and the role of the empire.

Text-making was one way of influencing the new king and those in whom he trusted, and gritty politics was another, as when the Massachusetts leadership sanctioned an expedition in 1690 against French Canada, a military disaster that temporarily ruined the colony's finances. Text-making was far less costly, but as the new government learned by the late spring of 1689, it was something enemies as well as friends were undertaking. Although officers of the Dominion were not in command, they still had the weapon of pen and paper. John Palmer, an experienced servant of the Crown who was put under arrest in April, turned at once to the medium of scribal publication. By June, copies were circulating of his attack on the new government, the anonymous "Impartial Account of the State of New-England." Almost as promptly, other royal officials were writing to agencies and officers of the Crown in London, Randolph in a letter of May 29, a navy captain and a less significant officer in mid-June. None of these were intercepted or suppressed. More remarkably, Palmer found a printer—probably William Bradford in

Philadelphia—willing to publish his account, attributed on the title page to "F. L." By November, the government was complaining that "many papers have been lately printed and dispersed tending to the disturbance of the peace and subversion of the governmt of this theire Maiesties Collonies King William & Queene Mary." Like its predecessor the Dominion, the Council ordered that "any person or persons . . . guilty of any such like Misdemeanor of printing, publishing or concealing any such like papers or discourses . . . shall be accounted enemies to theire Majesties present Gouvernment."[76] More steps of this kind followed, some of them aimed at curtailing rumor, others at the Boston trade.

The provisional government was also realizing that it had to do more than simply suppress what others were writing. Text-making had already accompanied the events of April 18 when the revolt had broken out, for early in the afternoon the notables who gathered at the Town House had in their hands a "Declaration of the Gentlemen, Merchants, and Inhabitants of Boston, and the Country adjacent" that someone read from the balcony to the excited crowd below. No name was on the printed broadside that Samuel Green issued a few days later. Highly rhetorical in its allusions to the "horrible brinks of Popery and Slavery" to which James II had brought England (and by implication, New England), the text may have been prepared before April 18, with a concluding section about William III added at the last minute. Soon, much more was called for at home and in England. There the burden of defending the revolt and responding to the counter-narratives published in London by Andros and Palmer fell upon a few of the colonists who were in the city. Increase Mather had been there since late 1687 agitating against Andros and pleading with the government of James II to restore some of the privileges of the old charter, a task he immediately resumed with the government of William III. Well informed by allies in London about discussions in Parliament and within the circles of William III, Mather faced the challenge of justifying a revolt that, as he was learning by mid-1689, persuaded many in Parliament and agencies like the Board of Trade that any new arrangement had to incorporate the authority of the Crown and Parliament. Meanwhile Andros and his allies had returned to the city and were rapidly issuing statements in their own defense.[77]

Back in Boston, rumor was flourishing in the absence of reliable news from London about Mather's negotiations with William III and Parliament about the status of the charter. In the London-printed version of his *Impartial*

Account, Palmer recalled the intense anxiety about news and publicity that affected how he published his defense of the Dominion:

> There was so much Industry used in New England, by those who had taken upon themselves the Government, that nothing should come abroad which might undeceive the People, already wrought to such a pitch of Credulity, easily to believe the most monstrous Lyes and Follies, that the ensuing Letter could not be Printed without excessive Charge and Trouble; the Press being forbid to any that were injur'd, to justifie themselves, though open to all that would calumniate, and abuse them; so that for several Months it appeared in Manuscript, by stealth, branded with the hard Name of a Treasonable and Seditious Libel; and would have been little better than Death, for any one, in whose Hands it should have been found.[78]

In this context of rumor and distrust, the new government took the step of printing in November 1689 a folio broadside, *The Present State of the New-English Affairs*, made up out of two recent news-filled letters from Increase Mather (one to Simon Bradstreet, the acting governor, the other to Cotton), together with an extract from a London-printed newsletter, all headed by the phrase, "This is Published to prevent False Reports."[79] Some months later, the government moved to *suppress* a broadside newssheet entitled *Publick Occurrences* on the grounds that it contained "sundry doubtful and uncertain Reports," insisting in the same order that nothing be "Set forth . . . in Print without Licence first obtained from those that are or shall be appointed by the Government to grant the same." Some of the leadership was probably involved in writing and publishing *An Account of the Late Revolution in New-England* (Boston, 1689), signed "A.B." and concluding with words that recalled the heading of *The Present State*: "The foregoing Account being very carefully and critically Examined, by divers very worthy and Faithfull Gentlemen, was advised to be Published for the preventing of False Reports." Presumably its assertions that Andros had given arms to the Indians to use against the colonists counted as true.[80]

Locally and in London, where Andros, Palmer, Randolph, and other officials of the Dominion arrived in early 1690, the manuscript and printed texts justifying or denouncing the rebellion rang changes on a small repertory of themes. Were the colonists the radical, seditious heirs of Cromwell and the regicides, as alleged by writers defending Andros, or were such connections entirely fanciful, as the colonists insisted? Were the disastrous effects of Indian raids in 1689 and 1690 the consequence of policies (and conspiracies) Andros had pursued, or the responsibility of the new government? Writing in their own defense, Andros and Palmer told a story of colonists refusing to volunteer for military service and of mishandled actions, as when the restored colonial government ordered the withdrawal of soldiers from the fort at Pemaquid. Writing in defense of the rebellion, the colonists spun out stories of Andros's complicity with the French, "fanciful Stories of Macquas, Subterranean Vaults, Fire-Works, French Frigats, poisoning the Soldiers to the Eastward" that Andros and company mocked as "monstrous Follies."[81] To give weight to the colonists' assertions about Andros and the Dominion, the Massachusetts government set in motion the collecting of depositions from towns and individuals that purported to detail abuses of power and law. In a replay of the Robert Child affair, the government also seized a collection of letters to and from Randolph. After a committee sorted through this material, excerpts from these letters were printed in the anonymous *An Appeal to the Men of New England, with a Short Account of Mr. Randolph's Papers* (undated, but probably 1690);[82] many of the depositions were reproduced in another pamphlet, *The Revolution in New England Justified* (Boston and London, 1691), also anonymous but signed with the initials E. R. and S. S. at the end of the preface, and known to be the work of Edward Rawson and Samuel Sewall, both then in London. Denying that the colonists had any connections with the "Commonwealth" tradition, the two compilers used the collection of depositions to replay the suppression of the Ipswich protest and the border wars that, from their vantage, Andros had encouraged.

Meanwhile, Increase Mather was turning out five separate imprints, each of them anonymous. The earliest, *A Narrative Of the Miseries of New-England, By Reason of an Arbitrary Government Erected there* (undated and with no colophon, but London, late 1688 or early 1689), had been drafted by Mather before the fall of James II but, as printed, acknowledged in the subtitle and an extra paragraph the presence of William III. In May 1689, still unaware of events in New England, he responded to a pamphlet (in the judgment of Samuel Sewall, a "virulent Libel")[83] asserting that the colonists wanted "Independence of this Crown" with the eight page undated and otherwise unidentified *New-England Vindicated*. The broadside *A Further Vindication* was followed by another brief pamphlet, *A Brief Relation of the State of New England*. In *A Letter to a Person of Quality* (1689), a text directed mainly to discussions in Parliament about the rechartering of corporations, he was finally able to incorporate parts of the printed *Declaration* of April 1689. Knowing, too, that Indian affairs were a key aspect of the campaign to defend the overthrow of Andros and the sincerity of the colonists, he inserted into *A Brief Relation of the State of New England* a previously printed letter extolling the history of the missions in New England.[84]

As always, anonymity invited exposure and the shifting sands of political allegiances, self-censorship. Moreover, every claim to speak the truth needed gestures of attestation. The writers of *The Revolution Justified* reprised the step Increase Mather had used in 1675 with *First Principles of New-England*, of advertising the availability of the documents they were printing: "Reader, There is such Notoriety as to Matter of Fact in the preceding Relation, that they who Live in New-England are satisfy'd concerning the Particulars contained therein. If any in England should Hesitate, they may please to understand that Mr. Elisha Cook, and Mr. Thomas Oakes . . . have by them Attested Copies of the Affidavits (at least-wise of most of them) which are in this Vindication published, and are ready (if occasion serves) to produce them."[85] Back in London and anxious to mask his connections with the Stuarts, John Palmer omitted twenty pages of diatribe against rebellion as a sin from the version of the *Impartial Account* he forwarded to a London printer, though what he had said in the first version was pounced upon by the colonists.[86] Local factionalism figured in the narrative strategy of another Boston-initiated text, *A Narrative of The Proceedings of Sir Edmund Androsse and his Complices, Who Acted by an Illegal and Arbitrary Commission from the Late K. James, during his Government in New England*, attributed on the title page to "several Gentlemen who were of his Council. Printed in the Year 1691," with their names appended at the end. Readers were told this was a commissioned text, brought into being at the request of the government. But in counter-point to other texts defending the revolt, the "gentlemen" insisted that "those Great Jealousies and Suspicions of Sinister Designs in the Governour as to our Troubles by the Indians" were in part "too uncertain, if not untrue [to] have been too easily reported and spread concerning him."[87]

The revocation of the Massachusetts charter and the rebellion against the Dominion brought about a political crisis unlike anything the colonists had experienced before. Its outcome was a new political structure and elements of a new political system. Another consequence was the damage done to long-lasting means of extolling consensus and curtailing publicity. Still favoring the traditional constraints against publicity and dissent, the political and religious elite were finding those constraints severely weakened—weakened because the divisions within that elite could not be covered up and because the rebellion *was* a Commonwealth-style event, an uprising of the people that, like the radical edge of English politics in the 1640s, drew on popular fears of tyranny and Catholicism. Beyond 1690, everyone had to take sides for and against the new charter and for and against William Phips, the first governor under its provisions. As the everyday weight of the culture of deference diminished, so did the political influence of Cotton and Increase Mather—and of William Phips, whose time as governor went badly. Anonymity remained a vital practice, but the availability of a printer in the middle colonies made it possible for *political* dissent to appear in printed form for the first time: two treatises by the Connecticut royalist Gershom Bulkeley denouncing the colonists and Palmer's *Impartial Account*.

The crisis of 1689 did not bring about a legitimizing of dissent. In 1692 the Baptist William Milborne was sharply censored for petitions the provincial Council characterized as "seditious and scandalous papers or writings" (Milborne was insisting that some of the persons convicted in the Salem witch-hunt were "Innocent"), shortly thereafter the Quaker Thomas Maule was indicted for libel (though the jury refused to convict), governors continued to claim the right to license publications, and petitions were variously received.[88] What the turmoil of 1689 accomplished was to reshape the middle ground on which dissent had persistently been voiced, a middle ground that, under Winthrop, had been bounded by a rough consensus that authority had to be respected, unity preserved, and the due "liberties" of the people acknowledged. Yet even in Winthrop's day there had been an elasticity about what constituted "seditious libel." Now, however, that elasticity was putting the old system out of joint.

More crises lay ahead, as did more bursts of surreptitious criticism, as when the elite writer Thomas Brattle circulated his criticism of the witch-hunt in an unsigned handwritten letter and Samuel Willard his of the same event in an un-attributed book with a false imprint (Philadelphia, when the actual printer was Samuel Green, Jr.).[89] To refer to any of these texts or situations as marking the "birth" of democratic politics or a "public sphere" seems pointless. Amidst the turmoil of 1689–92 the old rules remained precious to many. "Obedience to lawful authority I evermore accounted a great duty," Brattle wrote in his letter,

> and willingly I would not practise any thing that might thwart and contradict such a principle. Too many are ready to despise domin-

ions, and speak evil of dignities; and I am sure the mischiefs, which
arise from a factious and rebellious spirit, are very sad and notorious;
insomuch that I would sooner bite my finger's ends than willingly
cast dirt on authority, or any way offer reproach to it: Far, therefore,
be it from me, to have any thing to do with those men your letter
mentions, whom you acknowledge to be men of a factious spirit . . .
declaiming against men in public place.[90]

These were words John Winthrop would have welcomed, though he might
have swallowed hard once he realized that Brattle the conservative was also
Brattle the critic of high-placed judges. Yet Brattle knew what Winthrop had
reluctantly acknowledged, that criticism was compatible with authority. Be
it in handwritten or printed texts, petitions or remonstrances, sermons or
rumor, criticism and dissent were a persistent feature of the political culture
of seventeenth-century New England.

ABBREVIATIONS

Amory and Hall, *Colonial Book*

Hugh Amory and David D. Hall, ed., *The Colonial Book in the Atlantic World*, vol. 1 of *A History of the Book in America* (New York: Cambridge University Press, 2000; repr., Chapel Hill: University of North Carolina Press, 2007)

Coll. MHS

Collections of the Massachusetts Historical Society

Hall, *Antinomian Controversy*

David D. Hall, *The Antinomian Controversy, 1636–1638: A Documentary History* (Middletown, Conn.: Wesleyan University Press, 1968; repr., Durham: Duke University Press, 1990)

Holmes, *Cotton Mather*

Thomas J. Holmes, *Cotton Mather: A Bibliography of His Works*, 3 vols. (Cambridge, Mass.: Harvard University Press, 1940)

Holmes, *Increase Mather*

Thomas J. Holmes, *Increase Mather: A Bibliography of His Works*, 2 vols. (Cleveland: privately printed, 1931).

Jantz, *First Century*

Harold Jantz, *The First Century of New England Verse* (Worcester, Mass.: American Antiquarian Society, 1944)

Mather, *Magnalia*

Cotton Mather, *Magnalia Christi Americana*, 2 vols. (1702; repr., Hartford, Conn., 1853–54)

NEHGR

New England Historical and Genealogical Register

PCSM	*Publications of the Colonial Society of Massachusetts*
Proc. AAS	*Proceedings of the American Antiquarian Society*
Proc. MHS	*Proceedings of the Massachusetts Historical Society*
Recs. Mass.	*Records of the Governor and Company of the Massachusetts Bay in New England*, ed. N. B. Shurtleff, 5 vols. (Boston, 1853–54)
Shepard, *Works*	*The Works of Thomas Shepard*, ed. John A. Albro, 3 vols. (Boston, 1853)
Walker, *Creeds*	Williston Walker, *The Creeds and Platforms of Congregationalism* (New York, 1893)
Winthrop, *Journal*	*The Journal of John Winthrop, 1630–1649*, ed. Richard S. Dunn, James Savage, and Laetitia Yeandle (Cambridge, Mass.: Harvard University Press, 1996)
Winthrop Papers	*Winthrop Papers*, 6 vols. (Boston: Massachusetts Historical Society, 1929–)

NOTES

CHAPTER I. CONTINGENCIES OF AUTHORSHIP

1. The allusion to "hundreds" is prompted in particular by the breadth of versifying revealed in Jantz, *First Century*, and the extent of sermonizing.

2. The minister Rowland Cotton, who graduated from Harvard in 1685, "would never suffer any of his works to come out in print." John L. Sibley, *Biographical Sketches of the Graduates of Harvard University*, 3 vols. (Cambridge, Mass., 1873–85), 3: 325.

3. Many of the manuscripts I describe in Chapter 2 do not correspond in size or other material features to what we conventionally think of as a book, and the chapters that follow also cite printed broadsides and brief pamphlets that sit uneasily within this category.

4. The project of excavating a native literary tradition, broadly questioned by William C. Spengemann in *A New World of Words: Redefining Early American Literature* (New Haven: Yale University Press, 1994), is questioned on bibliographical grounds in Hugh Amory, *Bibliography and the Book Trades: Studies in the Print Culture of Early New England*, ed. David D. Hall (Philadelphia: University of Pennsylvania Press, 2004), and, in terms of imported books, reading practices, and material form, in Matthew P. Brown, *The Pilgrim and the Bee: Reading Rituals and Book Culture in Early New England* (Philadelphia: University of Pennsylvania Press, 2007).

5. Some historians of text-making during the English Renaissance incorporate readers into the story of transmission or remaking, a step I omit. But see Stephen B. Dobranski, *Readers and Authorship in Early Modern England* (Cambridge: Cambridge University Press, 2005), ch. 1.

6. Larzer Ziff, "Upon What Pretext? The Book and Literary History," *Proc. AAS* 95 (1985): 297–315; Gerard Genette, *Paratexts: Thresholds of Interpretation*, trans. Jane E. Lewin (Cambridge: Cambridge University Press, 1997), an account that is not historically specific.

7. As Margaret J. M. Ezell emphasizes in *Social Authorship and the Advent of Print* (Baltimore: Johns Hopkins University Press, 1999), writers were not considered to be really writers if their texts were not printed.

8. Udo J. Hebel, "Sanctioned Images: Court Orders, Legal Codes, Synodal Resolu-

tions, and the Cultural Contestation of Seventeenth-Century Puritan New England," *REAL Yearbook of Research in English and American Literature* 11 (1995): 43–74. See also David Cressy, *Coming Over: Migration and Communication Between England and New England in the Seventeenth Century* (New York: Cambridge University Press, 1987), ch. 1.

9. Nathaniel Morton, *New Englands Memoriall* (1669), ed. John Davis (Boston, 1826), 205n.

10. Self-censorship shaped *The Orthodox Evangelist* (Cambridge, 1654), which embodies John Norton's careful compromise of two different theological positions, as pointed out in Janice Knight, *Orthodoxies in Massachusetts: Rereading American Puritanism* (Cambridge, Mass.: Harvard University Press, 1994), 123–25. For John Winthrop and John Cotton as self-censoring, see the case histories that follow in Chapters 3 and 4 and the discussion of the Antinomian controversy in Chapter 2.

11. D. F. McKenzie, *Bibliography and the Sociology of Texts* (London: British Library, 1986), 56; Leah Marcus, *Unediting the Renaissance: Shakespeare, Marlowe, Milton* (London: Routledge, 1996); Stephen Orgel, quoted in the editor's introduction to *Crisis in Editing: Texts of the English Renaissance*. Papers Given at the Twenty-fourth Annual Conference on Editorial Problems, ed. Randall McLeod (New York: AMS Press, 1994), xii.

12. David Scott Kastan, *Shakespeare and the Book* (Cambridge: Cambridge University Press, 2001), 5.

13. A process superbly described in Margreta De Grazia, *Shakespeare Verbatim: The Reproduction of Authenticity and the 1790 Apparatus* (Oxford: Clarendon Press, 1991).

14. Though it could be argued that the recurrent anthologizing of certain authors and texts has created a de facto canon.

15. See Chapters 2 and 4 for case studies of Hooker, Edward Taylor, and Anne Bradstreet, writers who in quite different ways may have tried to control their oeuvre.

16. Compare Ezell, *Social Authorship*, ch. 6, "Making a Classic." H. R. Woudhuysen comments on the same phenomenon in *Sir Philip Sidney and the Circulation of Manuscripts, 1558–1640* (Oxford: Clarendon Press, 1996), 387.

17. Holmes, *Increase Mather* and Holmes, *Cotton Mather*; Sargent Bush and Winfried Herget's studies of Thomas Hooker's imprints, included in *Thomas Hooker: Writings in England and Holland, 1626–1633*, ed. George H. Williams et al. (Cambridge, Mass.: Harvard University Press, 1975). For other scholarship on which I have relied, see Amory and Hall, *Colonial Book*, chs. 3–4.

18. As David McKitterick has pointed out in *Print, Manuscript and the Search for Order 1450–1830* (Cambridge: Cambridge University Press, 2003), "Authors complained, sometimes bitterly, of their printers' incompetence; yet it is noticeable how few appreciated the importance of differences between copies. That, it seems, was assumed" (p. 111).

19. John N. King, *English Reformation Literature: The Tudor Origins of the Protestant Tradition* (Princeton, N.J.: Princeton University Press, 1982); John R. Knott, *The Sword of the Spirit: Puritan Responses to the Bible* (Chicago: University of Chicago Press, 1980); Barbara Kiefer Lewalski, *Protestant Poetics and the Seventeenth-Century Religious Lyric* (Princeton, N.J.: Princeton University Press, 1979); Barbara A. Johnson, *Piers Plowman*

and The Pilgrim's Progress: Reception and the Protestant Reader (Carbondale, Ill.: University of Illinois Press, 1992).

20. As Alexandra Halasz argues in *The Marketplace of Print: Pamphlets and the Public Sphere in Early Modern England* (Cambridge: Cambridge University Press, 1997).

21. Peter Lindenbaum has calculated that Thomas Parkhurst, the most important Nonconformist bookseller in late seventeenth- and early eighteenth-century London, published at least 1,015 books by 275 authors, of whom a mere six were Anglicans. He also shows that Nonconformist publishing was fragmented; Parkhurst published Independents, but his sometime ally and competitor, the more conservative Brabazon Aylmer, did not, though publishing a number of moderate Anglicans. I am grateful to Peter Lindenbaum for sharing this data with me.

22. Cressy, *Coming Over*, ch. 9.

23. Sargent Bush, Jr., *The Correspondence of John Cotton* (Chapel Hill: University of North Carolina Press, 2001), 183–84.

24. *Winthrop Papers*, 3:76; see also the long letter of 1637 (pp. 397–402) warning of "dangerous passages" in letters from New England.

25. Nathaniel Ward, *The Simple Cobler of Aggawam*, 3d. ed. (London, 1647), 3.

26. David D. Hall, *The Faithful Shepherd: A History of the New England Ministry in the Seventeenth Century* (Chapel Hill: University of North Carolina Press, 1972), ch. 10; and see Chapter 5.

27. "The Autobiography of Increase Mather," ed. Michael G. Hall, *Proc. AAS* 71 (1961): 289.

28. Nigel Smith, *Literature and Revolution in England, 1640–1660* (New Haven, Conn.: Yale University Press, 1994), 2.

29. Thomas Cobbet, *A Practical Discourse of Prayer* (London, 1654), 315–16.

30. Mather, *Magnalia*, 1, 256.

31. Kari Konkola, "The Production of Theological Texts in Early Modern England," *Papers of the Bibliographical Society of America* 94 (2000–2001): 5–34; for a broader overview, see Ian Green, *Print and Protestantism in Early Modern England* (Oxford: Oxford University Press, 2000).

32. Just how close the orthodox colonists were in their understanding of the Holy Spirit to those on their left is demonstrated in Geoffrey Nuttall, *The Holy Spirit in Puritan Faith and Experience* (Oxford: Blackwells, 1946).

33. Winthrop, *Journal*, 570 (Mrs. Hopkins was subsequently treated for mental illness by John Winthrop, Jr.); *Records of the Colony or Jurisdiction of New Haven*, ed. Charles J. Hoadly, 2 vols. (Hartford, 1857–58), 2: 234; and for another case of intra-family editorial interventions, Clayton Chapman, "Benjamin Colman's Daughters," *New England Quarterly* 26 (1953): 169–92. But the Mather family preserved (and valued) a substantial collection of manuscript texts by Increase's mother. Kenneth Silverman, *The Life and Times of Cotton Mather* (New York: Harper & Row, 1984), 20.

34. Russell was ridiculed by Samuel Willard in *Ne Sutor Ultra Crepidam* (Boston, 1681); Cotton Mather, *Memorable Providences, Relating to Witchcrafts And Possessions* (Boston, 1689), 45.

35. Quoted in James A. Goulding, "The Controversy Between Solomon Stoddard and the Mathers: Western Versus Eastern Massachusetts Congregationalism" (Ph.D. diss., Claremont University, 1971), 426. Increase did eventually endorse Stoddard's sermons.

36. As calculated by George Selement, "A full 66 percent of the practicing clergymen in New England never published anything, an additional 11 percent of them wrote only a single publication, and a mere 5 percent published ten or more tracts during their lives" (p. 223). Selement, "Publication and the Puritan Minister," *William and Mary Quarterly*, 3rd ser. 37 (1980): 219–41. Note: this data encompasses some of the eighteenth century.

37. Edward Holyoke, *The Doctrine of Life* (London, 1658), sig A2v. "Generation" probably refers to his sister's children, and the "you" were his kin in England.

38. Quoted in Amory and Hall, *Colonial Book*, 97–98.

39. John Norton, *Orthodox Evangelist*, sig. A1v.

40. Dobranski, *Readers and Authorship*, 6–7; see also the case study of Anne Brad-street that follows in Chapter 4. To cite another English example, the minister Richard Rogers declared in the preface to *The Practice of Christianitie* (1618) that "finding of late that I could not call in the copies I had given and lent abroad, and fearing lest some (which is a common practice in these dayes) might have thrust it forth with wrong to me . . . I gave way . . . to the publishing thereof." Quoted in H. S. Bennett, *English Books & Readers 1603 to 1640 Being a Study in the History of the Book Trade in the Reigns of James I and Charles I* (Cambridge: Cambridge University Press, 1970), 9.

41. B. R. Burg, *Richard Mather of Dorchester* (Lexington: University of Kentucky Press, 1976), 61; *Coll. MHS* 4th ser. 8 (1868), 32–33; Nathaniel's efforts with his brother Samuel's book are described in subsequent letters (pp. 43, 45, 50).

42. For copies, see Chapter 2; George Parker Winship, *The Cambridge Press, 1638–1692* (Philadelphia: University of Pennsylvania Press, 1946), 53–54.

43. *Recs. Mass*, 5: 279, 378, 394–95. Two handwritten versions of the manuscript survive (Massachusetts Historical Society). The rougher and presumably earlier may be in Hubbard's own handwriting; the second, in the hand of two or more copyists, contains corrections by Hubbard. "Explanations," in William Hubbard, *A General History of New England* (Boston, 1848), after title page.

44. *Coll. MHS* 4th ser. 8 (1868): 630.

45. Mather, *Magnalia*, 1: 300; and see the case study in Chapter 4.

46. Mss., Massachusetts Historical Society.

47. *Letter-book of Samuel Sewall*, 2 vols., *Coll. MHS* 6th ser. 1–2 (Boston, 1886–88), 1: 321.

48. Frederick Gookin, *Daniel Gookin, 1612–1687* (Chicago: privately printed, 1912)), 161, 165. The outline of Gookin's history of New England is printed in ibid, 162–64. Lord Culpepper was passing through Boston, which is why he could be "affected." The manuscript of "Indian Converts" is at Massachusetts Historical Society; the manuscript copy (a nineteenth-century copy of an older manuscript of "Historical Account of the Doings and Sufferings" printed by the American Antiquarian Society is in the AAS library and was printed in *Archaeologia Americana. Transactions and Collections of the American Antiquarian Society* 2 (1836).

49. *Coll. MHS* 4th ser. 8 (1868): 375.

50. Davenport, *The Power of Congregational Churches* (London, 1672), sig. A3r. The "M.N." could be Nathaniel Mather of Dublin, concealing himself at a time of political difficulties; Davenport's papers had passed to the Mather family. Paget's defense of Presbyterianism had been published in 1641.

51. Michael G. Hall, *The Last American Puritan: The Life of Increase Mather* (Hanover, N.H.: Wesleyan University Press, 1988), 103, noting that ignorance of these sequences has misled modern readers. As Peter Stallybrass pointed out to me, the English book trade relied heavily on "old" books. For eighteenth-century re-printings in the context of evangelical revivals, see Susan O'Brien, "Eighteenth-Century Publishing Networks in the First Years of Transatlantic Evangelicalism," in *Evangelicalism: Comparative Studies of Popular Protestantism in North America, the British Isles, and Beyond, 1700–1900*, ed. Mark A. Noll, David W. Bebbington, and George A. Rawlyk (New York: Oxford University Press, 1994), 38–57.

52. As noted by Brown, *Pilgrim and the Bee*, 95, referencing mainly eighteenth-century imprints.

53. Amory and Hall, *Colonial Book*, ch. 3. A more specific analysis of Mather's imprints follows in Chapter 4.

54. This argument is influenced by recent scholarship on censorship and licensing in seventeenth-century England; for citations, see David D. Hall and Alexandra Walsham, "'Justification by Print Alone'? Protestantism, Literacy, and Communications in the Anglo-American World of John Winthrop," in *The World of John Winthrop: Essays on England and New England 1588–1649*, ed. Francis J. Bremer and Lynn A. Botelho (Boston: Massachusetts Historical Society, 2006), 381 n. 108. That licensers could approve a text while altering its contents is superbly demonstrated in Anthony Milton, "Licensing, Censorship, and Religious Orthodoxy in Early Stuart England," *The Historical Journal* 41 (1998): 625–51.

55. Bartholomew Green, *Printers Advertisement* ([Boston, 1700]; [Benjamin Colman et al.], *Gospel Order Revived* ([New York? 1700?]); Clyde Augustus Duniway, *The Development of Freedom of the Press in Massachusetts* (New York: Longmans, Green, 1906), 74–75. The reference is to Solomon Stoddard, *The Doctrine of Instituted Churches* (London, 1700); *A Manifesto or Declaration* was anonymous and printed without colophon (Boston, 1699?).

56. *Acts of the Commissioners of the United Colonies of New England, 1643–1679*, ed. David Pulsifer, vols. 9–10 of *Records of the Colony of New Plymouth*, ed. N. B. Shurtleff, 11 vols. (Boston, 1855–61), 10: 176–77.

57. *Some Seasonable Considerations for the Good People of Connecticut* (1694); the place of printing was not identified; reprinted in *Collections of the Connecticut Historical Society* 1 (1860): 84; the two writers are indicated by initials at the end of their "To the Reader."

58. As members of Third Church Boston was doing (they also gave away books in abundance); Mark A. Peterson, *The Price of Redemption: The Spiritual Economy of Puritan New England* (Cambridge, Mass.: Harvard University Press, 1997), 90–92.

59. Hall, *Last American Puritan*, 166; *Coll. MHS* 4th ser. 8 (1868): 90, 95–96, 97–98, among many other references.

60. Cotton Mather, *Magnalia Christi Americana Books I and II*, ed. Kenneth B. Murdock (Cambridge, Mass.: Harvard University Press, 1977), 89.

61. "Gods Controversy with New England," mss., Massachusetts Historical Society; the visual difference is not reproduced in *The Poems of Michael Wigglesworth*, ed. Ronald A. Bosco (Lanham, Md.: University Press of America, 1989), but see p. 311.

62. Their own term for the style they preferred, but one that must not exclude the richly symbolic and baroque modes of writing (and art) they also practiced.

63. [Increase Mather], *The Life and Death . . . of Richard Mather* (Cambridge, Mass., 1670), 31; Samuel Willard, *The Truly Blessed Man* (Boston, 1700), 6.

64. [John Lilburne], *A Worke of the Beast* ([London], 1638), reprinted in *Tracts on Liberty in the Puritan Revolution 1638–1647*, ed. William Haller, 3 vols. (New York: Columbia University Press, 1934), 2: 21–22.

65. Kenneth Murdock, *Handkerchiefs from Paul Being Pious and Consolatory Verses of Puritan Massachusetts* (Cambridge, Mass.: Harvard University Press, 1927), 25; James Fitch to Increase Mather, May 1679, *Coll. MHS* 4th ser. 8 (1868): 473.

66. Murdock, *Handkerchiefs from Paul*, 25; Thomas Cobbet, *A Fruitfull and Usefull Discourse* (London, 1656), sig. A3r. See also Hall, *Worlds of Wonder*, ch. 1; Brown, *Pilgrim and the Bee*, ch. 1.

67. Referring to late sixteenth-century English writers, Harold O. White notes that most of them "opposed only what classical critics had pointed out as incorrect: piracy, secrecy, perversity, servility, superficiality. And of all those who demanded originality of invention, not one used the term in its modern sense of individual fabrication. All sought originality . . . through individual adaptation, reinterpretation, and, if possible, improvement of the best." White, *Plagiarism and Imitation During the English Renaissance* (Cambridge, Mass.: Harvard University Press, 1935), 119.

68. Davenport, *The Saints Anchor-hold, in All Storms and Tempests* (London, 1661), sig. A3r.

69. As Thomas Fugill, the secretary of New Haven Colony, was when he gave himself a larger allotment of land, reworking documents to do so. *Records of the Colony or Jurisdiction of New Haven*, ed. Hoadly, 1: 221–24.

70. Increase Mather, *The First Principles of New-England* (Cambridge, 1675), sig. a2r.

71. Were this a fuller rendering of authorship and writing, it would be impossible to ignore the continuing presence of the classical tradition and its consequences for how both were understood. The Michael Wigglesworth who incorporated the voice of the living God into his verse was also the Michael Wigglesworth who, for his master's thesis at Harvard, described "Eloquence" as the sum of rhetorical strategies that owed nothing to the Bible or the Holy Spirit. The thesis is printed in Samuel Eliot Morison, *Harvard College in the Seventeenth Century*, 2 vols. (Cambridge, Mass.: Harvard University Press, 1936), 1: 180–83.

CHAPTER 2. NOT IN PRINT YET PUBLISHED

1. The single manuscript copy (New-York Historical Society) is not in Winthrop's handwriting and may have an English provenance. Hugh Dawson, "John Winthrop's Rite of Passage: The Origins of the 'Christian Charitie' Discourse," *Early American Literature* 26 (1991): 219–31.

2. The seventeenth-century minister-historian William Hubbard attributed it to John White of Dorchester, an early supporter of the Massachusetts Bay Company and author of the promotional tract *The Planters Plea* (London, 1630); Hubbard, *A General History of New England* (Boston: Massachusetts Historical Society, 1848), 126.

3. *The Letter-book of Samuel Sewall, Coll. MHS* 6th ser. 2 (1888): 39.

4. "General Observations for the Plantation of New England," *Winthrop Papers*, 2: 111–49; 3: 188; 4: 25; Winthrop, *Journal*, 443.

5. In what follows I ignore the material and technological aspects of handwriting. As Peter Stallybrass pointed out during the course of the lecture series in Philadelphia, important changes occurred in the seventeenth century in the instruments used for writing. Some of this story is told in Harold Love, *Scribal Publication in Seventeenth-Century England* (Oxford: Clarendon Press, 1993); H. R. Woudhuysen, *Sir Philip Sidney and the Circulation of Manuscripts, 1558–1640* (Oxford: Clarendon Press, 1996), ch. 2; and Peter Beal, *In Praise of Scribes: Manuscripts and their Makers in Seventeenth-Century England* (Oxford: Clarendon Press, 1998).

6. See also David D. Hall, "Scribal Publication in Seventeenth-Century New England: An Introduction and a Checklist," *Proc. AAS* 115 (2006): 29–80, for descriptions of other scribal texts not cited in what follows.

7. Manuscript Book of Records, Guilford, Connecticut, quoted in William K. Holdsworth, "Law and Society in Colonial Connecticut, 1636–1672" (Ph.D. diss., Claremont Graduate School, 1974), 125; William Brigham, *The Compact with the Charter and Laws of the Colony of New Plymouth* (Boston, 1836), 121.

8. Francis C. Gray, "Remarks on the Early Laws of Massachusetts Bay; with the Code adopted in 1641, and called The Body of Liberties, now first printed," *Coll. MHS* 3rd ser. 8 (1843): 191–237; *Recs. Mass.*, 1: 344.

9. Roger Williams, *The Bloudy Tenent, of Persecution, for cause of Conscience, discussed* ([London], 1644), 118–239; J. Hammond Trumbull, ed., The *Public Records of the Colony of Connecticut*, 3 vols. (Hartford, 1850–59), 1: 302.

10. *Coll. MHS* 1st ser. 5 (1798): 61–79; *Coll. MHS* 3rd ser. 1 (1826): 126–33. The manuscript of the Brattle letter cannot be located at the present time.

11. Too many to enumerate, sermon notes survive in many research collections, the most famous set being Robert Keayne's notes on sermons preached in Boston in the late 1630s, which he had bound up in leather (Massachusetts Historical Society). Several book-length collections of sermon notes are preserved in the Gratz Collection, Historical Society of Pennsylvania; John Cotton (Jr.)'s notes of 1648 on sermons in Boston are preserved in a $5^{1}/_{4} \times 3^{3}/_{4}$ leather bound book with clasps (New York Historical Society). See also

Winfried Herget, "The Transcription and Transmission of the Hooker Corpus," in *Thomas Hooker: Writings in England and Holland, 1626–1633*, ed. George H. Williams et al. (Cambridge, Mass.: Harvard University Press, 1975), 253–70; Herget, "Writing After the Ministers: The Significance of Sermon Notes," *Studies in New England Puritanism*, ed. Winfried Herget (Frankfurt: Lang, 1983), 113–38.

12. *Winthrop Papers*, 5: 33, 39, among many examples.

13. A paper bill of credit of 1690 is reproduced in *Proc. MHS* 6 (1863), between pages 428 and 429.

14. Woudhuysen, *Sir Philip Sidney*, 147–49.

15. Peter Lake and David Como, "Puritans, Antinomians and Laudians in Caroline London: The Strange Case of Peter Shaw in its Contexts," *Journal of Ecclesiastical History* 50 (1999): 4.

16. A fuller description of such texts appears in Chapter 5.

17. *Proc. MHS* 9 (1866–67): 485–501; ibid., 12 (1872–75): 419–27.

18. Love, *Scribal Publication*, ch. 5.

19. Ibid., 70–79.

20. Ibid., 83–89.

21. Henry Wolcott of Windsor, Connecticut took notes on sermons in shorthand; Douglas H. Shepard, "The Wolcott Shorthand Notebook Transcribed" (Ph.D. diss., State University of Iowa, 1957).

22. William Aspinwall, *Aspinwall Notorial Records, Records Relating to the Early History of Boston* 32 (Boston: Boston Record Commissioners, 1903); "Note-book kept by Thomas Lechford, Esq.," *Archaeologia Americana: Transactions and Collections of the American Antiquarian Society* 7 (1885); Sargent Bush, Jr., *The Correspondence of John Cotton* (Chapel Hill: University of North Carolina Press, 2000), 68–70; for John Higginson, see below and the case study of Thomas Hooker in Chapter 4. In the late 1630s Lechford was making copies of petitions, instruments of debt, letters, deeds, and other kinds of documents.

23. "Note-book kept by Thomas Lechford, Esq.," 237, 244.

24. See below, note 41.

25. As emphasized by Love, *Scribal Publication*. See also Margaret P. Lannay, "The Countess of Pembroke's Agency in Print and Scribal Culture," in *Women's Writing and the Circulation of Ideas: Manuscript Publication in England, 1550–1800*, ed. George L. Justice and Nathan Tinker (Cambridge: Cambridge University Press, 2002), 17–49.

26. Peter Lake and Michael Questier, "Puritans, Papists, and the 'Public Sphere' in Early Modern England: The Edmund Campion Affair in Context," *Journal of Modern History* 72 (2000): 603–4.

27. John Cotton, *The Way of the Churches . . . Cleared* (London, 1648), reprinted in Larzer Ziff, *John Cotton on the Churches of New England* (Cambridge, Mass.: Harvard University Press, 1968), 217.

28. Winthrop, *Journal*, 423; 443; John Cotton, *Sermon . . . Delivered at Salem, 1636* (Boston, 1713), reprinted in Ziff, *John Cotton on the Churches*, 43.

29. *Coll. MHS* 4th ser. 8 (1868): 82–84 (one of several examples).

30. *Letter-book of Samuel Sewall*, passim.

31. Otho T. Beall, Jr., "Cotton Mather's Early 'Curiosa Americana' and the Boston Philosophical Society of 1683," *William and Mary Quarterly*, 3rd ser. 18 (1961): 360–72.

32. Thomas Hutchinson, *A Collection of Original Papers Relative to the History of the Colony of Massachusets-Bay* (Boston, 1769), 477–503.

33. *The Complete Works of Anne Bradstreet*, ed. Joseph R. McElrath and Allan P. Robb (Boston: Twayne Publishers, 1981), 526.

34. Mss., Houghton Library, Harvard University, printed in Kenneth B. Murdock, *Handkerchiefs from Paul Being Pious and Consolatory Verses of Puritan Massachusetts* (Cambridge, Mass.: Harvard University Press, 1927).

35. Mss., Thomas Shepard Papers, Houghton Library, Harvard University. Shepard mentioned manuscripts in his will, printed in John Albro, "Life of Thomas Shepard," Shepard, *Works*, 1: clxxviii. William Greenhill and Samuel Mather used language so similar in their preface to the posthumously published *Subjection to Christ* (London, 1652) that I surmise Shepard had shared a copy with Greenhill.

36. The history of this text remains elusive; no record survives of a seventeenth-century printing; the earliest to survive dates from 1770.

37. [Joshua Scottow], *A Narrative Of The Planting of the Massachusetts Colony Anno 1628* (Boston, 1694); reprinted in *Coll. MHS*, 4th ser. 4 (1858): 293.

38. Everett Emerson, *Letters from New England: The Massachusetts Bay Colony, 1629–1638* (Amherst: University of Massachusetts Press, 1976), 67, 167; Paul S. Seaver, *Wallington's World: A Puritan Artisan in Seventeenth-Century London* (Stanford: Stanford University Press, 1985), 207.

39. "Letter-book of William Bradford," *Coll. MHS* 1st ser. 3 (1810): 27–76.

40. Winthrop, *Journal*, 393–94; the relation has apparently not survived.

41. Frank Thistlethwaite, *Dorset Pilgrims: The Story of West Country Pilgrims Who Went to New England in the 17th Century* (London: Barrie & Jennings, 1989), 41; Bush, *Correspondence of John Cotton*, 141–49, 347.

42. For these titles, see the case study of Cotton in Chapter 4.

43. B. R. Burg, *Richard Mather of Dorchester* (Lexington: University Press of Kentucky, 1976), 176 n. 11; 177 n. 26; Walker, *Creeds*, 289–90.

44. Emerson, *Letters*, 224.

45. Samuel Rutherford, *The Due Right of Presbyteries* (London, 1644).

46. Winthrop, *Journal*, 608–9.

47. Ibid., 343–44; *Collections of the Connecticut Historical Society* 2 (1870): 73–81; Hamilton Andrew Hill, *History of the Old South Church*, 2 vols. (Boston, 1890), 1: 50–89.

48. Israel Stoughton's letter is printed in *Proc. MHS 58* (1925): 446–58; for Saltonstall, see Chapter 5.

49. *The Andros Papers*, ed. W. H. Whitmore, 3 vols. (Boston: Prince Society, 1868–74), 1: 23–24. Also printed in Boston (anonymously) as *The Present State of New England, impartially considered in a Letter to the Clergy*, signed F. L. without printer or date.

50. John Coffey, *Politics, Religion and the British Revolutions: The Mind of Samuel Rutherford* (Cambridge: Cambridge University Press, 1997), 26 and n. 142.

51. *Thomas Hooker Writings*, ed. Williams, 4.

52. [Cotton Mather], *The Temple Opening* (Boston, 1709), 30–31.

53. Jonathan Mitchell, *A Discourse of the Glory To which God hath called Beleevers By Jesus Christ* (London, 1671), second pagination, 1–21; *Mr. Mitchel's Letter to His Brother* (Boston? 1732?), 19–22.

54. Robert Trent, "'The Deuil Came Upon me like a Lyon': A 1697 Cambridge Deathbed Narrative," Connecticut Historical Society, *Bulletin* 48 (1983): 115–19.

55. John Whiting drew on a biography by Davenport (possibly an extended sermon) for his life of Cotton; Alexander Young, *Chronicles of the First Planters of the Colony of Massachusetts Bay* (Boston, 1846), 419; Thomas Hutchinson had seen a "life of John Wilson." Hutchinson, *The History of the Colony and Province of Massachusetts-Bay*, ed. Lawrence S. Mayo, 3 vols. (Cambridge, Mass.: Harvard University Press, 1936), 1: 54 n.

56. Cotton Mather, *Early Religion, Urged* (Boston, 1694), 96, 85–95.

57. Mss., Connecticut Historical Society.

58. Murdock, *Handkerchiefs from Paul*, 25.

59. Timothy Alden, *A Collection of American Epitaphs* (New York, 1814), 3: 42–49 (a reference I owe to Jantz, *First Century*, 273).

60. Walker, "Captan Perse & his coragios Company," ed. Diane Bornstein, *Proc. AAS* 83 (1973): 65–102; Jantz, *First Century*, 211–12; *PCSM* 10 (1904–6): 191–205.

61. *The Diary of Samuel Sewall*, ed. M. Halsey Thomas, 2 vols. (New York: Farrar, Straus and Giroux, 1973), 2: 213 and passim; *Letter-book of Samuel Sewall*, 2: 175; Jantz, *First Century*, 226–27, 218, 219. Sewall's commonplace book (mss., New-York Historical Society) incorporates texts he received in printed and manuscript form.

62. Jantz, *First Century*, 287, 219.

63. [Bartholomew Green], *The Printers Advertisement* (Boston, 1700); *Winthrop Papers*, 5: 103–5; "Note-book of Thomas Lechford," 48–49; for Hooker, see Chapter 4.

64. The several drafts are compared in a model of comparative text study, *Winthrop Papers*, 2: 106–49.

65. *Edward Taylor vs. Solomon Stoddard: The Nature of the Lord's Supper* volume 2 of *The Unpublished Writings of Edward Taylor*, ed. Thomas M. and Virginia L. Davis (Boston: Twayne, 1981), 12; the Davises point out that subsequent manuscript critiques by Taylor were not shared with Stoddard or Increase Mather (p. 30).

66. Common-place books require a fuller analysis than I am able to provide in this chapter.

67. Mss, Connecticut State Library.

68. George Selement, "John Cotton's Hidden Antinomianism: His Sermon on Revelation 4: 1–2," *NEHGR* 129 (1975): 278–94.

69. *The Notebook of the Reverend John Fiske, 1644–1675*, ed. Robert G. Pope, *PCSM* 47 (Boston: Colonial Society, 1974): 162; John L. Sibley, *Biographical Sketches of Graduates of Harvard University*, 3 vols. (Cambridge 1873–85), 1: 311–12.

70. Roger Thompson, *Sex in Middlesex: Popular Mores in a Massachusetts County, 1649–1699* (Amherst: University of Massachusetts Press, 1986), 180–82, 185–86.

71. Frederick Gookin, *Daniel Gookin, 1612–1687* (Chicago: privately printed, 1912), between pages 154–55.

72. *Collections, Historical and Miscellaneous: and Monthly Literary Journal*, ed. John Farmer and J. B. Moore, 3 (1824): 30–32.

73. *Edward Randolph*, 7 vols. (Boston: Prince Society, 1898–1909), 3: 277. See also *Coll. MHS* 4th ser. 8 (1868): 483.

74. English practice is richly described in David Colclough, *Freedom of Speech in Early Stuart England* (Cambridge: Cambridge University Press, 2005), 199–238; see also the scholarship cited on p. 217, n. 13.

75. Thomas Knoles and Lucia Zaucha Knoles, "'In Usum Pupillorum': Student-Transcribed Texts at Harvard College Before 1740," *Proc. AAS* 109 (1999): 333–472; quote, 335. See also Rick Kennedy, ed., *Aristotelian and Cartesian Logic at Harvard: Charles Morton's A Logick System & William Brattle's Compendium of Logic*, PCSM 67 (Boston: The Society, 1995); *Charles Morton's Compendium Physicae*, PCSM 33 (Boston: The Society, 1940).

76. William C. Lane, "Manuscript Laws of Harvard College," *PCSM* 25 (1924): 244–53; *Coll. MHS* 4th ser. 8 (1868): 516.

77. Samuel Willard, *Brief Directions to a Young Scholar Designing the Ministry* (Boston 1735), i; the two editors, Joseph Sewall and Thomas Prince, remarked that they had compared "several copies."

78. Glenn W. LaFantasie, ed., *The Correspondence of Roger Williams*, 2 vols. (Hanover, N. H.: University Press of New England, 1988), 2: 479. Bulkeley's "Will and Doom" is printed in *Collections of the Connecticut Historical Society* 3 (1895): 79–269, from the one surviving copy (Public Record Office, London, forwarded by Lord Cornbury, the royal governor of New York, in 1704).

79. *Coll. MHS* 6th ser. 5 (1892): 35.

80. Mather thanked Hubbard in the preface to *Johannes in Eremo* (Boston, 1695).

81. Hugh Amory, "A Boston Society Library: The Old South Church and Thomas Prince," in Amory, *Bibliography and the Book Trades: Studies in the Print Culture of Early New England*, ed. David D. Hall (Philadelphia: University of Pennsylvania Press, 2004), 146–62.

82. William A. Saunders, "Correspondence Relative to 'The History of Massachusetts Bay,' Between Its Author, Gov. Thomas Hutchinson, and Rev. Ezra Stiles," *NEHGR* 26 (1872): 162, 164; the history of printed versions is noted in Hall, *Antinomian Controversy*, 153.

83. As Ronald Huebert points out in "Privacy: The Early Social History of a Word," *Sewanee Review* 105 (1997): 20–38, privacy and private overlap but are not identical, though used indifferently by sixteenth- and seventeenth-century writers. My emphasis falls on private. I owe this citation to Claire Preston, *Thomas Browne and the Writing of Early Modern Science* (Cambridge: Cambridge University Press, 2005); see also her discussion of the private, pp. 19–23.

84. John Cotton, *The Bloudy Tenent, Washed, And made white* (London, 1647), 2.

85. [Mary Rowlandson], *The Sovereignty & Goodness of God* (Cambridge, 1682), sig. A3 r.

86. I.H., "To the Christian Reader," in John Cotton, *The Powring Out of the Seven Vials* (London, 1642), sig A2r, v.

87. Hall, *Antinomian Controversy*, 319; Walker, *Creeds*, 227; the next verse indicates the possibilities for discipline becoming public.

88. Ibid., 289.

89. "The Commonplace Book of Joseph Green," ed. Samuel Eliot Morison, *PCSM* 34 (Boston: The Society, 1943): 233.

90. Woudhuysen, *Sir Philip Sidney*, 147.

91. William Prynne, John Lilburne, and other dissidents of the 1630s also relied on surreptitious printing; for the colonists' awareness of their activities, see Chapter 5.

92. The textual history of this sermon is discussed in Chapter 4.

93. J. W. Saunders, "The Stigma of Print: A Note on the Social Bases of Tudor Poetry," *Essays in Criticism* 1 (1951): 139–64; but see Steven W. May, "Tudor Aristocrats and the Mythical 'Stigma of Print'," *Renaissance Papers* 10 (1980): 11–18.

94. Increase Mather, *The Mystery of Israel's Salvation* (London, 1669), sig. A2r, v.

95. See Chapter 5.

96. On Child, see Chapter 5; Winthrop, *Journal*, 484.

97. *Coll. MHS* 1st ser. 1 (1792): 106.

98. *Winthrop Papers*, 4: 403.

99. E.g., ibid., 3: 190–91.

100. Walker, *Creeds*, 92. Handwritten copies of the Massachusetts Bay Company charter of 1629 are described in *The Founding of Massachusetts: Selections from the Sources* (Boston: Massachusetts Historical Society, 1930), 19–30, evidence that bears on how the charter was employed in political situations.

101. Some of Mather's citations are corrected in Cotton Mather, *Magnalia Christi Americana Books I and II*, ed. Kenneth B. Murdock (Cambridge, Mass.: Harvard University Press, 1977).

102. Morse's testimony is printed from the original manuscript in David D. Hall, *Witch-hunting in Seventeenth-Century New England: A Documentary History, 1638–1692* (Boston: Northeastern University Press, 1991), 231–33; the headnote (p. 231 n. 2) indicates a key difference.

103. *The Hutchinson Papers*, ed. W. H. Whitmore, 2 vols. (Albany, N.Y.: Prince Society, 1865), 2: 205.

104. For this letter and the errors in it, see Chapter 3.

105. Mss., Massachusetts Historical Society; "Letter-book of William Bradford," 1 *Coll. MHS* 3 (1798): 48.

106. Hill, *History of the Old South*, 1: 33, 44–45.

107. Burg, *Richard Mather*, 176 n. 14.

108. John Mason, *A Brief History of the Pequot War: Especially Of the memorable*

Taking of their Fort at Mistick in Connecticut In 1637 (Boston, 1736), v; Mather, *Magnalia*, 1: 330, referring to *A Discourse about Civil Government in a New Plantation Whose Design is Religion* (Cambridge, 1663), with John Cotton's name on the title page.

109. *Coll. MHS* 4th ser. 8 (1868): 100–110; Holmes, *Cotton Mather*, 3: Appendix A.

110. John Cotton, *A Sermon Preached by the Reverend Mr. John Cotton Deliver'd at Salem 1636* (Boston, 1713); Hall, *Antinomian Controversy*, 263, 412.

111. Winthrop, *Journal*, 193–95, 197; 200, 203; *Winthrop Papers*, 3: 326–32.

112. Hall, *Antinomian Controversy*, 210–11.

113. Winthrop, *Journal*, 206. The "Elders Reply" and Cotton's "Rejoynder" were printed for the first time in Hall, *Antinomian Controversy*, from a manuscript at the Massachusetts Historical Society.

114. Ibid., 249–50; John Wheelwright, *A Brief, and Plain Apology by John Wheelwright* (London, 1658), quoted in Sargent Bush, Jr., "John Wheelwright's Forgotten *Apology*: The Last Word in the Antinomian Controversy," *New England Quarterly* 64 (1991): 31, 33; Sargent Bush, Jr., "Revising what we have done amisse': John Cotton and John Wheelwright, 1640," *William and Mary Quarterly*, 3rd ser. 45 (1988): 745.

115. Winthrop, *Journal*, 219; Hall, *Antinomian Controversy*, 283, 251.

116. For the locations and nineteenth-century printings, see Hall, *Antinomian Controversy*, 153.

117. Hall, *Antinomian Controversy*, 283; Bush, "John Wheelwright's Forgotten *Apology*," 31 n. 4; Samuel Groom, *A Glass For the People of New England* ([London?], 1676), 6–8. Groom also had a copy of Wheelwright's fast day sermon, from which he quoted (pp. 19–21).

118. *Winthrop Papers*, 3: 392.

119. Three manuscript versions of Cotton's answers to the sixteen questions survive, one at the Massachusetts Historical Society, another in the British Library, and a third in the Hartlib Papers, Rylands Library, University of Manchester (a reference I owe to Francis Bremer).

120. The minister-antiquarian Thomas Prince had seen "An ancient Record of the first New-England Synod, viz. at Cambridge, 1637." Thomas Prince, *A Chronological History of New-England*, ed. Samuel G. Drake (1746; Boston, 1852), xvii.

121. Hutchinson, *History of . . . Massachusetts Bay*, 1: 63; Hall, *Antinomian Controversy*, 301–3, 305, 351–52; the reference to a "Recantation" in Hooker's letter (quoted in Hutchinson) is amplified as being "under her hand" in Cotton's *Way . . . Cleared*, in ibid., 423.

122. *Winthrop Papers*, 4: 23; Winthrop, *Journal*, 254; Hall, *Antinomian Controversy*, 280–82; Valerie Pearl and Morris Pearl, eds. "Governor John Winthrop on the Birth of the Antinomians' 'Monster': The Earliest Reports to Reach England and the Making of a Myth," *Proc. MHS* 102 (1990): 21–37.

123. "Conclusions" refer to the arguments of the Antinomians.

124. Hutchinson, *History of . . . Massachusetts-Bay*, 1: 60–61.

125. Hall, *Antinomian Controversy*, 174.

126. Or six if we count the texts arising out of the disputed law of 1637 concerning who could be received as immigrants into the colony; these were printed for the first time in Hutchinson, *Collection of Original Papers*.

127. See *Winthrop Papers*, 4: 8–9 (the dating of this document remains in doubt).

128. *Winthrop Papers*, 3: 326–32, 415–16; Hall, *Antinomian Controversy*, 400 (a document that does not seem to survive).

129. *Winthrop Papers*, 3: 324.

130. Hall, *Antinomian Controversy*, 284; Bush, "John Wheelwright's Forgotten *Apology*," 32–33; Winthrop, *Journal*, 216.

131. Hall, *Antinomian Controversy*, 321, 327.

132. The comparison may be followed in Hall, *Antinomian Controversy*, 46–59; the Charles Deane copy (John Carter Brown Library) of *Severall Questions* has his note suggesting Cotton's authorship.

133. Hall, *Antinomian Controversy*, 173–98.

134. A detailed analysis may be found in Mary Jane Lewis, "A Sweet Sacrifice: Civil War in New England" (Ph.D. diss., Syracuse University, 1986), with findings (of possible changes in words and certainly of omissions) too complex to be cited in detail; she may overlook Winthrop's routine practice of writing entries retrospectively. Lewis has also analyzed other documents emerging from the controversy—for example, comparing the two versions of the "examination" of Anne Hutchinson for evidence of alterations or suppression. Her work is a significant complement to my own description. See also Selement, "John Cotton's Hidden Antinomianism," 281 n. 18, pointing out changes between the two reports of the examination.

135. A conclusion put more hesitantly in Bush, "John Wheelwright's Forgotten *Apology*," 42–44.

136. Quoted in John Gorham Palfrey, *History of New England*, 5 vols. (Boston, 1858–90), 1: 173 n.

137. Modern historians have usually ignored the "some" and attributed the text to a single author, Winthrop.

138. George H. Moore, "Work and Materials for American History—Continued," *Historical Journal*, 2nd ser. 3 (1868): 26–27. "Mr Higginsons petition is thus answered: Wee can find no record about the matter of this petition, but that the petitioner might have liberty to print it, & make his best of it, which is the answere now to this petition; if any particular person disswaded him from the printing of it, and thereby occasioned his losse, they, and not the Court, are to give him satisfaction." *Recs. Mass.* 2: 52.

139. Giles Firmin, quoted in Moore, "Work and Materials," 27. Several decades later, the Boston minister Charles Chauncy had seen an ""ancient Manuscript Copy" of the synod of 1637's deliberations, and perhaps much more, from which he quoted in *Seasonable Thoughts on the State of Religion in New-England* (Boston, 1743) a passage not otherwise available (p. vi).

140. "Authorship of the 'Short Story'," *Historical Magazine* 1 (1857): 321–24. Charles Francis Adams, Jr., who personally knew the participants, told the story of Savage's cam-

paign and the responses it provoked in his introduction to *Antinomianism in the Colony of Massachusetts Bay, 1636–1638* (Boston: Prince Society, 1894); citing attributions to Winthrop by Robert Baillie and Samuel Rutherford, Adams agreed with Savage's critics that Winthrop prepared the book (pp. 37–64).

141. Bush, "John Wheelwright's Forgotten *Apology*," 24, 30, 39, 40. Cotton Mather attributed the book to Weld, as did Samuel Groom.

142. Winthrop, *Journal*, 107, 109.

143. Winthrop, *Journal*, 460; *Winthrop Papers*, 3: 146–49; Winslow, *Hypocrisie Unmasked*, 57.

144. *Baptist Piety: The Last Will & Testimony of Obadiah Holmes*, ed. Edwin S. Gaustad (New York: Arno Press, 1980), 85–92.

145. Rufus M. Jones, *The Quakers in the American Colonies* (London: Macmillan, 1911), 78.

146. Ibid., 30–31.

147. George Bishop, *New England Judged* (London, 1661), 8; Joseph Felt, *The Ecclesiastical History of New England,* 2 vols. (Boston, 1855–62), 2: 145–46.

148. Jones, *Quakers in the American Colonies*, 67, 69; James Bowden, *The History of the Society of Friends in America*, 2 vols. (London, 1850–58), 1: 90–91.

149. Mss., Buffum Family Manuscripts, Massachusetts Historical Society.

150. The verse autobiography has never been published (mss., New England Historical and Genealogical Society); the prose version was printed in *NEHGR* 8 (1854): 147–56.

151. Mather's indifferent memory is noted in Jantz, *First Century*, 258.

152. The indispensable source of information on poetry writing remains Jantz, *First Century*; for problems of attribution, see pp. 184, 185, 203, 213, 216, 228–230, 242.

153. Quoted in Peter White, *Benjamin Tompson, Colonial Bard: A Critical Edition* (University Park: Pennsylvania State University Press, 1980), 30.

154. Ibid., 57; mss., Massachusetts Historical Society; Peter White names this the "Edward Tompson manuscript" after the donor of 1895.

155. Joseph Tompson filled a blank unbound book with copies of eleven poems written in Massachusetts before 1715, five by his sister Anna Hayden and three by Benjamin Tompson, together with religious reflections of his own. For a fuller analysis, see Matthew P. Brown, *The Pilgrim and the Bee: Reading Rituals and Book Culture in Early New England* (Philadelphia: University of Pennsylvania Press, 2007), 60–67.

156. White, *Benjamin Tompson*, 157–58.

157. Ibid., 168–75.

158. I rely on Thomas M. Davis, *A Reading of Edward Taylor* (Newark: University of Delaware Press, 1992), 15–17; ch. 2. Donald E. Stanford, ed., *The Poems of Edward Taylor* (New Haven, Conn.: Yale University Press, 1960), describes the contents of this manuscript and others in "Appendix 2: Manuscripts." Taylor took similar pains to preserve what amounts to a fair copy, bound in vellum, of his sermon series on the nature of Christ, the "Christographia." Norman Grabo, ed., *Edward Taylor's Christographia* (New Haven: Yale University Press, 1962), xlv–xlvi. The manuscripts themselves are in the Beinecke Library, Yale University.

159. Thomas M. and Virginia L. Davis, *Edward Taylor's Minor Poetry volume 3 of The Unpublished Writings of Edward Taylor* (Boston: Twayne, 1981), xxi.

160. Thomas M. Davis, "Edward Taylor's Elegy on Deacon David Dewey," *Proc. AAS* 96 (1987): 75–84.

161. Elegies and this verse appear in initial pages of the manuscript (Beinecke Library, Yale University), but Stanford excluded most of them from his edition of the poems.

162. *NEHGR* 5 (1851): 385.

163. The second dialogue has not survived. The third is available as Charles Deane, "Governor Bradford's Dialogue between Old Men and Young Men, concerning 'The Church and the Government thereof'," *Proc. MHS* 6 (1870): 407–64.

164. For general information, see "The Bradford Manuscripts" in William Bradford, *History of Plymouth Plantation*, 2 vols. (Boston: Massachusetts Historical Society, 1912), 2: 431ff.

165. It is possible that Willett's copy text was someone else's transcription from the "booke," but the proximity of Bradford's death and the dating of Willett's version makes this unlikely.

166. Michael Gracen Runyan, "The Poetry of William Bradford: An Annotated Edition with Essays Introductory to the Poems" (Ph.D. diss., University of California, Los Angeles, 1970), 259–62; these manuscripts are at the Massachusetts Historical Society.

167. *Plymouth Church Records*, 2 vols. (Boston: Colonial Society of Massachusetts, 1920), 1: 62–63, a poem composed c. 1626, the year of Robinson's death.

168. Nathaniel Morton, *New Englands Memoriall* (Cambridge, 1669), sig A3v.

169. Edward Arber, *The Story of The Pilgrim Fathers 1606–1623 AD* (London, 1897), 432.

170. For example, the writer refers (p. 83) to "here in England" and, alluding again to England (p. 77) "our bridges." Charles Deane shared my doubts that Bradford wrote this poem; Deane, "Governor Bradford's 'Dialogue'," 466n.

171. Douglas Anderson, *William Bradford's Books Of Plimmoth Plantation and the Printed Word* (Baltimore: Johns Hopkins University Press, 2003), suggests that Bradford intentionally withheld the manuscript from the book trades as "the best way to ensure its immediate survival" (p. 247), a speculation linked to another, that Bradford was alarmed by the suppression of William Pynchon's book.

172. Richard S. Dunn, introduction, Winthrop, *Journal*, xx–xxi; *Winthrop Papers*, 2: 157.

173. Henry Dunster Notebook, mss., Massachusetts Historical Society; *Winthrop Papers* 3: 338–44.

174. *Winthrop Papers*, 3: 327.

175. Richard S. Dunn, "John Winthrop Writes His Journal," *William and Mary Quarterly*, 3rd ser. 41 (1984): 185–212.

176. Hall, *Worlds of Wonder*, ch. 2.

177. *Winthrop Papers*, 4: 183 (endorsed "Mr Shepard about the History").

178. G. H. Turnbull, "Robert Child," *PCSM* 38 (1943): 53.

CHAPTER 3. SOCIAL AUTHORSHIP AND THE MAKING OF PRINTED TEXTS

1. Winthrop, *Journal*, 402; Cotton, *The Powring out of the Seven Vials* (London, 1642).

2. The letter was quoted by Giles Firmin, *The Real Christian* (London, 1670), and is quoted anew in John A. Albro, "Life of Thomas Shepard," in Shepard, *Works*, 1: clxxxvi.

3. H. S. Bennett, *English Books & Readers 1603 to 1640 Being a Study in the History of the Book Trade in the Reigns of James I and Charles I* (Cambridge: Cambridge University Press, 1970), ch. 4.

4. David Scott Kastan, *Shakespeare and the Book* (New York: Cambridge University Press, 2001), ch. 2.

5. Margaret J. M. Ezell, *Social Authorship and the Advent of Print* (Baltimore: Johns Hopkins University Press, 1999), where the phrase is introduced with particular reference to handwritten texts; Stephen B. Dobranski, *Milton, Authorship, and the Book Trade* (Cambridge: Cambridge University Press, 199), ch. 1.

6. I. H., "To the Christian Reader," Cotton, *Powring Out of the Seven Vials* (London, 1642), sig. A2r, v.

7. A phrase Thomas Shepard transferred to the spiritual condition of his congregation: "for every Christian is not a fair copy." Shepard, *Works*, 1:138.

8. "Note-book kept by Thomas Lechford, Esq.," *Archaeologia Americana: Transactions and Collections of the American Antiquarian Society* 7 (1885): 48–49.

9. John Cotton, *The Way of the Churches* (London, 1645), sig A3 r.

10. "To the Reader," James Noyes, *Moses and Aaron* (London, 1661).

11. "To the Reader," John Cotton, *A Brief Exposition With Practical Observations Upon . . . Canticles* (London, 1655), sig. [B1r]; John Wilson and Jonathan Mitchell, "To the Reader," Samuel Whiting, *A Discourse of the Last Judgment* (Cambridge, 1664).

12. Sargent Bush, Jr., *The Correspondence of John Cotton* (Chapel Hill: University of North Carolina Press, 2002), 436–38.

13. Increase Mather, *Five Sermons on Several Subjects* (Boston, 1719), preface. In the 1680s notes were being taken by his son Cotton, though whether for the purpose of future publication is unclear.

14. Samuel Willard, *A Compleat Body of Divinity in Two Hundred and Fifty Expository Lectures* (Boston, 1726), ii.

15. William L. Joyce and Michael G. Hall, "Three Manuscripts of Increase Mather," *Proc. AAS* 86 (1976): 116; Gookin, "Indian Converts," mss., Massachusetts Historical Society. Robert St. George has compared Gookin letters with the manuscript and is certain it was the doing of a clerk or scribe.

16. Kasten, *Shakespeare and the Book*, 35, 44; Marcy L. North, *The Anonymous Renaissance: Cultures of Discretion in Tudor-Stuart England* (Chicago: University of Chicago Press, 2003), 3, 14. See also Robert J. Griffin, introduction to Griffin, ed., *The Faces of Anonymity: Anonymous and Pseudonymous Publications from the Sixteenth to the Twentieth Centuries* (New York: Palgrave Macmillan, 2003).

17. North, *Anonymous Renaissance*, ch. 5.

18. *Recs. Mass.*, 3: 215–16; 4, pt. 1: 29–30.

19. Walker, *Creeds*, 135 n. 4.

20. The connections between anonymity and writers who were women are pursued more thoroughly in Margaret J. Ezell, *The Patriarch's Wife: Literary Evidence and the History of the Family* (Chapel Hill: University of North Carolina Press, 1987) and North, *Anonymous Renaissance*, ch. 7.

21. The coyness about anonymity in Mather, *Decennium Luctuosum* (Boston, 1699) is neatly exposed in Kenneth Silverman, *The Life and Times of Cotton Mather* (New York: Harper & Row, 1984), 200.

22. Increase Mather, *The Great Blessing of Primitive Counsellours* (Boston, 1693), 4. Nearly twenty years after the fact, he also revealed his authorship of a diatribe against Anglicanism. Holmes, *Increase Mather*, 1: 54.

23. See Chapter 2; I owe the example of Spenser to North, *Anonymous Renaissance*, 100–104.

24. *Coll. MHS* 4th ser. 8 (1868): 54.

25. The anonymous *Miscellaneous Observations*, published in 1692 with a false imprint, was included in the list of Samuel Willard's publications in *A Compleat Body of Divinity* (Boston, 1726).

26. Franklin B. Williams, Jr., *Index of Dedications and Commendatory Verses in English Books Before 1641* (London: The Bibliographical Society, 1962).

27. A point made by Dustin H. Griffin, *Literary Patronage in England, 1650–1800* (Cambridge: Cambridge University Press, 1996), 21, in the context of noting immaterial benefits of the practice; and by contributors to *Patronage, Politics, and Literary Traditions in England, 1558–1658*, ed. Cedric C. Brown (Detroit: Wayne State University Press, 1993).

28. If the Anglican priest and early resident of New England William Morrell is included in the larger story, then his is the exception that proves the rule, for he dedicated *New England. Or A brief enarration of the ayre, earth, water fish and fowles of that country* (London, 1625), to Charles I.

29. Two of Hooker's books contained dedications written by intermediaries; see Sargent Bush, "A Bibliography of the Published Writings," *Thomas Hooker Writings in England and Holland, 1626–1633*, ed. George H. Williams et al. (Cambridge, Mass.: Harvard University Press, 1975), 409, 413.

30. See Chapter 5.

31. Winslow's role is described more fully in Richard W. Cogley, *John Eliot's Mission to the Indians before King Philip's War* (Cambridge, Mass.: Harvard University Press, 1999), 66–70.

32. William Hubbard, *The Happiness of a People In the Wisdome of their Rulers Directing And in the Obedience of their Brethren Attending Unto what Israel ought to do* (Boston, 1676), sig. A2 r.

33. Greenhill, "To the Christian Reader," in Shepard, *The Sincere Convert* (London, 1646).

34. As is ably demonstrated in Kevin Dunn, *Pretexts of Authority: The Rhetoric of Authorship in the Renaissance Preface* (Stanford: Stanford University Press, 1994), chs. 1–2.

35. Arthur Hildersam, *Lectures upon the Fourth of Iohn* (London, 1629), sig. A2r; Shepard, *Works*, 3: 22–23; Mather, *The Summe of Certain Sermons* (Cambridge, 1652), sig. A2r; Willard, *Mercy Magnified on a Penitent Prodigal* (Boston, 1684), sig. A3v.

36. Thomas Wheeler, "Christian Reader," *A Thankefull Remembrance of Gods Mercy* (Cambridge, 1676); James Allen, *New-Englands choicest Blessing* (Boston, 1679), sig. A2r; Increase Mather, *Wo to Drunkards* (Cambridge, [1673]), sig. A2r, v.

37. Shepard, *Works*, 2: 9–10; [Rowlandson], *The Sovereignty & Goodness of God* (Cambridge, 1682), sig. [A3]v; and see in general, Brown, *Pilgrim and the Bee*, ch. 2.

38. *Wine for Gospel Wantons* (Cambridge). The account that follows omits a few other Shepard publications.

39. Albro, "Life of Thomas Shepard," Shepard, *Works*, 1: clxxviii.

40. Based on comparing copies owned by Houghton Library, Harvard University.

41. Shepard, *Works*, 3: 22–23, 280.

42. Shepard, *The Parable of the Ten Virgins Opened & Applied* (London, 1660), sig. A3v, r.

43. Shepard, *Subjection to Christ* (1652; London, 1657), "To the Christian Reader"; William Greenhill and Samuel Mather, "To the Reader," sig. A2r.

44. *Coll. MHS* 4th ser. 8 (1868): 50, 53, 55; Mather, *The Doctrine of Divine Providence* (Boston, 1684), sig. [A4r]. Contrary to his brother's wishes, Increase (or the printer) put Nathaniel Mather's name on the separate title page for his sermon.

45. These connections are richly evident in Thomas Shepard's autobiography, reprinted in Michael McGiffert, *God's Plot: The Paradoxes of Puritan Piety* (Amherst: University of Massachusetts Press, 1972).

46. See in general Francis J. Bremer, *Congregational Communion: Clerical Friendship in the Anglo-American Puritan Community, 1610–1692* (Boston: Northeastern University Press, 1994), which contains much information not carried over into my account.

47. *A Letter of Mr. John Cotton, Teacher of the Church in Boston in New-England, to Mr. Williams a Preacher There* (London, 1643); Bush, *Correspondence*, 212.

48. Bush, *Correspondence*, 374 n. 1; Chapter 4.

49. Shepard, *Subjection to Christ* (1657), sig. A4r.

50. *Winthrop Papers*, 3: 327.

51. Mather, *Life of Thomas Dudley*, ed. Charles Deane (Cambridge, Mass., 1870); for Colman, see Chapter 1, n. 33.

52. Shepard, *The Sound Believer* (London, 1645), sig. A4v; Bush, *Correspondence of John Cotton*, 437; *NEHGR* 5 (1852): 242; Thomas Thorowgood, *Jews in America* (London, 1660), 27.

53. Percy Simpson, *Proof-Reading in the Sixteenth Seventeenth and Eighteenth Centuries* (London: Oxford University Press, 1935), 50–51. See especially ch. 3, "Correctors of the Press."

54. Dobranski, *Milton, Authorship, and the Book Trade*, 157.

55. John Davenport, *The Knowledge of Christ* (London, 1653), "To the Reader." But see Holmes, *Increase Mather*, 1: 286; and as noted in the case study of Cotton Mather, he issued a Boston-printed errata for the London-produced *Magnalia Christi Americana*.

56. The following paragraphs are informed by David McKitterick, *Print, Manuscript and the Search for Order, 1450–1830* (Cambridge: Cambridge University Press, 2003), chs. 3 and 4.

57. Hugh Amory, "Under the Exchange: The Unprofitable Business of Michael Perry, a Seventeenth-Century Boston Bookseller," *Proc. AAS* 103 (1993): 31–60, reprinted in Amory, *Bibliography and the Book Trades*, ch. 4.

58. The title was changed from *A Defence of the Answer* (London, 1648) to *A Treatise on Liturgies* (London, 1653).

59. Randolph G. Adams, "William Hubbard's 'Narrative,' 1677: A Bibliographical Study," *Papers of the Bibliographical Society of America* 33 (1939): 25–39; quotations, pp. 26, 28.

60. Hugh Amory, "'Gods Altar Needs Not Our Pollishings': Revisiting the Bay Psalm Book," *Printing History* 12 (1990): 2–14, reprinted in Amory, *Bibliography and the Book Trades*, ch. 2.

61. Robert K. Diebold, "A Critical Edition of Mrs. Mary Rowlandson's Captivity Narrative" (Ph.D. diss., Yale University, 1972), cli–clxviii.

62. William Frederick Poole, introduction to Edward Johnson, *Wonder-Working Providence of Sions Saviour* (Andover, Mass., 1867), iv–v.

63. Hall, *Antinomian Controversy*, 174 n. 3.

64. Holmes, *Cotton Mather*, 3: 973; for another example, see 988.

CHAPTER 4. TEXTURES OF SOCIAL AUTHORSHIP

1. Foster would publish a new printing of John Wilson's *Songs of Deliverance* (originally 1626; Boston, 1680).

2. Samuel Green, *John Foster The Earliest American Engraver and The First Boston Printer* (Boston, 1879), 34. The elegies, which are not by Danforth, also circulated in manuscript.

3. Thomas A. Ryan, "The Poetry of John Danforth," *Proc. AAS* 78 (1968): 129–93; he corrects the list of poems in Jantz, *First Century*, noting that some were of English origin.

4. John Danforth, *A Sermon Occasioned by the Late Great Earthquake* (Boston, 1728).

5. "Autobiography [of Michael Wigglesworth]," in John Ward Dean, *Memoir of the Rev. Michael Wigglesworth*, 2nd ed. (Albany, 1871), 64–65. I follow Hugh Amory's argument as found in Amory and Hall, *Colonial Book*, 107–8. It has sometimes been argued that the first printing occurred in London, and an early London printing would certainly make the sales figure more understandable.

6. The sequence and number of editions remain uncertain because complete copies

do not survive of some. Amory's census differs from that of Ronald A. Bosco, *The Poems of Michael Wigglesworth* (Lanham, Md.: University Press of America, 1989), 305–6.

7. Cotton Mather, "Life of Thomas Dudley," ed. Charles Deane (Cambridge, Mass., 1870), 19.

8. Quotations from *The Complete Works of Anne Bradstreet*, ed. Joseph R. McElrath, Jr., and Allan P. Robb (Boston: Twayne Publishers, 1981).

9. The evidence is reviewed with care in ibid., xxxii–xxxiv.

10. Ibid., xviii.

11. Philip H. Round comments interestingly on their identities and also on the choice of London bookseller/printer in *By Nature and By Custom Cursed: Transatlantic Civil Discourse and New England Cultural Production, 1620–1660* (Hanover, N. H.: University Press of New England, 1999), ch. 4.

12. Ramona Wray, *Women Writers of the Seventeenth Century* (Horndon, Tavistock, Devon: Northcote House, 2004), ch. 3. I agree with Wray when she argues (p. 43) that "the formative role of mothers' advice books suggests that . . . it was perfectly possible for women to construct a legitimate and authoritative speaking voice," though she limits this possibility to women who were dying. For a local expression of maternal responsibilities, see Richard Mather, *A Farewel-Exhortation to the church and people of Dorchester in New-England* (Cambridge, Mass., 1657), 13.

13. See Chapter 2 for this imprint.

14. Mss., Houghton Library, Harvard University (on deposit from the North Andover Historical Society); printed in many places, including McElrath and Robb, *Complete Works*.

15. *The Letters of John Davenport Puritan Divine,* ed. Isabel MacBeath Calder (New Haven, Conn.: Yale University Press, 1937), 54.

16. Sargent Bush, Jr., *The Writings of Thomas Hooker Spiritual Adventure in Two Worlds* (Madison: University of Wisconsin Press, 1980), 31, a circumstance that holds for sermon series printed in the early 1640s as well.

17. Mather, *Johannes in Eremo* (Boston, 1695), reprinted in *Magnalia*, 1: 330, 347. The minister Giles Firmin had lived briefly in New England; for his comments on Shepard, see Chapter 3.

18. Winfried Herget, "The Transcription and Transmission of the Hooker Corpus," *Thomas Hooker Writings in England and Holland, 1626–1633*, ed. George H. Williams et al. (Cambridge, Mass.: Harvard University Press, 1975), 260. Sixteen years later a fuller version of this sermon appeared in a collection of sermons by another minister, William Fenner, found, it seems, after his death among his papers by the man who edited the posthumous collection.

19. Sargent Bush, "The Growth of Thomas Hooker's *The Poor Doubting Christian*," *Early American Literature* 8 (1973): 5–13; Herget, "Transcription and Transmission," 265–66.

20. Mather, *Magnalia*, 1: 347; George L. Walker, *History of the First Church in Hartford, 1633–1883* (Hartford, 1884), 493–94.

21. Ibid., 493. Possibly this subsidy was used to support the publication of *A Comment upon Christ's last Prayer In the Seventeenth of John* (London, 1656), "Printed from the Authors own Papers, written by his own Hand. And attested to be such, in an Epistle" (title page). The book had previously been printed in 1637.

22. Goodwin and Nye, "To the Reader," in Hooker, *The Application of Redemption* (London, 1656).

23. Z. S., "Epistle Dedicatory," in Hooker, *The Christians Two Chiefe Lessons* (London, 1640), sigs. A2v, A3r, A4r. That Symmes would play such a role, with Hooker very much alive and well and traveling back and forth between Hartford and Boston/ Cambridge, strikes me as quite odd. The "Epistle Dedicatory" implies that the manuscript had been prepared in England.

24. Thomas Hooker, *A Survey of the Summe of Church-Discipline* (London, 1648), sig. c2r.

25. Walker suggested that the gap was meant to be filled by another treatise by John Cotton defending the Congregational Way. *History of the First Church in Hartford*, 440.

26. Mather, *Magnalia*, I: 342; books attributed to him falsely are identified in Sargent Bush, Jr., "Bibliography of The Published Writings of Thomas Hooker," in Williams et. al., *Thomas Hooker*, 390–425.

27. Bush, *Correspondence*, 20. The only careful study of Cotton's imprints is Julius H. Tuttle, "Writings of Rev. John Cotton," in *Bibliographical Essays A Tribute to Wilberforce Eames* ([Cambridge, Mass.: Harvard University Press], 1924), 363–80. Much information about variants and re-printings is not carried over into my account.

28. William Twisse, *A Treatise of Mr. Cottons Clearing Certaine Doubts Concerning Predestination, Together with an Examination Thereof* (London, 1646).

29. Mather, *Magnalia*, I: 268.

30. One of these (dated 1635) was published as *A Coppy of a Letter of Mr. John Cotton of Boston . . . Directed to a Friend* (London, 1641); almost a century later, *A Treatise I. Of Faith . . . IV. Questions and answers upon Church-Government* (dating from about the same time) was printed in Boston in 1713.

31. Larzer Ziff, *John Cotton on the Churches of New England* (Cambridge, Mass.: Harvard University Press, 1968), 56–57, 58.

32. John Cotton, *The Way of the Churches in New England Cleared* (London, 1648).

33. *The First Book of Records of the Town of Southampton* (Sag Harbor, N.Y., 1874), 18–22; *The Hutchinson Papers*, ed. William H. Whitmore, 2 vols. (Albany, N.Y.: Prince Society, 1865), I: 181–205, indicating the variants.

34. Based on comparing copies in the Houghton Library, Harvard University.

35. George Selement, "John Cotton's Hidden Antinomianism: His Sermon on Revelation 4:1–2," *NEHGR* 129 (1975) 278–94; Michael McGiffert, *God's Plot: The Paradoxes of Puritan Piety* (Amherst: University of Massachusetts Press, 1972), 74. John Winthrop also had notes on a Cotton sermon. *Winthrop Papers*, 3: 351.

36. Cotton, *Way . . . Cleared*, in Hall, *Antinomian* Controversy, 400.

37. Preface to *The Way of the Churches* (London, 1645).

38. Nathaniel Holmes, "A Pacificatory Epistle," *Way . . . Cleared*, sig. A2r, [a3v].

39. William Morton, "To the Reader," in Cotton, *The way of Life* (London, 1641), sig. A4r, v.

40. "To the Christian Reader," in Cotton, *Gods Mercie* (London, 1641), sig. A2r.

41. Cotton, *Some Treasure Fetched out of Rubbish* (London, 1660), sig A2r; Tuttle, "Writings of John Cotton," 376. These were also sermons from his English years.

42. Charles Scott, "To the Reader," *A Practical Commentary . . . upon the First Epistle Generall of John* (London, 1656); Mather, *Magnalia*, 1: 280. Scott also asserted that someone familiar with Cotton's preaching had confirmed the sermons as his.

43. To these five should possibly be added the catechism *Milk for Babes. Drawn Out of the Bresats of both Testaments* (1646), which was reprinted in Cambridge in 1656 and would have many more printings on both sides of the Atlantic well into the eighteenth century.

44. Tuttle, "Writings of John Cotton," 375; the copy in Houghton Library, Harvard University, has errata apparently corrected by Cotton.

45. Thomas Allen, "To the Reader," Cotton, *An Exposition upon the Thirteenth Chapter of the Revelation* (London, 1655).

46. Allen, "To the Reader," *The Covenant of Grace* (London, 1655).

47. Thomas Allen, "To the Reader," Cotton, *A Practical Commentary* (London, 1656). A second edition (London, 1658), advertised as "much corrected and inlarged," begins with a note from one Roger Drake extolling the book and noting that he "perused it to correct the many and manifold errours of the former impression."

48. Allen, "To the Reader," *The Covenant of Grace*.

49. John Allen, "The Stationer to the Reader," in Cotton, *A Treatise of the Covenant of Grace* (London, 1659), sig. A3r, v.

50. Cotton, *The way of Life*, sig. [A4]r; Mather, *Magnalia*, 1: 280.

51. Holmes, *Cotton Mather*, 2:729–35 (reprinting the prospectus of 1714).

52. *The Diary of Cotton Mather, 1681–1724*, ed. Worthington C. Ford, 2 vols. (Boston: Massachusetts Historical Society, 1911–1912), 1: 97; Samuel Mather, *The Life of . . . Cotton Mather* (Boston, 1729), 48.

53. Although its purpose is not author's portraits per se, Kenneth B. Murdock, *The Portraits of Increase Mather* (Cleveland: privately printed, 1924), is informative. The earliest author portrait of which I am aware is of John Norton in *A Discussion of that Great Point in Divinity* (London, 1653; printed by Giles Calvert). A portrait of Increase appeared in the London printing of *An Essay for the Recording of Illustrious Providences* (1684).

54. Silverman, *Selected Letters*, 190.

55. Mather, *Diary*, 2: 331.

56. *Coll. MHS*, 4th ser. 8 (1868): 407; Silverman, *Selected Letters*, 77. When Mather's imprints are arranged by page length, their brevity becomes strikingly evident. I am indebted to a table of this evidence, prepared for me by Alan DeGutis and Kathleen Haley of the American Antiquarian Society. In summary, it shows that 89 imprints were of twenty-four pages or less, 78 of thirty-eight or less, and 91 of forty to forty-eight, making

a total of 258 imprints, or approximately 65 percent of Mather's full bibliography (somewhere in the range of four hundred imprints).

57. *Coll. MHS* 4th ser. 8 (1868): 448.

58. Mather, *Diary*, 1: 122.

59. Matthew Mead, "To the Reader," Mather, *Early Piety, exemplified*, 2nd ed. (London, 1689), sig. A3r, v; Samuel Mather, "To the Reader," ibid., sig. A4v.

60. Silverman, *Selected Letters*, 111–13.

61. Ibid., 43, 44–45.

62. Holmes, *Cotton Mather*, 3: 1236–66, a brilliant reconstruction of how the book was written.

63. Mss., Mather Family Papers, American Antiquarian Society; mss., Massachusetts Historical Society; see also Holmes, "The Surreptitious Printing of One of Cotton Mather's Manuscripts," in *Bibliographical Essays: A Tribute to Wilberforce Eames*, 149–60.

64. Silverman, *Selected Letters*, 27; *Coll. MHS* 3rd ser. 1 (1825): 126–33. For more on these texts and events, see Chapter 5.

65. Robert Calef, *More Wonders of the Invisible World* (London, 1700), reprinted in Samuel G. Drake, *The Witchcraft Delusion in New England*, 3 vols. (Roxbury, Mass., 1865), 3: 151.

66. Silverman, *Selected Letters*, 76–77.

67. Ibid., 296, 163.

68. Chester N. Greenough, "A Letter Relating to the Publication of Cotton Mather's Magnalia," *Pub. CSM* 26 (1927): 296–312. The attempted abridgement is in the library of the Massachusetts Historical Society. Mather was not the only colonist at the end of the century to imagine making it big within the London book trade; for a Virginian with the same hopes, see Amory and Hall, *Colonial Book*, 79–80.

69. Holmes, *Cotton Mather*, 3: 1103–4.

70. Silverman, *Selected Letters*, 147–49; *Coll. MHSC* 4th ser. 8 (1868): 446, 448 (on cost).

71. Silverman, *Selected Letters*, 170; and see D. N. DeLuna, "Cotton Mather Published Abroad," *Early American Literature* 26 (1991): 145–72. The "Biblia Americana" was far from being the only manuscript of his that the trade ignored or that intermediaries misplaced. When Benjamin Harris returned to London in 1694, Mather entrusted him with "certain Manuscripts" that Harris "carelessly left . . . in the Hands" of another bookseller, whereupon they vanished, only to turn up some years later and pass into print. Mather had no such luck with a manuscript of 1716 he entitled "Boanerges, or Work of the Day." Ford, *Diary*, 1: 402; Holmes, *Cotton Mather*, 1: 84–85.

72. Silverman, *Life and Times*, 161.

73. Shepard, *Works*, 3: 275. Many other remarks of this kind appear in prefaces.

CHAPTER 5. BETWEEN UNITY AND SEDITION

1. As David Zaret has pointed out, the practice of petitioning was acceptable because it met the condition of deference and made no "claims about the supremacy of popular

will over petitioned authority." Zaret, "Petitions and the 'Invention' of Public Opinion in the English Revolution," *American Journal of Sociology* 101 (1996): 1499; see also Zaret, *Origins of Democratic Culture: Printing, Petitions, and the Public Sphere in Early Modern England* (Princeton, N.J.: Princeton University Press, 2000), 90–91. His emphasis on printing and the emergence of printed petitions in 1640s England is significantly different from my own, as is the importance in his narrative of "secrecy."

2. *The Hutchinson Papers*, ed. W. H. Whitmore, 2 vols. (Albany, N.Y.: Prince Society, 1865), 1: 72; Hall, *Antinomian Controversy*, 249–50.

3. *Recs. Mass.* 1: 207–12.

4. See, e.g., Perry Miller, *Orthodoxy in Massachusetts, 1630–1650* (Cambridge, Mass.: Harvard University Press, 1933), a telling of the story much reiterated in recent work.

5. *Recs. Mass.* 1: 213.

6. That is, whether admitted to freemanship or not; that this distinction was waived is itself significant.

7. William H. Whitmore, *The Colonial Laws of Massachusetts* (Boston, 1889), 35, 49.

8. Rather than contributing to the elasticity of the term "public sphere," I take for granted the elements that were critical to Jurgen Habermas's frame of reference: the presence (emergence) of the bourgeoisie, understood as an urban social formation; the technology of printing; a domestic culture centered on the family; and—in political philosophy—a critical appropriation of "reason" or rationality, always in the context of an absolutist civil state. With the possible exception of domestic culture, none of these conditions recurred in early New England, and as others have noted, religious practice is absent from Habermas's account. I have also avoided the term "public opinion" in order not to give the impression that the leadership in the colonies routinely referred to or acknowledged as authoritative the "clamours" reaching them from the people. Referring to the news books being printed in 1640s England, Nigel Smith is less cautious: "public opinion . . . was being born, and its consent had to be sought." Nigel Smith, *Literature and Revolution in England 1640–1660* (New Haven: Yale University Press, 1994), 56.

9. Hall, *Antinomian Controversy*, 260; *Hutchinson Papers*, 1: 74–78 (the text does not survive; this is a response to it).

10. Hall, *Antinomian Controversy*, 212–13, 209; the magistrates were also accused of being "Ahabs, Amiziahs, Scribes and Pharisees, enemies to Christ, led by Satan" (211).

11. See in general Adam Fox, *Oral and Literate Culture in England 1500–1700* (Oxford: Oxford University Press, 2000), ch. 7.

12. As did the Massachusetts General Court, or so William Aspinwall claimed. Hall, *Antinomian Controversy*, 258.

13. Philip Hamburger, "The Development of the Law of Seditious Libel and the Control of the Press," *Stanford Law Review* 37 (1985): 661–765, shows how imprecise and politicized the term "seditious libel" was in English practice under Elizabeth I and the Stuarts. See also David Colclough, *Freedom of Speech in Early Stuart England* (Cambridge: Cambridge University Press, 2005).

14. A point strongly made by Julian Davies, *The Caroline Captivity of the Church: Charles I and the Remoulding of Anglicanism, 1625–1641* (Oxford: Clarendon Press, 1992), 14.

15. Zaret, *Origins of Democratic Culture*, ch.3; Alexandra Walsham, *Charitable Hatred: Tolerance and Intolerance in England, 1500–1700* (Manchester: University of Manchester Press, 2006), ch. 2.

16. Anthony Fletcher, *Reform in the Provinces: The Government of Stuart England* (New Haven: Yale University Press, 1986), a remarkable account of local muting of royal policies and mandates. Walsham, *Charitable Hatred*, is equally lucid on circumstances that limited the suppression of dissent.

17. Love, *Scribal Publication*, 9–22.

18. *Winthrop Papers*, 3: 357–60; for the context, see William Haller, *Liberty and Reformation in the Puritan Revolution* (New York: Columbia University Press, 1955).

19. *Winthrop Papers*, 3: 175–76; *Proc. MHS* 58 (1925): 450–51.

20. *Winthrop Papers*, 5: 44–45.

21. Walker, *Creeds*, 236.

22. *Winthrop Papers*, 5:91; Thomas Shepard to Hugh Peter, 1645, *NEHGR* 39 (1895): 371.

23. *Recs. Mass.* 1: 117; a printed broadside of the oath was possibly the first publication of the newly-established press in Cambridge. Similar laws and requirements for oath-taking were enacted in Plymouth and Connecticut.

24. Hall, *Antinomian Controversy*, 292–93.

25. See, e.g., *Winthrop Papers* 3: 54, 76, 94, 100–101, 112.

26. Winthrop, *Journal*, 107, 149.

27. For example, John Pratt, who was required to recant his comments; *Coll. MHS* 2nd ser. 7 (1818): 126–29, 255–77.

28. *Winthrop Papers*, 3: 8–9, 54.

29. *Collections of the Connecticut Historical Society* 1 (1860): 20, 12; *Winthrop Papers*, 4: 81–82.

30. Winthrop, *Journal*, 314–15; David D. Hall, *The Faithful Shepherd: A History of the New England Ministry in the Seventeenth Century* (Chapel Hill: University of North Carolina Press, 1972), 116–17.

31. Winthrop, *Journal*, 390–91.

32. Winthrop, *Journal*, 395–98; *Winthrop Papers*, 4: 359–61; Robert E. Wall, Jr., *Massachusetts Bay: The Crucial Decade, 1640–1650* (New Haven, Conn.: Yale University Press, 1972), 50–59.

33. Winthrop, *Journal*, 455–57; *Winthrop Papers*, 4: 347–52; The negative vote had already contested in 1630s by figures such as Israel Stoughton; see *Proc. MHS* 58 (1925): 446–58.

34. In these paragraphs on political debate I have ignored the participation of the ministers and the texts they were contributing to the process; for more on their role, see Hall, *Faithful Shepherd*, ch. 6. My account of the disputes of the 1640s has benefited from the close analysis given to them by Wall, *Massachusetts Bay*.

35. Winthrop, *Journal*, 452, 454–55; Arthur Prentice Rugg, "A Famous Colonial Litigation: The Case Between Richard Sherman and Capt. Robert Keayne, 1642," *Proc. AAS* 30 (1920): 217–50.

36. *Hutchinson Papers,* 1:130–37; *Winthrop Papers,* 4: 394–95, 397–401, 402–3; Winthrop, *Journal,* 440, 443.

37. Winthrop, *Journal,* 514–15.

38. *Recs. Mass.* 3: 17, 19–26; Winthrop, *Journal,* 579. The minister John Wilson may have harangued the people gathered in Cambridge for the fateful election of May 1637.

39. Winthrop, *Journal,* 584–89.

40. Ibid., 590–91; *Winthrop Papers,* 4: 468–82.

41. Winthrop, *Journal,* 592, 593.

42. Ibid., 617.

43. *Recs. Mass.,* 3: 64; Winthrop, *Journal,* 592, 611–12, 617–18, 629. Interestingly, the petition favoring the Baptists evoked the debate about the law against strangers passed in 1637, a sign of how political memory was at work. Hitherto a fugitive group on the outer margins of English Nonconformity, Baptists were benefiting from the chaotic politics of civil war England in being able to publish openly through the London trade.

44. *Winthrop Papers* 5: 55–56; the remonstrance itself is printed in John Child, *New-Englands Jonas Cast Up* (London, 1647).

45. *Winthrop Papers,* 5: 125; *Recs. Mass.* 2:162; Edward Winslow, *New-Englands Salamander, Discovered* (London, 1647), reprinted in *Coll. MHS* 1st ser. 2 (1793): 116; see also George Lyman Kittredge, "Dr. Robert Child the Remonstrant," *PCSM* 21 (Boston: The Society, 1935): 1–146.

46. Wall, *Massachusetts Bay,* 184.

47. G. H. Trumbull, "Robert Child," *PCSM* 38 (1947–51): 52.

48. *Records of the Colony of Connecticut 1636 to 1663,* ed. J. Hammond Trumbull, 3 vols. (Hartford, 1850–59), 1: 87, 90, 91, 97 (hereafter, *Recs. Conn*); Sylvester Judd, *History of Hadley* (Northampton, 1863), 7–8.

49. *Recs. Conn,* 1:302; *Collections of the Connecticut Historical Society* 2 (1870), 77–78.

50. *Records of the Colony or Jurisdiction of New Haven, From May, 1653 , to the Union,* ed. Charles J. Hoadly, 2 vols (Hartford, 1858), 2: 24, 52–57.

51. *Records of the Colony of New Plymouth in New England,* ed. N. B. Shurtleff, 11 vols. (Boston, 1855–61), 3: 130, 149–50; Samuel Deane, *History of Scituate, Massachusetts* (Boston, 1831), 245–48.

52. *The New England Company of 1649 and John Eliot* (Boston: Prince Society, 1920) 108; *Proc. MHS* 5 (1860–62): 376–77.

53. Shurtleff, *Records of . . . New Plymouth, Acts of the Commissioners of the United Colonies of New England,* ed. David Pulsifer, 10: 255–59.

54. James C. Pilling, *Bibliography of the Algonquian Languages* (Washington, D.C., 1891), 136.

55. John Tully, *An Almanac* (Boston, 1687), 15–16.

56. See Chapter 3.

57. *Hutchinson Papers,* 2: 113–14.

58. Mss., Massachusetts Historical Society; printed in *Coll. MHS* 2nd ser. 8 (1819): 46–112. For other commentary on the Danforth manuscript, see Chapter 2.

59. See Chapter 2.

60. *Recs. Mass.* 4, pt. 2, 62.

61. *Coll. MHS* 4th ser. 8 (1868): 205–6.

62. Davenport, *Another Essay for Investigation of the Truth* (Cambridge, 1663), sig. A3r.

63. Michael G. Hall and William L. Joyce, "The Half-Way Covenant of 1662: Some New Evidence," *Proc. AAS* 87 (1977): 97–110. The Henry Martyn Dexter Papers, Beinecke Library, Yale University, also contain transcripts (by David Pulsifer) of documents written by the minority.

64. John Allin, *Animadversions upon the Antisynodalia Americana* (Cambridge, 1664), 82, 1, 2–3, sig. A2v, 5, 16. A near-book-length study would be necessary to survey the echoes of this debate, notably the turmoil that surrounded the founding of Third Church Boston in 1670.

65. The connections among imperial authority, local politics, and Indian-colonist relations are described much more fully in Jenny Hale Pulsipher, *Subjects unto the Same King: Indians, English, and the Contest for Authority in Colonial New England* (Philadelphia: University of Pennsylvania Press, 2005); in particular, Pulsipher provides important details on the role of Edmund Andros during King Philip's War and on the colonists' pleas for assistance from England.

66. [Saltonstall], *Present State*, repr. in *Narratives of the Indian Wars 1675–1699*, ed. Charles H. Lincoln (New York: Scribner's, 1913), 35, 28, 39, 26, 49; he also incorporated into his text a statement published by the Massachusetts Council on September 17, 1675, justifying the war. A fuller listing of texts prompted by the war appears in Jill Lepore, *The Name of War: King Philip's War and the Origins of American Identity* (New York: Knopf, 1998), ch. 2, though in the interest of a different question than mine.

67. John Easton, "A Relacion of the Indyan Warre," in Lincoln, *Narratives,* 7–8, 12, 14–16, 10.

68. Ibid., 53, 54, 82, 83.

69. Benjamin Tompson, *New Englands Crisis* (Boston, 1676); *New-Englands Tears For Her Present Miseries* (London, 1676).

70. [Rowlandson], *The Sovereignty & Goodness of God* (Cambridge, 1682), 6, 7, 32, 50.

71. Hubbard, *A Narrative of the Troubles with the Indians In New-England* (Boston, 1677), 9–11, 13, 30, 61, 28.

72. Mather, *An Earnest Exhortation To the Inhabitants of New-England, To hearken to the voice of God in his late and present Dispensations* (Boston, 1676), 13, 15; Michael G. Hall, *The Last American Puritan: The Life of Increase Mather* (Hanover, N.H.: Wesleyan University Press, 1988), 125.

73. "To the right honorable the Lords of his Majesties most honorable Privy Council appointed a committee for trade and plantations," *Hutchinson Papers,* 2: 225, 227–28, 243–44, 219. A manuscript version in a clerk's hand survives (American Antiquarian Society).

74. Ibid., 247–48.

75. John G. Palfrey, *History of New England*, 3 vols. (Boston, 1858–65), 3: 547, 547n; *The Andros Tracts*, ed. W. H. Whitmore, 3 vols. (Boston: The Prince Society, 1868–74), 1: 79. The events in Ipswich and Watertown were narrated in *The Revolution in New England, Justified* (London and Boston, 1691); for Wise's statement, see 1: 84. Increase, not Cotton, had written the attack on Anglicanism, but he was safely in England at the time.

76. *Andros Tracts*, 3: 107.

77. All of the printed materials, and much that circulated in manuscript, are brought together in the three volumes of the *Andros Tracts*; my account is selective.

78. *Andros Tracts*, 1: 23, 24.

79. Albert Matthews, "An Alleged Boston Newspaper of 1689," *PCSM* 10 (1907): 310–20.

80. *Andros Tracts*, 2: 201, 193–94, 13.

81. *Ibid.*, 1: 54–55, 58 (from Palmer's *Impartial Account*). Such stories were pervasive in *The Revolution in New England Justified.*

82. That Cotton Mather abridged the letters is demonstrated in *Andros Tracts*, 3: 208n. This tract was probably written by Charles Morton of Charlestown.

83. Holmes, *Increase Mather*, 2:376.

84. For this letter, see *Andros Tracts*, 2: 163–70. The contexts for these publications are more fully sketched in Holmes, *Increase Mather* (see under title); see also Hall, *Last American Puritan*, 230–34.

85. *Andros Tracts*, 1: 132.

86. Ibid., 1: 128–29.

87. Ibid., 2: 137, 1: 145.

88. George H. Moore, "Notes on the History of Witchcraft in Massachusetts, with Illustrative Documents," *Proc. AAS*, n.s. 5 (1887–88): 171, 171 n, 246–47.

89. [Willard], *Miscellaneous Observations* ([New York, 1692]). A broader description of communication and empire after 1690 is provided by Ian K. Steele, *The English Atlantic, 1675–1740: An Exploration of Communication and Community* (New York: Oxford University Press, 1986).

90. *Coll. MHS* 1st ser., 5 (1798): 61.

INDEX